MW01231612

SECURITY AND CRIME PREVENTION IN LIBRARIES

Security and crime prevention in libraries

Edited by
Michael Chaney
and
Alan F. MacDougall

Routledge
Taylor & Francis Group

LONDON AND NEW YORK

First published 1992 by Ashgate Publishing

Reissued 2018 by Routledge
2 Park Square, Milton Park, Abingdon, Oxon OX14 4RN
52 Vanderbilt Avenue, New York, NY 10017

Routledge is an imprint of the Taylor & Francis Group, an informa business

Publisher's Note
The publisher has gone to great lengths to ensure the quality of this reprint but points out that some imperfections in the original copies may be apparent.

Disclaimer
The publisher has made every effort to trace copyright holders and welcomes correspondence from those they have been unable to contact.

A Library of Congress record exists under LC control number: 92025849

Typeset by P Stubley, Sheffield

ISBN 13: 978-1-138-34634-5 (hbk)
ISBN 13: 978-0-429-43733-5 (ebk)

Contents

List of contributors

Colin Baddock is a Training Consultant

Dr Philip Bean is Director of the Midlands Centre for Criminology and Criminal Justice and Reader in the Department of Social Sciences, Loughborough University

Harry Faulkner-Brown is an Architect and Library Planning Consultant

Michael Chaney is Senior Assistant Librarian (Administration) Loughborough University

J Eric Davies is Senior Assistant Librarian (Information) Loughborough University

John Hinks is Deputy Director of Libraries, Leicestershire Libraries and Information Service

Inspector John Houlgate is a crime prevention consultant in the Metropolitan Police Crime Prevention Service

Marie Jackson is National Preservation Officer, National Preservation Office

Andrew McDonald is Deputy Librarian, University of Newcastle upon Tyne

Dr Alan MacDougall is Director of Library Services, Dublin City University

John Parsons is Marketing Manager, Sun Alliance International

Dr Fred Ratcliffe is The Librarian, Cambridge University

Dr Raymond Wall is a Copyright Consultant

Stephen J Wrigley is a Partner in Thomas Solicitors

Preface

Crime is increasing at a spectacular and frightening rate in all sections of society, and criminal activity of one sort or another is now affecting every type of library and information service.

Vandalism, mutilation, defacement, theft, verbal and physical abuse, harassment, arson and other criminal activities are problems regularly encountered by staff working in libraries and information services today. It is vital, therefore, that today's library managers are in a position to be able to confront these new concerns in an objective, analytical and professional manner.

Surprisingly perhaps, crime as a management issue in libraries and information services has, on the evidence of the scant literature available, received relatively little attention by the profession, and what has been written is mainly anecdotal and noticeably lacking in a management-oriented approach. Since there has been no full-scale treatment of the subject in the UK, we thought that it was the right time to publish a wide-ranging book on library crime for managers which would be both descriptive and prescriptive. The basic intention of the resulting book is, therefore, to be a source of practical information for library and information service managers, to which they may have recourse whenever a particular problem arises.

We thought that what library managers need to know would be best conveyed by inviting a series of experts from different, though related, professional backgrounds to examine and evaluate specific areas, thereby providing a multi-faceted perspective on the subject.

The contributors were asked to consider library crime in its various manifestations in libraries and information services, and the related security measures, under two separate headings:

a) physical issues (buildings, including fabric and fittings, and materials, including stock); and,

b) personnel issues: staff, users etc.

Within these two broad headings contributors have considered the subject of library crime and security from various standpoints, including the legal process, crime prevention and protection, constraints of one kind or another, and equipment. As a result, dilemmas have been highlighted, solutions suggested, guidelines proposed and a range of practical advice proffered.

Contributors were encouraged to discuss their subjects from the viewpoint of their own beliefs and convictions within the context of their individual professional backgrounds and expertise. This has produced a pattern of broadly similar advice throughout the volume, but opposing opinions on some aspects of library crime have not been suppressed. The editors thought that this was a legitimate approach to a complex subject and that the library or information manager would be best left to draw his or her own conclusions from the broad range of opinions presented, according to his or her own individual circumstances.

The editors would like to thank all the contributors to this volume for the hard work which they have put into their individual chapters. All of them are busy professionals, and many are pursuing careers in sectors of working life far removed from the world of libraries and information services.

We wish to reserve a special word of thanks for Peter Stubley, of Sheffield University Library. His expertise in the intricacies of desktop publishing, and his invaluable advice on the art of producing camera-ready copy from original typescripts and disks have been indispensable in the collation of the final draft of the book.

Michael Chaney
Alan MacDougall
June 1992

1

Changing times? Crime and security as a major issue in libraries

DR F W RATCLIFFE

Crime seems to be endemic in society. Libraries, despite the cloistered air which surrounded them in earlier times, have not been exempt from it. Its corollary, security, soon followed and has been enforced or neglected in varying degrees across the centuries. Today the situation is such as to give rise to alarm not simply because thefts cost money but in terms of their cost to scholarship and, all too frequently, to the nation's heritage.

The earliest surviving catalogue of the holdings of Cambridge University Library dates from 1424 and lists 122 volumes. All of these manuscripts appear to be donations, as was customary at that time, and theology, religion and canon law predominate, as might be expected.

Oates (1975; 1986) noted in his history of the Library that the Library of today possesses only four of the items listed there. The second earliest extant catalogue was compiled in 1473 and 'shows 330 volumes disposed in seventeen lectern cases, each of which had hanging at its end a written table of the books it contained'. Of these, 73 are thought to be still in the Library today but Oates points out that already in 1557 when Cardinal Pole's commissioners drew up their catalogue, they recorded fewer than 200 volumes. Oates, with the tumultuous events of the times in mind, comments that 'the survival of so many [volumes] is emphatically more remarkable than the loss of the remainder'. Fuller (1655), writing over 300 years earlier expresses a different opinion: 'This Library formerly was furnished with plenty of choice books, partly at the costs of the aforesaid Archbishop Rotherham, partly at the charges of Cuthbert Tunstall

... But these books by the covetousness of some great ones and carelessness of the Library Loosers (for Library Keepers I cannot call them) are for the most part imbezzled to the great losse of the University, and Learning in Generall'.

The addition of security to the brief of the National Preservation Office (NPO) underlines the reason why preservation rather than conservation is the preferred term in dealing with conservation in general (for further information about the work of the NPO, reference should be made to chapter 12 by Jackson). Looking after the stock certainly extends beyond conservation measures as they are now widely understood and in the context of a university library like Cambridge which has survived, if at times with difficulty, over 600 years of continuous existence, it can be clearly demonstrated. The chaining of the books in the fifteenth century, the employment of night-watchmen, the use of grating or grilles in the library room of 1471, the earliest records of the Library leave no doubt that crime and security was as much a major issue for the Library's administration then as it is today. On the face of it, given the losses, it may be thought it was not all that effective but, as Oates indicated, the Reformation and Counter-Reformation have much to answer for, not simply in Library but in University terms. It should perhaps also be added that unlike many of the books which disappear today, the whereabouts of many of those absent early volumes is known. Some are in Trinity College Cambridge, some in the Bodleian, some in the British Library, some in the Vatican, among sundry other places.

Theft, mutilation of stock, disasters, these are certainly not new to libraries. There is, however, today a growing sense of urgency and concern about such matters which is quite new among librarians and archivists. Immediate reactions to the unmasking of T. J. Wise's activities some 55 years ago, for example, were that they were unscholarly, even ungentlemanly, rather than downright criminal as they undoubtedly were. Successful forgery as we know from the art world and the late Tom Keating may be dishonest but it is also grudgingly admired, even collectable at high prices. Understandable as that may be, mutilation of manuscripts, that other part of Wise's activities, can only be regarded as theft of the worst kind. Yet it was not greeted with the same kind of outrage in the library world of the 1930s as it certainly would be today. Moreover, in such cases, the world outside libraries in Britain still seems to be not altogether decided as to their criminal nature, certainly if the response of the courts to thefts from libraries is any guide (see chapter 3 by Wrigley). It is somehow a different sort of theft from shoplifting, even an explicable form of theft, some kind of aberration. The Cambridge Magistrates Bench, of which I am a member, illustrates this all too well. Thefts from bookshops are clearly shoplifting and are punished accordingly, usually by significant fines; if persistent, by a custodial sentence. Yet, when an overseas postgraduate research student appeared before the Court having stolen systematically new books on community medicine to the tune of several thousand pounds, she was put on probation for nine months and counselling was advised. The books were all exported for instant reproduction by her printer husband for sale to the trade. There was not even an order made as to compensation for the library. It would have been treated very differently today in the United States, where attitudes to theft from libraries have hardened sharply in the last fifteen years or so (see chapter 2 by Bean).

The growth of conservation awareness in Britain during the last decade found its origins in the concern generated in the United States. Whilst in this country the preservation issue really came to the fore in the '80s, the USA was already warning about embrittlement and deterioration of collections in the '60s. Much the same pattern of delayed response may be discerned in regard to crime and security. In the UK it was as late as June 1987 that the first British Library (BL) seminar on library security was held in Novello House, London, under the Chairmanship of Alex Wilson with a carefully selected audience, which included a strong BL representation (see also chapter 12 by Jackson). Its three sessions dealt with the collections and their storage, the users, and the staff. Its proceedings were not published. Two papers, both American, were circulated to the participants, namely, *Conditions for the security of rare books, manuscript and other special collections* prepared by the Rare Books and Manuscripts Section of the Association of College and Research Libraries (compare this with Guidelines ..., 1982) and *Bookline alert: missing books and manuscripts*, an online database compiled by the American Book Prices Current. The latter is a more sophisticated version of the arrangements made between the Rare Books Group of the Library Association and the Antiquarian Booksellers' Association in the 1970s. In the UK towards the end of 1989 another conference on security was held in London, this time organised by SCONUL and the NPO (Quinsee and McDonald, 1991).

The published literature on conservation increased rapidly in Britain during the 1980s, though not to the level evident in the USA in the late

1960s and '70s to which inevitably much reference was made. At present, not surprisingly, much of the research into security in libraries and archives is also to be found published in the USA, relatively little appearing so far in this country (see also chapter 2 by Bean). In one obvious respect the literature takes up anew an age old theme, one very familiar to librarians and archivists alike, that of preservation versus access, of custody versus exploitation. It comes as no surprise that special collections, rare books and manuscripts were the starting point of the security debate both because of their high value and collectability and because of a number of spectacular thefts.

The literature from the viewpoint of the librarian is in general dispiriting when it is not simply alarming. If the trends in the USA are realised here, the outlook is bleak. The American situation is best conveyed by Zeidberg (1987) who begins his article on collection security in libraries:

> 'Between 1979 and 1986, American libraries reported thefts and missing materials, including: rare books valued at $500,000 from Harvard's zoological library; 400 books worth $6,000 from the University of New Hampshire; $20,000 in rare science books from the deGolyer collection at the University of Oklahoma; $1.1 million in plates, engravings, maps, books and manuscripts from the University of Georgia Library in two separate cases; $130,000 in rare books and manuscripts from George Washington University; more than $100,000 in incunabula from Boston College; $200,000 in rare documents from the Thomas A. Edison National Historical Site; $25,000 in books from the general collections at Berkeley; $50,000 in rare numismatic books from UCLA – to name the more widely reported examples. During these years, the Crerar Library thefts were also discovered, and James Shinn was 'flourishing' at most of the major research libraries in the country.
>
> 'Who were the thieves? Those who have been identified run the gamut, beginning with outside professionals, such as Shinn, and lesser amateurs, such as Michael Kinashko, apprehended in the Berkeley case. My colleagues and I are more concerned, saddened, and perplexed, however, by the number of students, professors, staff members, and librarians who are implicated in these cases. The University of New Hampshire thief was a graduate student, for example. In the first case at the University

of Georgia, a professor of history was apprehended; in the latter case, just now unfolding, a former rare books librarian appears to be a suspect. The head of special collections at Boston College offered incunabula from his library's collection for an unauthorised sale at Sotheby's in New York... The case of missing books at George Washington University involved the University Librarian himself.'

The case of James Shinn, referred to in the quotation, is worth a special mention: 'he was an expert in rare books and took only the best, specialising in lavishly illustrated works on travel, and flora and fauna printed in the 18th and 19th century. He used rare book lists to help find hot titles' (*News*, 1982). His treatment in the American courts is also worth noting: 'his sentence was the maximum: two consecutive ten-year terms'.

Although the American awareness and much of the resulting literature grew in the first instance out of concern for special collections, many other factors have subsequently contributed to its growth. Wyly (1987/88) traces the transition from 'the confidence and security' of 1957, despite Lawrence Thompson's *Bibliokleptomania* of ten years earlier, to the 'much more acute problem' of 1987 in the context of the changed library environment. During these 30 years there have been many significant changes – in the methods of teaching history and literature, in the great increases in numbers of users, especially of those seeking access to primary sources, in the huge growth of libraries, in particular of rare books and archives, and not least in the rocketing value of rare books, which become national news items all too often. Pressure on library and archival services arose not from more liberal policies of admission but from the presence of so many more eligible users.

The patterns of use and growth of collections are reflected·no less clearly in the UK although not as yet to the same extent in the literature. University populations, students and staff, have increased by many times in the post Second World War period, to say nothing of the populations of polytechnics and other institutions of higher education. Special collections departments, formerly havens of rest, are now hives of industry. Local Record Offices, at one time backwaters of solid industry, now measure their success by the bodies coming through their doors. Nowhere, however, have staffing quotas risen proportionately. As in the USA, there have been some striking examples of theft. In Newcastle upon

Tyne in the early 1960s a considerable number of important items were recovered by the University Library which had been stolen by a visiting research scholar; other repositories in the North East were also plundered. In 1971, in the University Library of Manchester, the Donner Copy of the Shakespeare First Folio was stolen at approximately 2.30 in the morning from its 'burglar proof' exhibition case. The police believed that the whole operation took less than four minutes, well within the response time of any standard alarm system, that it was highly professional and that the security locks to the building, which had not been forced, posed no problem to any burglar of standing. The book was never recovered and since it is virtually unsaleable on the open market, the theft was almost certainly commissioned by a wealthy collector. In Cambridge in the late '70s a research student, introduced and vouched for by a Senior Member, stole oriental manuscript material of great value from various libraries in the University. Although the University Library items were recovered, it cannot be said for certain that all College material was retrieved. At the beginning of the 1980s a detailed inspection of the Map Department in the University Library revealed that a number of valuable items had disappeared since the last inspection a decade or so earlier. These were not recovered, although replacements have been secured. It underlined the importance of regular inspections of all special collection materials (see chapter 15 by McDonald). Many more instances from other institutions could be cited. In all those known to me, some element of blame attaches to library staff whose impeccable but naive standards of honesty put them very much at risk when dealing with plausible thieves (see chapter 4 by Houlgate and Chaney).

Vulnerability of stock is not confined to special collections materials: stock on open access is today even more at risk. The cost of new books and the unavoidable presence in a library on open shelves of many expensive books in regular use by readers have contributed to, some might say encouraged, significant losses. There are many other contributory factors, not least the limits of student grants, the high cost of books, the costs of photocopies, the pressures on researchers, the comparative ease of shoplifting in libraries which do not employ store detectives. Mutilation of stock, the removal of articles from periodicals, of illustrations and, at times, the whole text block from monographs is becoming an unfortunate fact of library life. In the USA, where it is deeply entrenched, a number of studies have been made and their findings published. Among the earliest, that by Hendrick and Murfin (1974)

6

establishes a pattern and practice which is all too clearly confirmed by subsequent published studies. Responses to the questionnaire which they issued to students in introductory psychology and social psychology at Kent State University suggest that necessity rather than criminal intent motivates most student mutilations and that much of it could be prevented by a security audit so as to ensure adequate surveillance, warning signs, improved and cheaper copying, reader education and the like (see chapter 15 by McDonald). It is not enough, say Hendrick and Murfin (1974) simply 'to suffer the problem of mutilation in silence' or reject it as 'an insult to the storehouse of civilization': it 'drains badly needed financial resources but also frustrates and frequently infuriates [the library's] patrons'.

Serious and disheartening as this kind of mutilation is – and it would be a mistake to attribute all such acts of mutilation to students – the American experience suggests that it is a disease which can be contained if never quite eradicated. The greater problem lies in dealing with the genuine thief, the person who is motivated by gain. Wyly (1987/88) quotes Belanger's views expressed at the Oberlin Conference (1983) that thieves 'are more likely to be students, professors, librarians, staff members, or custodians rather than professional criminals', that 'staff, who are insiders, have been held accountable for all but 25% of major library thefts'. This echoes the views of Zeidberg (1987), already quoted, and Mason (1975) who states 'Bona fide researchers, students and faculty members with impeccable credentials have been thieves, con artists posing as scholars, both dealers, librarians, archivists and even clergymen have been caught stealing... There is strong evidence that many other major thefts have involved insiders.' Wyly's (1987/88) account of 'Major cases of rare book theft' and 'Thieves and their methods' are as readable as they are instructive. The losses recently uncovered at the Chester Beatty Library, Dublin, say all that needs to be said in this context.

Not all book losses are deliberate theft: in my experience, at least, books have been removed from the library because the scholar genuinely felt they were more secure in his hands than in the library. This was stated to me by a great benefactor to the University Library in Manchester who returned all library books with interest when he retired from his chair. In Glasgow I was called to the room of a distinguished professor on his retirement to ask how to deal with the books lining his room. I thought he wanted to present them to the library: in fact, he wanted to return them. The professorial executor to a deceased professorial colleague in Manchester rejected my offer to purchase the library of his dead friend because, as he pointed out, none of the books were to be found in the library. When I explained to him why that was, he hastened to accept the money. The founder librarian of Keele University was embarrassed to find that he had purchased books from a retiring Keele professor, many of which the professor had inherited from his father, a former Manchester professor. Over 250 books belonged to Manchester University, where his father, a close friend of my predecessor there, had been chairman of the Library Committee for very many years. In a different category, I still possess a book which I borrowed from an army library over 40 years ago. When I returned from leave, they had 'posted the library' and no-one wanted to know.

It is the real theft by the professional thief which has to be our concern. For the non-professional, who would make off with the odd volume, electronic devices have proved a major deterrent although they are hardly affordable in the large library, even if selectively applied to a proportion of the stock, or acceptable in buildings which are heavily listed (McDonald covers electronic security systems in chapter 16). Boss (1984/85) has noted that 'electronic theft detection in libraries has become a growth industry with vendors selling or leasing 500 new electronic detection systems annually'. He continues: 'while of value in controlling losses, theft detection systems can instill a false sense of security because they protect only the entrances at which they are placed... A number of the libraries that suffered losses at the hands of Shinn and Freeman had electronic security systems in place and operational'. Moreover, as Zeidberg (1987) pointed out, 'James Shinn had among his burglary tools an electronic sensing device to detect tattletapes in books, which he simply removed in the stacks prior to taking the books away'. Before his arrest at Oberlin College, he had allegedly stolen stock worth approximately $500,000 from such libraries.

Helpful as these and other devices, televisual surveillance, alarms and suchlike are, the security of the library depends essentially on the quality of the staff and will reflect their attitudes towards it. This is no less true of the senior library staff than it is of the cleaners and porters. When a thirteen-volume encyclopaedia disappeared from the Reading Room in Cambridge, it had to be a member of staff and when action was taken, a sigh of relief went through immediate colleagues. The chances of finding delinquent users among the 30,000 registered to use a university library have to be high and that is generally accepted as an unavoidable risk; in a public library the risk must be present at all times. The chances of recruiting a potentially delinquent member of staff may be significantly lower but the thought has to be ever present if the library is to be protected. In my rather long period as a University Librarian, I have managed to avoid such recruitment – as far as I know – but I have inherited staff whose services eventually proved altogether too costly.

In one great rare books library, very rare books on witchcraft began to disappear from high security closed stacks and the police were brought in to investigate. Within half an hour the crime had been solved.

> 'Do you watch television?' the Keeper of Printed Books was asked.
> 'Infrequently', was the reply.
> 'Last night this book-duster appeared on a witchcraft programme; he is the Chief Witch of Britain.'

The books were recovered, the book-duster was dismissed and the Keeper, who is now in his 80s, has begun to believe that the curse wished on him by the Chief Witch is that he must live forever!

Much effort in the past decade has been put into promoting conservation awareness. A similar input is now essential if crime is to be combated and the necessary level of security awareness is to be achieved. It now features in induction courses for staff as well as for readers in Cambridge and a Security Sub-syndicate of the Library Syndicate has been established. Security has received stimulus from other quarters too. The Health and Safety at Work Act has spawned committees in every major University department. Not only access to stock is in conflict with security, so all too often is health and safety also. Increasingly the staff member now designated Safety Officer is also involved in matters of crime and security. Ideally, a Library Security Officer should also be appointed but in a reducing staffing situation there are limits to what staff may be invited to do. At the moment, the responsibility falls principally on myself, my deputy and my personal administrative assistant.

Terrorist attacks on public buildings and main line stations are uncomfortably near to staff who must frequently travel to London. This unhappy phenomenon too has injected a salutary dose of security awareness into the library staff. Crime and security are now recognised as extending beyond personal possessions and stock in a way that theft and mutilation of stock alone could never have promoted. Staff are much less reluctant to challenge people they regard as suspicious, although with the occasional exception, they often turn out to be visiting professors. Staff are also clearly aware of the potential dangers to be found in very large buildings with considerable open access provision. Staff protection is more a matter of security than of safety and in my librarianship in Manchester, there were instances of assault on staff and attempted rape which brought the police into the building and which were all too reminiscent of incidents reported from large urban American libraries. Before the Rylands merger with the University of Manchester Library, a fire bomb was thrown in the cloisters of the Rylands Building destroying a number of copies of ordinary standard works and filling the ventilation shafts with smoke which spread through the building. In the post-mortem a senior member of staff described the immediate exodus of staff from the building and was asked: 'What about the books?'. The reply was instant: 'B***** the books'. Strange things can happen in libraries. I suppose he had his priorities right.

I was asked to write this introductory chapter because, I suspect, of my long experience as a University Librarian. At the risk of becoming a bore, if I were prone to worry about my work, I would say there is much more to worry about today than when I first embarked on librarianship. For example, the massive growth in and widespread abuse of photocopy machines has led to a quite new kind of surveillance in the context of the new Copyright Act (see chapter 6 by Wall). Again, we are far advanced in online techniques – the catalogue, the issue system, the order files, the union catalogue and periodicals lists of the university's libraries, and so much more, flash up on terminals on demand. This new technology has brought its own security problems and various steps have had to be taken to secure files from hackers, and from those seeking to introduce computer viruses. The automated issue system has to live with the Data Protection Act. Librarians have generally sought to safeguard the privacy of users, not to disclose who reads what. Having said that, borrowing records and faculty cooperation brought two very senior members to book in Manchester, enabling the library to pinpoint the individuals, both 'in' for chairs, responsible for the mutilation of certain books. In the United States the police and government have sought access to records for quite different purposes. To anyone who doubts the significance of this, Kennedy's (1989) article is recommended reading. He states: 'privacy, like other legal values, is not an absolute right; it must be balanced against competing legal interests. The interests of the library record seeker must be weighed against the privacy interests of the library user'.

I am in no doubt that crime and security is a major issue in libraries and in a way in which it has not been before in the twentieth century. It has to be an all embracing theme in librarianship today and I apologise for leaving so much out and concentrating on the obvious at the expense of the detail. There is much to be said about microforms for example, and the report by Martin (1973) from the Kearney State College, Nebraska, in the context of the mutilation of periodicals, shows that microforms escape attacks of any kind. This complements the microfilming of periodicals as a preservation measure and suggests that part of the answer to mutilation may be an increased use of this medium. Again, I have omitted completely any reference to architectural considerations which have been another major concern in my librarianship (but see chapter 5 by Faulkner-Brown), and to insurance matters (see chapter 11 by Parsons). At most it only shows what a massive subject crime and security is.

In such changing times in such a volatile world, I look to my colleagues, senior and junior, cataloguers and cleaners and to professional experts of the kind in this book, to ensure our collective security. We are developing new standards of trust in what is a constant educational exercise. It presupposes new attitudes and a preparedness to ask and be asked questions, to carry out audits and formulate strategies. Wurzburger (1988) begins her paper with a quote with which I can conveniently end mine. The Public Record Office may find it particularly interesting.

'So you want to take a look at Civil War records at the National Archives? Is it worth a body frisk? They may be the next step as officials at the Archives and the Library of Congress assess whether tighter security is needed after the apparent theft of scores of historical documents recently from the two buildings in the nation's capital'.

I am sure you will find echoes of this and much else besides in the rest of this book.

REFERENCES

Boss, R. W. (1984/85), Collection security. *Library Trends*, vol. 33, Summer/Spring, p. 40.

Fuller, T. (1655), *Church history of Britain*. London: J. Williams.

Guidelines for the security of rare book, manuscript and other special collections – draft II, (1982). *College and Research Libraries News*, vol. 43, no. 3, (March), pp. 90–93.

Hendrick, C. and Murfin, M. E. (1974), Project library ripoff: a study of periodical mutilation in a university library. *College and Research Libraries*, vol. 35, no. 6, (November), pp. 402–411.

Kennedy, B. M. (1989), Confidentiality of library records: a survey of problems, policies and laws. *Law Library Journal, American Association of Law Libraries*, vol. 81, no. 4, pp. 733–804.

Martin, R. (1973), Comment and news. *Microform Review*, vol. 2, no. 1, (January), pp. 6–8.

Mason, P. P. (1975), Archival security: new solutions to an old problem. *American Archivist*, no. 38, (October) p. 485.

News (1982), *Library Journal*, vol. 107, no. 21, (December), pp. 2210–2212.

Oates, J. C. T. (1975), *Cambridge University Library: a historical sketch*. Cambridge: Cambridge University Library.

Oates, J. C. T. (1986), *Cambridge University Library: a history from the beginnings to the Copyright Act of Queen Anne*. Cambridge, C.U.P.

Oberlin Conference on theft makes history and headlines (1983), *Wilson Library Bulletin*, no. 58, (November), p. 171.

Quinsee, A. G. & McDonald, A. C. (1991), *Security in academic and research libraries*, proceedings of three seminars organised by SCONUL and the British Library, held at the British Library 1989/1990. Newcastle upon Tyne: University Library.

Wurzburger, M. (1988), Current security practices in college and university special collections. *Rare Books & Manuscripts Librarianship*, vol. 3, no. 1, (Spring), p. 43.

Wyly, M. (1987/88), Special collections security: problems, trends, and consciousness. *Library Trends*, vol. 36, no. 4, (Summer/Spring), pp. 241–256.

Zeidberg, D. S. (1987), 'We have met the enemy...': collection security in libraries. *Rare Books & Manuscripts Librarianship*, vol. 2, no. 1 (Spring), pp. 19–20.

2

An overview of crime in libraries and information services

PHILIP BEAN

The public image of libraries does not usually encapsulate the problem of crime – although library staff may know the reality is otherwise. That image is of a quiet respectable place, somewhere in which to read and study – an institution of social control perhaps. Indeed, the library's very existence presupposes reflection and contemplation far removed from the mainstream of social life in which crime flourishes. And yet as will be shown throughout this volume, libraries are places in which crimes are frequently committed. They may not experience levels which occur elsewhere, such as in schools, or on public transport, but they have not remained crime free either. Crime, once thought alien to the world of the library, has now become part of it. As the chapters throughout this volume demonstrate, the problem is a real one.

In this chapter however, I want to answer two questions of a more general nature: first, what is the level and nature of crime in England and Wales? and second, what levels and types of crime should libraries expect during periods of high crime rates nationally? Clearly libraries cannot insulate and isolate themselves from the outside world, nor should they expect to. The commodity they promote, books and reading material, are valuable and expensive, and likely targets for crime. Moreover, the framework of the institutions – what sociologists call the regime, easily lends itself to criminal activity – the library expects its assets to be taken off the premises free of charge and brought back at a later date without incurring costs. The more controls, safeguards, security levels there are the less it resembles a library. And yet the traditional library, if not actually iatrogenic as far as crime is concerned, nonetheless provides a *milieu* in which crimes can readily flourish.

But before looking at the library itself, let me look first at the crime problem generally in England and Wales and try and answer the first of those two questions. Here I want to show how the problem has grown, and show too the type of world in which the library must operate. After that I want to look at how crime in the library fits that general pattern.

CRIME IN ENGLAND AND WALES : AN ASSESSMENT

The period following the Second World War has seen an explosion in the crime rates where known or reported levels of crime have risen at about 10% per annum. Immediately after the war, or at least for the first 15 years or so, the increase was fairly gradual. But after 1960 crime rates began to take off – indeed 1960 can be said to be the watershed marking the end of the immediate post war era. Crime rates have continued to rise and remained remarkably impervious to change. From 1960 the sheer annual volume of crime is staggering, especially if compared with the inter-war or immediate post war period. During the inter-war period there were less than half a million indictable offences recorded annually: in 1990 there were well over 4 million. (Field, 1990). Table 2.1 provides data for selected offences for the year October 1989 to September 1990.

Table 2.1 is interesting in a number of respects. First it shows the high levels of reported crime – and if only to repeat the point levels which have grown steadily and relentlessly throughout. Second, it shows that the bulk of crime is against property, with theft and handling stolen property accounting for over 50% of the total. This is followed by burglary (21.8%) and criminal damage (16.2%). It is interesting that the types of offences causing the greatest public concern, violence against the person, sexual offences and robbery together account for only 5.7% – though of course even then this amounts to over 250,000 offences annually. As we shall see later, libraries are particularly prone to offences such as theft and criminal damage, whether of theft of reading materials or damage to library buildings. Hence the earlier assertion that libraries cannot expect to remain crime free during high crime periods. Finally

Offence Group	Estimated number	%	% increase over last year
Violence against person	182000	4.2	4
Sexual offences	29000	0.7	1
Robbery	35000	0.8	8
Burglary	945000	21.8	17
Theft and handling	2261000	52.3	15
Fraud and forgery	141000	3.2	6
Criminal damage	703000	16.2	14
Other offences	30000	0.8	17
Total	4326000	100.0	14

Table 2.1: Notifiable offences recorded in England and Wales (Source: Home Office Statistical Bulletin 1989/90)

Table 2.1 shows the percentage increase over the previous year – 14% over 1988 compared with an average annual increase of about 10%.

Whereas Table 2.1 provides the raw data of reported offences, Table 2.2 gives details of the rates of growth of selected forms of recorded crime given as an annual percentage growth over stated periods. Rates are measured as crimes per 100,000 of the population: the stated periods or intervals have been listed as 10 year periods – apart that is from those in the 1980s which are given as a 7 year period to 1987 (Field, 1990).

There are interesting differences in the rates for these selected offences over the 37 year period. For example sexual offences have increased rather slowly, by about 2% on average, whereas most other crimes have increased at a much larger rate: theft of vehicles by 10% and criminal damage by 14%. In contrast, other thefts and fraud have increased at a lower rate i.e. about 2% or 3%. Robbery and violence against the person

	1950–9	1960–9	1970–9	1980–7	Whole period 1950–87
Residential burglary	3	9	3	8	6
Non-residential burglary	4	8	2	4	5
Theft from person	2	7	12	3	6
Shop theft	5	9	8	2	6
Theft of vehicle	16	5	8	3	10
Theft from vehicle	10	10	5	11	8
Other theft	3	6	2	2	3
Robbery	7	10	7	12	9
Violence against person	10	9	9	5	9
Sexual offences	5	2	0	2	2
Criminal damage	9	12	24	12	14
Fraud	2	6	5	2	4

Table 2.2: Rates of growth in recorded crime for England and Wales (Source: Home Office Research and Planning Unit Report 119, 1990)

are different again. They show an above average increase; this compares with non-residential burglary which shows an increase only slightly below average.

Equally interesting are the fluctuations in the rates of offences throughout the 37 year period: none of which show a steady or even pattern. Criminal damage fluctuates widely, so too does theft of a vehicle and residential burglary. Similarly, sexual offences which first showed a 5% average annual increase between 1950–9 showed no increase at all during the 1970s.

The point could be made more dramatically by examining selected crimes in specific years. For example, theft of vehicle grew by 25% in 1974 but by only 5% in 1975. Burglary from a dwelling fell by 10% in 1973 only to rise by 23% a year later. Whether these variations reflect genuine differences or are created by the way crime is recorded still remains a mystery.

Clearly the data does not lend itself to simple or straightforward pronouncements. Moreover, these tables give details only of recorded crime: that is, crime known to the police. They tell us nothing of the full extent of crime. To know that we need to know the amount of hidden or of the dark figure of crime; that is, of crimes committed but not reported. This could be large, and indeed some criminologists suggest it could increase the level of recorded crime by a factor of ten. One can see why this could be so, to give but a few examples. Witnesses may not want to get involved with the police, or they may not regard the offence as sufficiently serious to report it, or they may even believe the police would not take matters seriously were it to be reported. Or there may not be a victim at all in the sense in which we usually speak of victims. Some crimes are victimless – defined as involving the willing exchange of prohibited goods and services: for example, selling heroin where buyer and seller agree to the sale. Or if there was a victim, the victim was unaware a crime had been committed; for example, theft of a small amount of money may go unnoticed. Or the victim may not want to discuss the crime with anyone, least of all the police, or may not report the offence because the victim did not want the offender prosecuted. These, and other examples show how the extent of hidden crime can be high.

Yet criminologists have wanted to be precise about crime figures. They have wanted to measure the full extent of crime which includes that of hidden crime rather than leave it to guesswork, however inspired those guesses might be. They have wanted precision, not just for its own sake, but because reported crimes may not reflect or fairly represent the extent of crime committed. Reported crimes may be an unrepresentative sample: they may be the least serious, or the most visible or contain some other element which sets them apart.

Without going into the various methods used, the most common form of research into the dark figures is what is called the self report study i.e. crimes committed are recorded on a questionnaire given to a sample of the population which are then checked against those reported to the police. The best and most comprehensive study of this type was the British Crime Survey where a representative group of adults in England and Wales were sampled (Hough, and Mayhew, 1983). Results show a considerably greater number of crimes committed than was reported, except for theft of a motor vehicle. There were twice as many burglaries, five times as many woundings, twelve times as many thefts, fifteen times as much vandalism, and five times as many sexual offences. Taken together the British Crime Survey found that overall, there were four times as many crimes committed than were reported. (The low dark figure for theft of motor vehicles is almost certainly due to insurance requirements whereby victims cannot claim unless the theft has been reported.)

One can see that a large number of crimes in libraries could, and probably do fall into this dark figure – though I know of no research which has tried to look closely at libraries in this way. If there is a high dark figure then it may have something to do with library policy which does not encourage library staff to report offences to the police. In the USA things are different. For example in a study of libraries in selected American cities nearly half (45%) called the police in any given year. In 6% of the libraries this happened more than once (Lincoln, 1984). There is of course a price to pay for police involvement. Lincoln concludes, 'on the one hand it reassures staff and patrons that they are protected when necessary. But it also indicates that danger may be present and the library may not be a safe place'. Clearly reporting offences to the police has implications far beyond the offence itself.

The data presented in Tables 2.1 and 2.2 is for the national figures. It tells us nothing of the variations between areas in England and Wales or within areas themselves. For recorded offences – and I stress again these are for recorded, not anything else – a closer examination of the data would show the following. First, that as a general rule cities have a proportionally larger amount of reported crime than do rural settings, and second, that the seriousness of the crime will vary according to the city size. That is, the larger the city the more serious the crime within its precinct. So the largest cities will, and do have the most serious crimes and indeed the most varied. However, this is only a general rule and there are some exceptions. For example whilst on the one hand London, Birmingham, Liverpool, Glasgow and Edinburgh have the highest crime rates they do not always have the monopoly of the most serious crime. Drug crime for example is proportionally more serious on the South

Coast and in the South West of England and in Edinburgh than Birmingham, whilst the murder rate is much more evenly spread over the UK. Yet overall the general rule applies: the Metropolitan district of London has the highest crime rate, followed by Merseyside, then by Nottingham – though this may too be an artefact created by the Nottinghamshire police recording practices.

It is possible to break down the data further and look at variations within areas, or within the cities themselves. If so, then we would see some interesting differences. Certain parts of London, for example, have consistently maintained high crime rates whilst others have not. Most surveys also show differences based on the social class composition of the residents. Working class areas have higher crime rates than middle class areas, and the larger the working class area the higher the crime rate. Moreover, middle class areas surrounded by working class areas have higher crime rates than when not. But as is often the case in criminology, matters are not that simple. There are also differences within areas even when there are no obvious variations between the social composition of the residents. For example, there are differences within streets: one part of the street having high rates, another with the same type of people having rates which are much lower.

However, that aside, in general terms the location of the library will be an important factor in the crime rates, though as we have seen there may be exceptions. If we refer again to that American study we can see examples of the general trend. The typical American high crime library was located in a city of 50,000 people or over. Only 1% of high crime libraries were in towns with less than 10,000 people. Or put another way libraries reporting low episodes of crime or disruption were almost always in towns with populations under 10,000. The same patterns were true for the social class composition of the area. High crime libraries were invariably in working class districts and low crime libraries were located in middle class areas (62%), or upper middle class (16%). Only 2% of low crime libraries were in locations described as lower class (Lincoln, 1984). Yet, there are the exceptions. Whilst high crime libraries were almost always in working class districts, an appreciable number of those libraries were also in middle class areas, especially those with the very highest rates, i.e. 39% of the highest crime libraries were in middle class districts. Clearly there is something odd going on here. Perhaps libraries themselves defy the usual criminological patterns and are unique in that the service they offer, their staff and patrons, set them apart from the main trends. Or these results are specifically related to the American situation and do not apply to Britain. Whatever the reason, it is a feature which would certainly repay more careful study.

The data provided in Tables 2.1 and 2.2 give information only on the offences reported. It tells us nothing about whether the offences led to a successful prosecution, or were what we call 'cleared up'. To be 'cleared up' an offence must be detected, followed by a successful prosecution. (There are other features such as where the offender dies before being convicted, or asks for offences to be taken into consideration but they need not concern us here.) Not surprisingly we find there are enormous variations in the clear up rate of offences. The clear up rate for murder is about 92% (reflecting in part the amount of police activity and in part that murders are often followed by the suicide of the offender and in part because about one third of those are family murders committed within the family). In contrast the clear up rate for burglary is about 30%, or 25% in London (compared with about 5% in New York). In some instances the clear up rate will be 100% – receiving stolen property for example – but this again is an artefact, for the only time the offence comes to the notice of the police and is recorded as a crime is when the offender is detected. The point about clear up rates is that they may not provide us with a representative sample of offences reported. The offences cleared up may be committed by the less successful offenders, or perhaps the unlucky ones, or there could be some other attribute which sets them apart. It seems that the closer one gets to the offender the further one gets from the true nature of the crime. This point can be illustrated diagrammatically in Figure 2.1.

Bearing this in mind we can now look at the offenders themselves. Immediately certain patterns begin to emerge. First, and most importantly, gender is a key factor. Male offenders outnumber female offenders by about 4 to 1 and do so at all ages, in all parts of the UK – and as far as I know in all countries in the western world. The ratio is dropping slightly; it was about 8:1 during the inter-war years and 7:1 after the war and has been falling steadily thereafter but even so the difference remains. Secondly, age. The peak age for offenders is 15 (the peak age for girl offenders is slightly higher): this has also remained so for a number of years. In the last 30 years or so it was 14 but has been steadily rising in the last decade. The peak age group is 15–18, followed by that of 18–21, and followed again by that of 21–24. Once past the age of 30 the numbers of offenders drop dramatically – though not for a small group

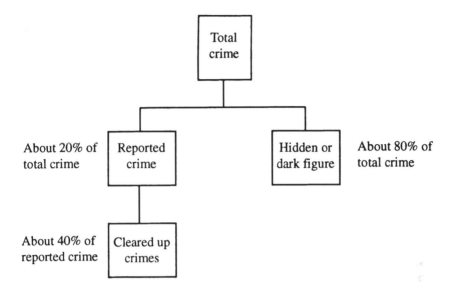

Figure 2.1: The pattern of crime

of offenders convicted for drunken driving and domestic violence. There is also a slight hiccup in the mid to late 50s offender age group which records a slight increase in offenders. The reason for this is not yet fully understood and will need more detailed research. Thirdly and finally, social class. If we use a 5 point scale based on the Registrar General's classification of social class, we find offenders from social classes 4 and 5 to be grossly over represented. This is so for almost all types of crime, especially for theft and personal violence (though not so for fraud) and for all areas of England and Wales. It is also true for all industrial societies throughout the western world. As a general rule the higher the social class the lower the crime rate.

Translating this information into types of offenders convicted before the courts then the model type of offender is likely to be young, aged 15 or so, male, from social classes 4 and 5 and convicted of a property offence – invariably theft. The amount of property will usually be small, less than £50 (small in an absolute sense, but not of course according to those from whom it was taken, especially if they are elderly). The offence itself will usually be opportunistic and spontaneous, where the opportunity presented itself to steal property and was taken. In contrast the type of person least likely to appear before the court will be an elderly woman from Social Classes I and II. Indeed so clear and obvious are those social characteristics of offenders that it can be confirmed any day and any time by a visit to any court throughout Britain. There one can see an endless procession of young male working class offenders involved in property offences – described incidentally by one criminologist as 'police property' – known to the police and recognised as such by police and offenders alike (Reiner, 1990).

In sketching the broad sweep of the argument concerning the extent and nature of crime I have wanted to show the milieu in which the modern library operates. In highlighting the nature and extent of crime, generally I am suggesting that much library crime remains hidden; library staff have not traditionally reported offences committed within the library to the police. I suggest too that the location of the libraries, and the types of clientele (or patron), have helped buttress them against the excesses of crimes committed elsewhere, or outside the building. That is, libraries are usually set in residential areas and the clientele are more likely to be middle class, older and less crime prone. This therefore would seem to be the picture: the crime data shows that for almost every crime the higher the proportion of patrons over the age of 55 the lower the rate of crime – and librarians have a large share of this type of patron (Lincoln, 1984).

They do of course have an increasing share of the others too. Yet as we keep saying, libraries cannot and have not remained separate from the world, and whilst they may take rather fewer of the typical offenders, they attract other clients who place the library and library staff at high levels of risk. These are the so called 'bag people', the vagrants, ex-mental hospital patients etc. It seems that what libraries gain in one direction they lose in another.

I want now to look at the second part of the argument and deal with crimes specific to the library itself. In doing so I wish to touch only briefly on the more detailed question of crime reduction and crime control for again these are dealt with in more detail throughout this volume.

CRIME WITHIN LIBRARIES

There has been no history of criminological research in Britain concerned with library crime, and little else in other parts of the world too for that matter. The main evidence, such as there is, remains anecdotal, though not to be dismissed out of hand because of that. Recently library crime seems to have received more attention: a trend I would regard as both welcoming and saddening: welcoming because it covers a neglected area well overdue for consideration, and saddening because it reflects a problem which most people hoped was not there. If, it has been said, 'libraries have evolved from temples for the learned elite to human service facilities' we nonetheless have wanted to believe those human service facilities have not strayed too far from their original function. That they have, has not always been accepted or recognised, nor has it been easy to adjust to the implications surrounding that.

Perhaps the first and most important area in which to concentrate is crime on the staff. Again there are no available or official figures which provide information on crimes against staff but much anecdotal evidence to suggest it is all too common. Indeed given the national trends described earlier it would be surprising if the staff escaped scot-free when social workers, sales assistants etc. are the victim of offences. Most library staff will doubtless recount incidents where they were victims or witnesses to crimes, some involving levels of personal violence, which were sometimes unprovoked and quite unexpected. More common in the UK are the frequent incidents of personal abuse which, though they fall short of assault or violence, are distressing and disturbing nonetheless. All the more so when one realises library staff may have had little training in how to cope with such abuse – nor did most begin their library careers with the expectation that something like this would ever happen to them. The saddening point however remains: any public place can now provide an opportunity for this type of incident, and libraries are not exempt.

Fortunately as yet the extent of crime committed on staff remains fairly small – though it must be emphasised the data on this is very patchy. In perhaps the only study on staff as victims of crime in UK libraries, Lincoln and Lincoln (1987) note that the majority of their respondents (59%) said they had not been the victim of a personal crime – nor indeed victims of crime against property while working in the library. However, about 25% had been the victim of a crime whilst working in the library, 11% mentioned being the victim of two crimes and 6% reported being the victim of three or more. Lincoln and Lincoln's study show men were more likely to be the victims than women – 44% male compared with 35% female – but women were more likely to be victimised more than once. These results, when compared with the USA, show the numbers of victims to be slightly lower in USA than England and Wales: only 21% said they had been the victims of crime while working in the library in America. (In Canada, they were about the same as in the USA.) There were similarities however: in the USA men were more likely to be victims than women, and again where they were victims more than once the victims were likely to be women (Lincoln and Lincoln, 1987).

It is difficult to know how to explain the discrepancy in the differences between the figures for the numbers of victims in England and Wales compared with the USA : evidence from other criminological studies comparing USA and Britain would suggest the USA would be much higher. Yet for library crimes it seems not so. Moreover in Britain library staff were more likely to call the police when they were victims than their American counterparts, perhaps suggesting they viewed the incident more seriously. Unfortunately, Lincoln and Lincoln give no details of the incidents themselves so direct comparisons are not strictly possible. These too would seem to be an area which warrants closer examination.

Incidents against staff do not of course end there. They leave a residue of fear, distrust and suspicion. They help reduce morale and lower the overall efficiency of the library. Lincoln's study of American library staff shows how staff changed their behaviour once they had been victims of crime: some began carrying protective devices, such as handguns, whistles, flashlights, clubs etc. (men and women alike) (Lincoln, 1984). Their fear was quickly communicated to colleagues so that others also began carrying protective devices and assumed the same suspicious manner. This amplification process continued. Staff began to be reluctant to work late, especially in winter evenings (more so among women library staff than men) and to insist that someone be available to pick them up at the end of the shift. Fear of crime quickly and easily became generalised extending far beyond the boundaries of the library itself. An attack on a staff member in a library seems to lead to fear of attacks outside the library. Once established these fears are not easily dispelled. The management are then required to meet these fears. This means extra staff are needed, in some cases double-staffing has to be introduced in order to make the staff feel safe.

Other problems soon develop. 'Not surprisingly,' says Lincoln, 'the problem of burnout, once restricted to social workers, teachers, and other service professionals, now is thought to affect public librarians as well' (Lincoln, 1984). The causes seem clear. As well as the more dramatic problems of violence against staff the less dramatic ones begin to take effect. In an interesting study Bold (1982) describes some of the sources of burnout in staff in American libraries:

> 'Readers of best sellers are especially apt to confront librarians with complaints regarding the long wait for popular items, and accusations of favouritism are common. Disputes with patrons over fines, unreturned and damaged material and the like also take their toll, even though the librarian is expected to remain outwardly calm. Los Angeles library workers have one of the highest sick-time rates when compared with other municipal workers.'

One recurring complaint amongst library staff is that they are not trained to deal with the type of patrons frequenting public libraries nowadays. One can see the point of course. Yet it is easy to over estimate the value of training and easy to see training programmes as the solution to a set of problems about which there is no solution. The truth is that libraries no longer attract the quietly studious patrons: they are home for the vagrants, the mentally ill, including those discharged from hospital under the recent Government package to reduce hospital expenditure (Bean, 1987; Bean and Mounser, 1991). They attract the lonely and the sometimes dangerous. One librarian said 'we are being asked to deal with problems that have nothing to do with our training. How far is our compassion supposed to go. How much damage can we do without training' (quoted in Lincoln, 1984).

It is difficult to believe training programmes could cope with these new style patrons for in truth no one is an expert in dealing with such people. The most that can be expected is that staff treat them with civility and receive respect and civility in return; and when they do not they call for aid. It is not so much training programmes that are needed, though they may help, but back up facilities to assist library staff who require instant assistance.

What is also becoming clear is that it is not simply the vagrants, the discharged mental patients, etc. who are troublesome but others who are more typically seen as traditional library clientele. Stories abound of the 'strange things' going on in libraries – the library being described by one American commentator as an 'erotic oasis' (Delph, 1980). Lurid accounts exist: an American librarian quoted by Delph (1980) complains that 'one of the populations that frequent the public library for unconventional goals is that of the homosexual public eroticist, i.e. males who engage in sex in public places such as toilets, streets, theatres, libraries and other such locations'. I suppose most library staff could relate stories of such strange goings on which if not exactly as extreme as this and not warranting the description of the library as the 'erotic oasis', at least provide evidence that the library is not the place it was once thought to be. Yet it is all too easy to fall into the trap of believing we are faced with entirely new phenomena. Perhaps libraries have always attracted a small number of the strange, the odd, and the disordered – if so we are not witnessing anything new though we may be seeing them in larger numbers. If so, that is the essential difference.

The whole issue of library security is at stake here – though as I said earlier I wish only to touch on this briefly. The point is well put by Paris (1984) when she says 'the public library administrator often faces a paradox: which should have priority, the open-door service ethic or enforcement of security and safety measures'. Unlike the university library, public libraries are not able to subject their patrons to security checks through the use of library membership cards. The public library is what it says: a library in a public place. This free right of access poses serious strain on the system: as Paris (1984) says, 'when the door of the urban library is wide open there will always be disruptive and problem patrons'. But why only urban I wonder? Doesn't the rural library have such patrons too? I suspect it does if the truth be known.

What can be the solution? One method, and there are many, is for libraries to resort increasingly to technology to solve the problems, as well, of course, as using more mundane measures such as a blacklist banning all known troublemakers. Such technology could be all embracing, directed towards internal and external security: the former to protect the staff, books, patrons; the latter to deal with the problems outside – graffiti and other forms of criminal damage which are no less important. Security involves protecting the whole environment not just the inside. Another method is to reinforce technology with greater levels of manpower, patrolling the reading rooms, checking the patrons before they come in – looking in their bags, asking about their reason for being in the library, covering the checkouts – and, just as important, patrolling outside the library. Again we are not talking of new ways of doing things, or of departing from a traditional way of life: there have always been technologies in libraries to control deviant behaviour, and there have always been security staff to enforce them. The difference is simply the extent and range. I think it likely, whether libraries want to or not, that the methods chosen will have to be in the form of greater surveillance i.e. using more and more technological devices supplemented by security staff aimed at controlling patrons yet maintaining the image of the library as a place for study and reflection.

Then there are the books themselves: the traditional *raison d'etre* of the library. There are two main forms of crime to discuss here: the theft of books and their mutilation. They are not separate. The type of checkout introduced will determine the type of crime committed. A sophisticated checkout system will produce less theft, though likely to increase the levels of book mutilation, and a less sophisticated checkout produce more theft and less damage. The choice is not an enviable one but has to be made nonetheless.

Lending books offers the greatest opportunity for theft. I suspect it takes two main forms. There is the systematic, carefully considered pre-planned type of theft, the other less preplanned where borrowers move house or no longer want to be library members; they have books on loan, may even promise to return them yet somehow never do. The latter is more numerous and includes large numbers of otherwise respectable or so called middle class citizens but no less blameworthy for that. (One is amazed how many people appear to have stolen books in this way, mostly when they were students but sometimes in later life.)

The American Library Crime Research Project (Lincoln, 1984) distinguished four kinds of theft:

a) theft of books
b) theft of reference material
c) theft of equipment
d) a category which they called other theft, including theft of magazines, or personal property of other readers or members of staff

Let us look briefly at these in turn. In the first, theft of books, research shows the numbers of books stolen from libraries to be enormous. One American study found there were 250,000 books stolen from 100 libraries per annum, which works out on average at about 250 books per library per year. (Lincoln, and Lincoln, 1987). In Britain a study by Souter (1976) showed the average annual rate of loss in British academic libraries to be 1.5% of the total collection. There were differences between institutions. Edinburgh University had a loss of less than 1% per year whereas Liverpool Polytechnic had losses about 5% per year and, for example:

> At University College Swansea library in 1970 it was found 773 items were newly missing – against 563 in 1969. At Strathclyde University library the figure for 1970–1 was 822 as against 696 for 1969–70 while Stirling University library's figure for 1970–1 was 985 more than double the 405 of the previous year.

Lincoln (1984) reports that the book losses of American universities may be higher than those in the UK. Quoting the Carnegie Report on Fair Practices in Higher Education, Lincoln says 'the undergraduate libraries at the University of California at Berkeley, Northwestern and the University of Washington reported annual loss rates of 2–5%. Tufts University found that almost 8% of the books in the library disappear after just one year on the shelves... and an inventory at the University of Maryland found losses of more than 30,000 volumes. For a three year period the University of California at Berkeley reported losses of 12% of the 150,000 volume undergraduate collection'. Apparently the Carnegie Report noted that it would cost about $63.7 million each year if 1% of library collections were stolen – presumably university collections.

These figures give some idea of the extent of the problem – and of course are for university libraries. Yet one should be careful at taking these figures at face value. It seems that librarians are not always clear about exact losses. According to the American study quoted above Washington University library reduced the losses over 3 years by about 40% by repeated searches of the shelves (Lincoln, 1984). It should be noted too that the data is for university libraries, traditionally catering for the less criminal groups (i.e. mainly middle class with a high proportion of women). Moreover, Lincoln also reports variations in thefts of books according to subject areas. Certain books are singled out: social science books and medical periodicals being the main target areas with those on English literature being slightly less preferred.

The second type of theft is theft of reference material. Included here is a special problem of the theft of rare books. This type of crime is more systematic in the sense it is probably more carefully planned involving selected books targeted by professional collectors. Unfortunately this type of crime is likely to increase as the value of those books continues to rise. I suspect there will soon be a time when rare books are no longer available for public use, or are placed under sophisticated forms of surveillance. Sadly, this seems an inevitable consequence of current trends. But other forms of reference material are stolen too: atlases, guide books etc., the loss of which may cause inconvenience, as well as being expensive to reproduce.

Theft of equipment, the third category, is of less significance overall though not likely to remain so as libraries move to more sophisticated monitoring and checkout devices as well as more sophisticated equipment for readers. Lincoln and Lincoln (1987) report that over 15% of British libraries had lost equipment at least once in the last year, and 3% lost it more than three times – those libraries losing the most equipment also experienced the highest levels of other crimes, including assaults on staff. Loss of equipment seems a key indicator of a high crime library.

The fourth category – other theft – is a difficult one to define and identify: it includes theft from staff, theft from patrons and various forms of criminal damage directed to the library premises. Little is known about these types of crimes except the extent is likely to vary according to the levels of other crime in the neighbourhood – including criminal damage to the library premises. It seems a good deal of this other theft, including theft from staff, goes unreported.

This massive catalogue of theft, with its attendant cost and inconvenience caused to readers is a problem all libraries including university libraries must face. As one commentator sagely suggested 'Books should be protected from the public': he could also have said library users should carry a Government health warning. Add to this the amount of book mutilation – whether of key pages torn out of books or papers, or the less serious but irritating form of mutilation which involves underlining or making comments in the margin of reading materials – and we can begin to see how dangerous library users have become. (The new Highlighter marker pens are used to devastating effect here.)

Nor can we comfort ourselves with the self righteous view that 'crime does not pay' or something to that effect. Sadly, it seems book mutilators profit from their activities. A study by Weiss on those who tore out the material found that they did better academically than their colleagues – at least that was their perception of themselves. Not only were they able to keep the material for themselves but by removing it they prevented other students having equal access to it (Weiss, 1981; see also Lincoln, 1984). Mutilators justified their actions by pressure of work and saw themselves in competition with colleagues and other readers. Rarely however were they reported. Other students seldom took action – even when they saw the books being mutilated and the reading material they wanted being torn out. The reasons given for such inactivity were identical to those given by people who fail to report other offences: 'I didn't have time'; 'it was none of my business'; or 'someone else will take care of it' (Lincoln, 1984).

Offenders involved in the less serious type of mutilation – for example, underlining, or writing in the margin – are probably acting from different motives. These less serious mutilators do not see themselves in competition with other students, they make assumptions that the books belong to them: that this library is part of their private collection. It is a curiously self-centred view which takes no account of the wishes or needs of others. Worse than that, it is sometimes justified on the basis that the offenders are helping others by emphasising key factors of the text. Reference or text books suffer the most, and university libraries are badly hit by this form of thoughtless criminal damage. We are not talking here just about the prevention of mutilation of scarce resources, we are talking of wider matters relating to the preservation and protection of the environment.

CONCLUDING REMARKS

Clearly the extent of hidden crime in the library is as great if not greater than that in the outside world. Crimes against staff, against other readers and against the books themselves, whether of theft or mutilation show there are no limits to the forms or type of criminal actions that can be taken. Add to these the amount of verbal abuse offered to staff, which although not criminal is often threatening and intimidating, and we get some idea of the type of problem the library staff now face. I have tried to do no more than outline some of the more obvious examples, rarely touching on the possible solutions for they will be covered throughout this volume. As I wish to emphasise, what is clear is that libraries can no longer see themselves separate from the world but have to recognise their problems are shared problems – part of and related to all public service industries. We may regret this change, and try to avoid recognising it, but once recognised we may then be able to begin to put it right.

REFERENCES

Bean, P. T. (1987), *Mental disorder and legal control*. Cambridge: Cambridge University Press.

Bean, P. T. and Mounser, P. (1989), Community care and the discharge of patients from mental hospitals. *Law Medicine and Health Care*, vol. 17, no. 2, pp. 166–173.

Bold, R. (1982), Librarian burn out. *Library Journal*, (November 1), pp. 2048–2049.

Delph, E. W. (1980), Preventing public sex in library settings. *Library and Archival Security*, vol. 3, pp. 17–26.

Field, S. (1990), *Trends in crime and their interpretation: a study of recorded crime in post war England and Wales*. Home Office Research and Planning Unit Report No. 119. HMSO.

Home Office (1990), *Statistical Bulletin*, 9/90.

Hough, M. and Mayhew, P. (1983), *The British Crime Survey first report*. HMSO.

Lincoln, A. J (1984), *Crime in the library*. Bowker.

Lincoln, A. J. and Lincoln, A. Z. (1987), *Library crime and security*. Haworth Press.

Paris, J. A. (1984), Internal and external responsibilities and practices for library security, in Brand, M. (ed) *Security for libraries*. Chicago: American Library Association.

Reiner, R. (1990), *Policing 2000*. Paper presented at the official opening of the Midlands Centre for Criminology and Criminal Justice. University of Loughborough, December 1990.

Souter, G. H. (1976), Delinquent readers: a study of the problems in community libraries. *Journal of Librarianship*, vol. 8, pp. 96–110.

Weiss, D. (1981), Book theft and book mutilation in a large university library. *College and Research Libraries* , vol. 42, (July), pp. 341–347.

3

A legal perspective on crime

STEPHEN J WRIGLEY

Crime affects us all. From the extra few pence we each pay in the department store to cover 'losses' to the fear of walking our city streets at night, we live in a society where the government's quarterly-published crime statistics continue to increase. There is no reason why the library environment should be isolated from the problems which beset society as a whole. It is therefore not just helpful but essential that the library manager should be able to identify when criminal acts are taking place or are about to happen and to deal with them swiftly and effectively.

A detailed study of English criminal law is not intended. However, some knowledge of the principles which apply, of the procedures for dealing with offenders, and of some particular offences with which the library manager is likely to have to deal, is essential to have a proper understanding of how to deal effectively (and within the law) with those who perpetrate (or attempt to perpetrate) criminal acts.

Although this chapter deals with the legal perspective on crime in libraries in an English context only, it is nevertheless true to assert that English law is a model for legal systems in other parts of the world, and many of the principles identified apply in other countries too.

It will be useful for the librarian to understand something of the essential requirements for particular offences, what action can be taken to prevent or remedy criminal acts, and what the consequences will be for the librarian for embarking upon a particular course of action. It would be impractical to try and give a legal answer to particular circumstances because of the infinite variation of such circumstances. The object therefore of the chapter is to help the librarian to understand what the law is, how it might apply to particular circumstances, and what the implications will be if criminal proceedings are to follow.

The chapter considers the sources of the criminal law, what constitutes a crime and how different crimes may be classified, and the essential elements which must be present for an act to be a crime. The relationship between civil and criminal responsibility is addressed in brief. Also considered are the general methods by which crimes are investigated and prosecuted, and an outline of general court procedures and the standard and burden of proof is given.

Although much of the content of this chapter is factual, much is also comment based on the author's own interpretation of the law which he accepts may not necessarily agree with the interpretation of others. The author also comments on many of the practical aspects considered in reliance upon many years experience as a practising solicitor.

THE SOURCES OF THE CRIMINAL LAW

The criminal law derives principally from:

a) the common law
b) statute
c) delegated legislation

The vast majority of the criminal law derives from statute, or from Statutory Instruments or bye-laws made under powers conferred by Parliament. Murder, however, although not a matter to be routinely expected by the library manager, remains undefined by statute, even though the penalty is prescribed by statute.

Where there is no statute altering the common law, by express terms or by implication, the common law remains in force. Many offences have been entirely codified, such as in the Theft Act 1968, and entirely new offences are often created, e.g. the Road Traffic Acts.

THE ANATOMY OF A CRIME

Definition of a crime

There have been numerous attempts by many distinguished lawyers and writers to define a 'crime'. The House of Lords, in a reported decision from 1957, adopted as a proper definition that contained in *Halsbury's Laws of England*:

> 'A crime is an unlawful act or default which is an offence against the public and renders the person guilty of the act liable to legal punishment.'

For the library manager, technical considerations are unlikely to be appropriate – the decision on what, if any, action to be taken in relation to a particular act or set of circumstances will usually need to be made swiftly A reasonable, practical, common-sense approach is often the best guide in such circumstances.

Elements of a crime

With the exception of a body of offences created by statute, or by statutory instrument, the law requires there to be two essential elements:

a) the physical act itself (the *actus reus*)
b) the mental element, or dishonest intention (the *mens rea*)

Thus, apart from the exceptions mentioned, the law as it has evolved over many centuries requires a criminal intent in the mind of the perpetrator. A physical act, capable in all other respects of being a crime, will not necessarily impart criminal liability. Perhaps one of the most common examples to illustrate this principle comes, not from the common law, but from the Theft Act 1968 (s. 1(1)):

'A person is guilty of theft if he *dishonestly* appropriates property belonging to another *with the intention of permanently depriving the other of it*; and *thief* and *steal* shall be construed accordingly.'

The above example is considered in more detail in the section below dealing with particular offences, but the general principle is clearly illustrated – the perpetrator must not only, for example, remove the book from the library, but must do so *dishonestly* and must also intend to *permanently deprive* the library of it. It is the concept of *dishonesty* that is most difficult to assess, both for the aggrieved and for the courts.

The inadvertent removal of property from a library by a forgetful user cannot be a crime, for in those circumstances there is genuinely no mental element. But what of the case where the university student removes a book from the university library without observing the proper formalities, but when approached outside the building claims that he is still on the campus and therefore has not actually removed the book? The difficulty for the library staff will always be to decide which is the genuine case, and which case is doubtful and ought to be the subject of further investigation. No advice can usefully be offered, and the library manager should have regard to his knowledge of the particular crime under suspicion, the elements necessary to fulfil the crime, and the burden and standard of proof required to convict.

The mental element will by definition always be the more difficult to assess, but sometimes the physical act is perhaps not as clear as might at first sight appear. An illustration of the difficulty is given in the decision in the case of *R. v. Easom* (1971) which turned on facts which might well occur within a library. In this case, the accused picked up and rifled through the contents of a handbag belonging to another. He had every intention of removing anything of value that took his fancy. In fact, nothing was taken and so he replaced the handbag, the contents intact if a little disturbed. The court held that his actions in taking but replacing intact the handbag was a conditional appropriation, which did not amount to theft under the definition provided under Theft Act 1968, s. l(1), as there was no intention to permanently deprive.

Exceptions

The general presumption that the mental element, or dishonest intent (the *mens rea*) must be present is usually only displaced by a strict liability imposed under statute, creating what is known to lawyers as an 'absolute' offence. Many obvious examples are contained in, for example, the Road Traffic Acts, which imposes many strict liabilities in relation to the use of motor vehicles: not to use without insurance; not to drive without a licence, etc. In these type of offences, a dishonest or criminal intent need not be shown, and the driver will be liable even if he, for example, honestly believed that he was insured/licensed to drive.

Often where statute excludes the necessity for the element of *mens rea*, it will also provide for a statutory defence. By way of example, it is a defence to a charge of being drunk in charge of a motor vehicle if, at the time of the alleged offence, the accused can prove that the circumstances were such that there was no likelihood of his driving the vehicle whilst still over the limit. This defence is prescribed by Road Traffic Act 1988, s. 5(2).

Parties to a crime

There will usually, but not always, be a victim. Clearly the perpetrator who commits the physical act (the *actus reus*) and does so intentionally or dishonestly (the *mens rea*) if applicable, is liable as principal. The net of criminal responsibility can spread wider:

> 'A person who aids, abets, counsels or procures the commission of an offence by another person may be tried as if he had committed the main offence.'
> Magistrates' Courts Act 1952, s. 35.

> 'A person who, knowing or believing another to have committed an offence, does any act with intent to impede the offenders apprehension, is guilty of an offence.'
> Criminal Law Act 1967, s. 4.

> 'If, with intent to commit an offence to which this section applies, a person does an act which is more than merely preparatory to the commission of the offence, he is guilty of attempting to commit the offence.'
> Criminal Attempts Act 1981, s. 1(1).

RELATIONSHIP BETWEEN CRIMINAL AND CIVIL LAW

We have looked at a definition of a crime, and one which has received judicial approval. Any definition of a crime has links with the general concept of morality, and suggests that a breach of the criminal law is a breach of duty imposed by law for the benefit of the community at large.

The civil law, too wide a subject to consider in any detail here, exists to regulate relationships not between individuals and the community at large, but between individuals and each other.

The criminal law will often have its parallel in the civil law – obvious examples are:

a) theft – a person guilty of theft is punished by the state for the anti-social act, and not necessarily to compensate the victim. The victim of a theft may, however, have a civil remedy for the wrongful removal and retention of goods rightfully his. He may sue the wrongdoer for the return of those goods and/or for damages – his remedy lies in the civil tort of conversion. This remains so even though recent years have seen an increasing emphasis within the criminal law system on recognising the victim of a crime and attempting, if only in an arbitrary way, to compensate him in some way

b) assault – in the criminal law, various different levels of assault are prescribed by statute – the civil equivalent is an action for damages for assault. Again, the courts generally have power, in addition to any penalty imposed on the wrongdoer, to award compensation to be paid by the wrongdoer to his victim. There is, in addition, the right to apply to the state for compensation through the Criminal Injuries Compensation Board

These differences need to be appreciated by the library manager. Take, for example, the case of the library assistant assaulted by a visitor to the library. The decision to bring criminal charges, and when brought to continue to prosecute, is generally taken elsewhere and not by the library manager, as will be seen later. If criminal charges are not brought, or are discontinued, it is useful to be aware that the victim may still wish to consider the options outlined above, namely of a civil action for damages, or an application to the Criminal Injuries Compensation Board. In considering the parties to a crime, we have noted that criminal responsibility is not limited to the perpetrator of the act. It is however not generally possible to incur criminal liability through another's acts. There are, of course, exceptions to the general rule. In civil law it could be said to be easier to incur liability, not least as the standard of proof required by the courts is not as great.

The standard of proof in criminal proceedings is *beyond reasonable doubt,* and the burden of proof rests squarely with the prosecution to discharge that burden. In civil law, the standard is generally *the balance of probabilities*, although the burden of discharging the same rests usually with the person bringing the proceedings – again there are exceptions to the general rule.

It is observed that there is often a considerable overlap between the two strands, and indeed, in an effort to prevent crime, the civil law may be invoked in a most obvious way. Membership of a library imposes a contractual relationship between the two parties, and in forming that relationship it is perfectly possible to introduce specific terms upon the library user, imposing, for example, conditions for the borrowing and return of books, and defining unacceptable forms of conduct both in relation to the library's property, and in relation to the use of the premises.

It is vital to note that such terms may not, as a general principle of contract law, be introduced subsequent to the formation of the contract without the agreement of both parties, and it would be wise to refer to, or preferably to recite in full, the terms of membership in writing on the membership application. Depending on the behaviour complained of, breach of such terms may well constitute a criminal offence, but might also entitle the library authority to impose its own, quite separate, sanctions on the wrongdoer, including disqualification from membership.

CLASSIFICATION OF CRIMINAL OFFENCES

Classification may be in one of several different ways. A convenient classification, used later in this chapter where particular offences are considered, is:

a) offences against the person
b) offences against property
c) offences against public order

The different classification now considered places offences in three categories according to the manner in which the law prescribes those offences to be dealt with. As a general rule, the further down the list of classifications given, the more serious the offence is considered, and because of the greater powers of punishment of the Crown Court the greater the penalty that may be imposed. The classifications are;

a) summary offences
b) offences triable either way
c) indictable offences

These classifications refer to the manner, and in particular the venue, for the proceedings. A brief explanation of the criminal courts structure is found below in the section dealing with procedural aspects.

Summary offences

These offences may only be tried by a Magistrates Court, and nearly always carry penalties defined by statute. The penalties prescribed are often financial, but may allow for a range of penalties, including imprisonment. The maximum penalty that may generally be imposed by the Magistrates, subject to the statutory penalties for particular offences under particular statutes, is six months imprisonment and/or a fine of £2,000.

Criminal damage of minor value (e.g. defacement of books or of other library property), and minor assault and disturbances are the more common example of summary offences.

Offences triable either way

Offences triable either way may be tried either by a Magistrates Court, or by the Crown Court. The prosecution may endeavour to persuade the Magistrates to refer the offence to the Crown Court, for example on the grounds of the particular seriousness of the offence charged. The accused generally retains the right to elect to be dealt with by judge and jury in the Crown Court. The maximum penalty for such an offence tried in the Magistrates Court is the same as for a summary offence – the Crown Court generally has greater powers of punishment, and in most cases the maximum penalty for any particular offence is prescribed by the statute creating the offence. Where the Magistrates try such an offence but, after hearing the case and hearing of the accused's previous record feel their powers of punishment insufficient, they may commit the accused to the Crown Court for sentence.

Theft, burglary, assault, and more serious criminal damage charges usually come into this category.

Indictable offences

Offences triable only on indictment must be tried by the Crown Court. By their very nature they are the more serious offences – murder, manslaughter, rape etc. – but generally the earlier stages of the procedure take the accused through the Magistrates Court in order for the evidence to be investigated and for the accused to be committed to the Crown Court for trial – the procedural aspects are considered later.

In addition to those examples given in the previous paragraph, arson and more serious assault charges fall into this category.

APPREHENSION, INVESTIGATION AND PROSECUTION OF OFFENCES

Offenders are usually apprehended and subsequently investigated by the police, but the prosecution of all offences on behalf of the state is now, since 1985, the function of the Crown Prosecution Service (CPS) (Prosecution of Offences Act 1985). This service was created as the result of increasing pressure to separate the functions of investigator and prosecutor, both of which had previously been carried out by the County or Metropolitan Councils through the police and the prosecuting solicitors department over which they exercised administrative control. The CPS is funded by central government and comprises both qualified lawyers and administrative staff. The head of the CPS is the Director of Public Prosecutions.

The function of the CPS is to consider and review evidence collated by the police as part of their investigative function, and to decide on whether sufficient evidence is available to present a prima facie case to the court. Although in most cases, the criminal proceedings will have been initiated by the police before the CPS has had the opportunity to consider the evidence, the existence of an independent body to exercise this function is considered advantageous to the just and efficient dispensation of justice. Although it is not the duty of the CPS to adjudicate on the offences in question, an independent and dispassionate view of the evidence available often results in the offence charged being altered to more particularly suit the circumstances of the case, or occasionally in proceedings being discontinued where, for example, the element of *mens rea* discussed above is absent from the evidence, or where the evidence is otherwise clearly unsatisfactory.

In theory, any member of the public may present evidence to the CPS to support the instigation of criminal legal proceedings, but in practice the investigation of offences, and the collation of evidence, is carried out by the police. Therefore, the entire criminal process of investigation, prosecution and trial takes place at the expense of the public purse, an important and significant factor considering the administrative and legal costs involved.

This is not to say that prosecutions may only be brought in this way. There are exceptions, but generally a member of the public, an organisation or a statutory authority may also investigate, institute and prosecute offences, and indeed in many cases particular authorities are charged with that responsibility, i.e. HM Factories Inspectorate under the Factories Acts.

The clear disadvantages of an individual or other bringing a prosecution have to be both lack of experience, and legal costs. The costs of bringing even a summary offence to trial are high, and in the event of an unsuccessful prosecution the prosecutor must be prepared to risk an order for payment of the successful accused's legal costs.

For the library manager, the choice will almost exclusively be to involve the police at the earliest stage and to allow matters to proceed in the way outlined above. Such a course has the particular advantages of protecting the library authority from legal costs whilst at the same time allowing the library authority to appear, as they in fact are, unconnected with and independent from the prosecution of the offence.

Having concluded that the investigation and prosecution process is best left with the appropriate authorities, at what point should the library manager commit those processes to the authorities, which in practice will mean to call the police? Again, the library manager will need to draw upon his own knowledge of the factors considered in this chapter with particular reference to the crime suspected.

Although the due process of investigation and prosecution will not normally directly involve the library manager, the ability to influence these decisions will in practice be present. The question of whether any influence should be brought will depend on the circumstances of each case, including the nature of the alleged offence, and will and should also depend on the policy of the particular library in each case. Are drunks politely tolerated, vandals requested not to use the facilities again, or is the policy always to seek prosecution if only for its deterrent effect? These are questions that cannot be answered here, as each authority will wish to formulate its own policy for dealing with crime. It is important that a policy does exist, is known to exist, is followed, but is sufficiently flexible to allow for all events.

PROSECUTION OF OFFENDERS: AN OUTLINE OF PROCEDURE

We have considered the classification of crimes into:

a) summary offences
b) offences triable either way
c) indictable offences

We will now look at how these offences are actually brought before the courts, and what part, if any, the library staff involved will be asked to play. The procedure differs in the different classifications under consideration, and areas of the legal process are constantly under review. The intention is therefore to provide a broad overview of how a case will proceed from apprehension and arrest to trial. It is assumed that the alleged offence is reported by the library manager to the police at the earliest opportunity, all facts concerning the alleged offence having been taken into account before deciding on this course of action.

Apprehension/arrest

The police are subject to certain, fairly rigid, statutory requirements when questioning an individual even before a formal arrest. Those requirements are set out in detail in the Police and Criminal Evidence Act 1984, and in the Codes of Practice made thereunder. Broadly speaking, an individual generally has the right to consult a solicitor before proceeding with an interview, and must be told in clear terms of that right. There are restrictions upon how long an individual may be held in custody before he must be charged, released or brought before a Magistrates Court to authorise further detention. All steps in the police procedures must be noted in writing by an officer unconnected with the investigation. It is now common practice to tape-record interviews, the tape being available to an accused or his legal representative, and of course to the court.

Having made the initial complaint, and probably having been asked to support the complaint by making a formal statement to the police, the library manager is unlikely to be involved in any of the stages referred to. From this point onwards, the police have the responsibility to investigate the allegation and to collect evidence in support, generally in the form of written statements from witnesses.

Having completed their investigations, the police will then either refer their file of evidence to the CPS for a decision as to whether to prosecute, or, more commonly, will charge the accused with an offence at that stage. The accused will then normally be granted bail pending the initial hearing of the case. From this point onwards, the procedures differ depending on the category into which the offence falls. An outline of those procedures is likely to be of help to the library manager whose attendance at court may eventually be required to give oral evidence of the matters of which he has knowledge and which presumably have formed the basis of the initial complaint.

A basic understanding of the criminal courts is useful.

Magistrates Courts

These are the lowest tier in the criminal court system, and sit in most towns and cities, and in centres which cover rural areas. The lay magistrates are persons appointed by the Lord Chancellor who in turn takes advice from local committees as to the suitability of individuals for the position. The court is generally composed of three lay Magistrates, but two, or occasionally only one, may hear different types of proceedings. In a trial, their function is to decide issues of fact. They are advised on procedure and questions of law by a legally qualified clerk.

In larger towns, stipendiary magistrates may sit. They are appointed to the bench by the Queen on the recommendation of the Lord Chancellor, and must be solicitors or barristers of at least seven years standing. They normally sit alone.

Magistrates Courts deal with the vast majority of criminal offences, whether summary only or either way offences (see above). In the event of a guilty plea, the attendance of witnesses for the prosecution is normally unneccessary, and the case proceeds by way of an outline of the facts and circumstances by the prosecution lawyer, followed by an address in mitigation by the defence lawyer or, if unrepresented, the accused himself. A plea of not guilty will involve the attendance at court of those prosecution witnesses, e.g. the library staff, whose evidence the defence may wish to test by cross-examination.

Crown Courts

The Crown Courts sit in the larger towns or cities, and cover much larger geographical areas than Magistrates Courts. They deal with the more serious criminal offences, and have considerably wider powers of punishment. Trials in the Crown Court are by Judge and Jury, the function of the latter being to decide issues of fact.

In respect of either way offences, an accused does of course have the right to choose to have his case heard by either the Magistrates Court, or by a Judge and Jury at the Crown Court. This right is occasionally limited, for example in the case of the Criminal Damage Act 1971 certain offences involving less than £2000 in value are triable only summarily.

Trial by Judge and Jury at the Crown Court will often not take place until many months after the incident complained of.

CONCLUSION

In this chapter, we have examined how our society defines crime, what elements are necessary before a particular act can be called a crime, the parties involved in a criminal act and the often close relationship between criminal and civil responsibility. We have considered how offences may be classified, and when a crime has been committed, how it is investigated and prosecuted, including a brief overview of the courts system.

What steps, therefore, can the library manager take to prevent crime and when crime has taken place, to act positively in the best interests of the library, its users, and the public in general?

Rules and regulations governing the membership and use of the library by its members can be an effective deterrent. To be enforceable, rules must be made widely known to the user, and indeed to the prospective user, but to be effective in practice should also be concise, readily understood, and not unnecessarily restrictive. If these basic principles are ignored, by the very nature of things rules will be bent, and a grey area will develop which may lead to abuse as a consequence of indecisive management.

Where crime has been committed or is suspected, there is no easy answer. The library manager must appraise himself or herself of all of the available facts before deciding, in consultation with his local authority or other superiors, whether to involve the police, or to prosecute privately. Many factors must be taken into account, varying enormously from case to case in the degree of influence which they will have on the final decision. The prospects of a successful prosecution is clearly a major factor, as indeed is the setting of example for others who might be tempted into criminal activities if there is a general feeling of immunity.

Library managers should develop a policy for dealing with crime, possibly in conjunction with rules of membership. A firm policy will help staff to understand how to deal with situations and will command respect.

Knowledge of the matters considered in this chapter will help the manager reach a proper decision. Do not be afraid to seek professional help. Advice offered by police officers will, from their experience, assist. Recourse will usually be available to a solicitor, either within the administration concerned or closely connected therewith. In many circumstances, an independent and dispassionate viewpoint, especially one with some professional expertise, is invaluable.

4

Planning and management of a crime prevention strategy

JOHN HOULGATE AND MICHAEL CHANEY

This chapter considers the question of library crime as perceived by the practising police officer. Not, it should be said, the perception of the bobby on the beat called in response to any emergency, but that of the professional Crime Prevention Officer, whose role in the modern police force is to take a pro-active stance on crime prevention and to analyse criminals and criminal activity in their wider social contexts. Advice will be offered on ways in which the criminal threat in libraries can be significantly minimised by judicious security planning and investment.

The emphasis throughout is on the concept of designing out crime. Library and information managers must face up to the contemporary reality of criminal activity in their organisations; it is one of the many facets of the job with which they must now concern themselves if they are to manage successfully a flourishing and efficient library or information service. Managers have to take full cognisance of this regrettable fact of life, and from the earliest germ of a new idea, whether concerning an initiative in an existing system or planning a whole new library or information service, the potential for crime must be addressed at the earliest possible stage, and then designed out.

SECURITY PLANNING

Library and information managers, in facing up to the unpleasant truth of crime in their organisations, must take the question of security planning seriously. There is no avoiding the fact that designing out crime can throw a lot of inconvenient spanners into the planning process; the cost implications cannot be overlooked either. Security is expensive, but in the long run it will prove to be a cost-effective investment. Clearly the level of that investment will depend very much on individual circumstances (and these will vary between organisations) but the need for that money to be spent is there and it cannot be avoided. If library and information managers can be persuaded to take the question of security seriously, the battle against library crime is already half-won.

Libraries have a head start in the battle against proliferating crime in that they are organisations where an ethos of order and a code of acceptable behaviour are already established; it should be relatively easy, therefore, to instil the concept of good security in libraries and information services, and managers should bear this in mind and capitalise on this advantage when devising their security plans. This is, however, just about the only plus-point in an otherwise rather gloomy picture.

Opportunism

For the most part, designing out crime in any organisation is all about reducing, or, if possible, removing the opportunity for criminal activity to occur. The simple truth about crime is that it can be reduced, or even eliminated, if the opportunity to commit wrongdoing is not present. Let us therefore consider the various facets of opportunism and criminal activity in the context of libraries and information services.

Who?

Criminals are people who are prepared to take chances, and the greater the likelihood of their being apprehended as a result of criminal activity, the less likely it is that he or she will take that risk. Libraries and information services are organisations which hold collections of publicly-owned property in buildings usually open to all and sundry, and given the criminal's disregard for the rules of society governing acceptable social behaviour, and his or her lack of respect for other people's property, libraries and information services present a 'soft' target. Weighing against this however, is the potential financial reward from criminal activity in libraries, which as regards theft is, for the most part low – although this is changing.

The criminal in the library or information service is unlikely to be of the hardened variety – at least as far as theft is concerned. The potential rewards for the pre-meditated criminal are generally insufficient to make it worth taking the risk, although there is no room for complacency.

The criminal in the library or information service is much more likely to be a member of the organisation's staff, since the chances of an insider getting away with substantial criminal activity are that much greater. Designing out crime must take full cognisance of this fact; library and information managers have to reduce the opportunities for their own staff to be tempted to take the risk. A figure of 30% of losses from libraries being attributable to premeditated theft by staff was quoted at a recent conference on library security (Quinsee and McDonald, 1991). This is a speculative figure, but the fact that it was made at all gives rise for concern.

Theft of materials by users is therefore generally unpremeditated – targeting of libraries and information services by sophisticated criminals for their nefarious activities is relatively uncommon, during opening hours at least. Prudent planning and investment are pre-requisites in any library planning exercise, and there are now in existence many admirable (and quite a lot of not-so-admirable) electronic devices through which the removal of opportunities for impulsive theft can be drastically reduced.

What?

A wide spectrum of potential criminal activity exists within the library or information service. This ranges from vagrancy and minor nuisance through petty vandalism and theft to burglary, criminal damage and physical assault. The criminal mind aims to exploit weaknesses either in property or in people, and in view of the fact that libraries and information services cannot easily reduce the vulnerability of their collections to theft and damage without proper planning and investment, it is this area of the broad range of criminal activity with which managers will realistically need to concern themselves.

Although theft and damage to library property are the major concerns, it is nevertheless vital to recognise that staff in libraries and information services have very real fears concerning crime against the person, and these fears can have a demoralising effect . Managers need to recognise this fact, and to plan their security strategies accordingly.

How?

Criminals measure risk against reward. Theft of, and malicious damage against, books are difficult to combat because the risk of getting caught is low, while the likelihood of success is high. However, libraries and information services are also ideal targets for other forms of opportunist crime which carry a high risk factor, in particular the theft of personal property (handbags, purses, wallets, keys etc.); the nature of library and information service use encourages concentration, and users can get distracted easily, thus presenting the potential criminal with the all-important opportunity.

The reduction of the opportunity for crime is what the manager must aim to achieve, and it is possible to deter the criminal by the introduction of relatively simple physical measures which will increase the risk factor for the criminal. Such measures will also deter the more pre-meditated type of criminal, because by incurring delay the risk of him or her being caught is increased.

The responsibility of the library or information service manager is to try to achieve a balance between security and access, and this is not an easy objective to achieve. While the logic of good security practice will be telling him or her that all high-risk property in the organisation should be in one place, the library and information professional in him/her will be saying the opposite. Striking the right balance in security disciplines is the ultimate aim.

When?

The vast majority of all crime is opportunistic in nature, and occurs when the equation of risk against reward tips in favour of the potential criminal. If the equation goes the other way, the opportunity is removed and the potential criminal will not be able to seize it.

Any security strategy must aim first and foremost to reduce criminal opportunity, and if that is not possible, then it must at the very least deter the potential criminal in other ways. Library and information managers must establish the right atmosphere in their organisations. Without the right attitudes amongst all involved (paymasters, staff and users alike), a strategy is unlikely to work effectively, so the grounding of that strategy in the right ethos is a pre-requisite in the process. If the perception in an organisation that theft is unacceptable is unequivocal, then the right ethos is being established for a successful security strategy. Equally, if management can persuade their staff that the real problem concerning personal safety is fear itself, and that violence is extremely unlikely, then the strategy is being adequately underpinned.

Crime prevention

Physical crime prevention

Designing out crime in libraries and information services encompasses various facets, and the traditional approach to crime prevention is the physical method. The aim is simply to guarantee the physical security of a building and its contents by means of whatever happens to be the state-of-the-art hardware at the time. The problem with this approach is that criminals become increasingly sophisticated, and there then arises a continuing obligation to upgrade the hardware in order to retain an effective deterrent. The result is a continual escalation and the development of a fortress mentality, and of course this runs counter to the basic ethos of libraries and information services. There is, however, no gainsaying the sad fact that if the aim is to actually prevent somebody stealing something from your organisation then it is only physical security measures which will guarantee this.

The advantages of physical methods of security are that they are easily costed and understood, and that they provide a deterrent which is clearly visible. If nothing else will do, physical measures ensure security.

However there are disadvantages too: physical security measures may well be expensive in terms of initial capital outlay and ongoing maintenance costs. They may also be obtrusive and inconvenient. To a greater or lesser extent, they will encourage the fortress mentality, and they may be perceived as intimidating to some users. Librarians and information personnel generally like to project an image of their organisations as friendly and welcoming places, for which reason the deployment of high-profile security hardware may be anathema.

Environmental crime prevention

Contrasting with the more traditional physical approach is an increasing recognition in recent years that the focus of attention should be on the environment in which a criminal is operating. In short, this entails devising a strategy which takes into consideration the psychology of criminal activity: the mental pressure of committing a crime, by way of excitement, anxiety, impatience, tension and fear.

The strategy for the manager here is to aim to increase this psychological pressure, and one relatively simple way to assist this process is to build in the maximum amount of potential natural surveillance in the new library or information service, particularly in vulnerable areas. Any criminal's anxiety level will be considerably heightened if it is likely that he or she is going to be seen – burglars generally take advantage of concealed means of entry where they are unlikely to be observed.

Managers do however need to be sensitive to that all-important balance here, for which reason it is vital that surveillance should strike a happy medium between the deliberate and the random. Making the criminal uneasy does not mean that the manager should at the same time intimidate his or her genuine clientele.

Designing in natural surveillance in libraries and information services should also take into account the value of integrating offices and other administrative functions into the public areas of these buildings. In this way random surveillance by the organisation's staff can occur in the normal course of their work in a way which is inconspicuous, but which raises the anxiety level in the mind of any potential criminal. It is ironic, but the old British Library Reading Room epitomises this principle, although more modern buildings where, for example, the administration offices have been designed to overlook the well of the building, exemplify the value of the idea.

In the wake of the creation of a secure environment, other things fall into place naturally which inhibit criminal activity. It is easy, for example, to use effectively barriers (e.g. rope barriers) which are no more than symbolic security devices. However, it will inhibit the potential criminal only if it is operating in a well-ordered, consistent and palpably security-conscious setting.

It is the role of the library or information manager to create and maintain that atmosphere of benign security which the genuine user perceives as both accommodating and efficient, but which at the same time induces anxiety and wariness in the villain.

Special difficulties

In planning for the introduction of a security strategy, library and information managers have to acknowledge that there are a number of concerns in library security which present special problems. All establishments have their own intractable difficulties, but the areas highlighted below are illustrative of the particular handicaps under which library and information service managers have to operate.

Public access

Public libraries are, by definition, available to all and sundry during opening hours, and there is no privacy while the public library's doors are open. It is a fact that anyone, be they genuine library users (as the vast majority undoubtedly are) or rather less desirable elements of the community, can walk in off the streets into a public library without let or hindrance. This is an established tradition.

However, librarians and information professionals also have to acknowledge that times change, and that we are now living in a society in which crime is increasing. Public library managers must therefore consider whether the proud tradition of open access is any longer the best way of operating, and thought must be given to methods of effective control on access to their organisations.

Regulating people does not necessarily have to cause offence, and it is obviously desirable that such a consequence does not result from the implementation of a security strategy. The vital first step is to create the right atmosphere of greater security awareness amongst the law-abiding majority. If that is successfully achieved initially, the appropriate levels of restrictions on access can be achieved without engendering antagonism from legitimate users.

Browsing and handling

A characteristic of libraries which distinguishes them from other publicly accessible places is the privilege of handling the materials themselves. Museums and art galleries, for example, protect or secure their exhibits, and in some shops it is not permitted for customers to touch goods on display. Visiting a library, in contrast, is very much a 'hands-on' experience. The notion of browsing is one of the distinguishing characteristics of libraries, but outside these organisations it is a form of behaviour which would often arouse suspicion.

Surveillance/supervision

Although things are constantly changing in libraries and information centres, with new developments in information technology occurring almost daily, the main sphere of activity in these organisations is still concerned with books. Books are bulky, and have to be accommodated on open access stacks, and stacks are a perfect haven for concealing illicit activity of whatever nature.

Any security strategy must take the concealment potential of library stacks into consideration, and their physical arrangement is crucial if the ability of library and information staff to supervise these vulnerable areas is to be maximised.

Vulnerability of the collection

Although individual items in library and information services are generally of a relatively low intrinsic value, it is still a unique act of trust by a librarian to lend an item to a member of the public, since all care and control over that item of property is surrendered at the point of lending. And if that is not enough, items can be damaged or destroyed with frightening ease without even being removed from the premises of the library.

Collections are very vulnerable to abuse of one sort or another and library managers need to keep this characteristic well to the forefront of their thinking in planning their security strategy.

Audits

It is possible for damage or theft to remain undiscovered for a long time in libraries or information services. While it is acknowledged that full-scale stock checking on a regular basis is not necessarily cost-effective these days, some means of appraising the problem is desirable in a good security strategy. Reliable and cost-effective methods of stock auditing, such as rolling programmes of stock checks and use of new technology in the process, are a managerial pre-requisite in the efficient, security-conscious library or information service. An added benefit will be the establishment of unequivocal evidence of the existence of a problem when the time comes to presenting a case to the paymasters for extra funds for security purposes.

Property identification

Museum managers are familiar with the various techniques available for the security coding of rare and precious items in their care. This option is not, however, available to library and information managers – apart, that is, from the ubiquitous and rather rudimentary library stamp, and the idea of marking every page and plate in every book is, of course, quite impractical. (Security tagging of library property using commercial security systems from companies such as 3M and Knogo is dealt with in chapter 16). Hardware, on the other hand, can be security coded.

Personal safety of staff

The last characteristic which library and information managers will recognise as a special problem in their type of organisation is the personal safety of staff.

The responsibility of supervising a large and perhaps remote premises late into the night is a burden with which some members of staff, especially females, may not be able to cope. However, library managers need to appreciate that the problem is usually fear itself – the chances of a real physical attack on a member of staff are not high, although it is incumbent upon library managers to take these fears, particularly amongst female staff and in certain locales, very seriously. It is the responsibility of the manager therefore to alleviate irrational fears by introducing appropriate training methods in their security plans; these will go a long way to reassure staff with regard to the reality of their personal security.

HOW TO DEVISE AND MANAGE A SECURITY STRATEGY

This section constitutes a broad-brush, selective framework by which the task of creating a security strategy for a library or information service may be approached. None of the individual elements is obligatory, and whilst some of the suggestions may be suitable in some circumstances, they will not necessarily be universally applicable. As much as anything, the suggestions here should be seen as triggers upon which to develop one's own ideas.

Nevertheless a structured approach to the subject of security management is presented, and the role of managers in adopting such an approach in devising their own security strategies cannot be over-stated. A checklist summarising the following sections is included as an

Appendix. (All matters concerning aspects of fire safety and prevention should be referred in the first instance to the local Fire Brigade.)

Stage 1: Appreciate the risk

The first major element in the formulation of an effective security strategy by library and information managers is to assess in a systematic manner the levels of potential risk to the library of the following areas of concern. Under each of these headings the manager should take into consideration the three big 'C's' which constitute crime: the Crimes, the Criminals and the Consequences.

Unwelcome users

Public libraries in particular are susceptible to potential criminal problems arising from various forms of undesirable and anti-social activity. This can range from the well established use of public libraries by vagrants looking for warm shelter, to the activities of rather more sinister intruders involving drug taking and dealing. It also encompasses other undesirable behaviour arising from alcohol abuse and simple rowdyism and hooliganism. Individual managers must consider the extent to which their own organisations are at risk, and plan accordingly.

Burglary

At a time when the incidence of burglary is increasing at a frightening rate, it is appropriate for library managers to assess the susceptibility of their own buildings to this form of criminal activity. Most burglars operate on a casual or opportunist basis, and a large part of the risk can be eliminated by systematic appraisal and planning. This element of the planning strategy should be arranged in such a way that the consequences of loss or damage to the organisation are ranked on a scale ranging from minor to serious.

This scale should also be used in assessing the consequences of loss or damage resulting from the activities of the premeditated or professional criminal, and from losses consequent upon vandalism and hooligan behaviour. The risk of premeditated burglary is likely to be much lower in libraries and information services than in other types of organisation, but it is important to bear in mind that apparently low value losses can have very serious organisational consequences. For example, the theft of computer software or the corruption of records can have disastrous long term financial and other implications for library managers.

Theft

Theft other than burglary will feature prominently in the risk assessment plans of library and information service managers. Library property, which includes furniture, fittings, computer hardware and peripherals, as well as the stock itself, is clearly vulnerable in an open access setting. But there are other elements of the library or information service set-up which are equally open to theft and which must therefore receive due weight in the risk assessment process. These include the personal property of library staff and library users – the latter being a particular hazard in libraries – and, increasingly, external concerns such as theft of or from vehicles in library car parks, and theft of pedal cycles from similarly adjoining locations.

Criminal damage

Library managers must recognise that wilful criminal damage to buildings and stock is a fact of life, and the risk assessment process should take that into account. Criminal damage may occur in a variety of forms which range from graffiti, through vandalism, to arson at the extreme end of the spectrum. However, library and information managers have also to contend with a grey area of damage risk assessment which concerns the very purpose of libraries: lending materials to users. It is an inevitable consequence of the lending process that items, some of which will be costly to replace, become damaged, either by accident or intent. Library managers must therefore assign priorities in assessing the likely risks of damage occurrence in the process of drawing up the right security strategy for their individual circumstances.

Personal safety

The last area of concern in this initial risk assessment stage of the security management strategy is to gauge the extent to which the personal safety of people in the library or information service may be in jeopardy. The safety of both staff and users should be assessed, and the process should encompass safety matters outside, as well as inside, the building under scrutiny. Libraries tend to be open for longer hours than other organisations and the safety implications for staff and users of this characteristic alone are considerable. The consequences of compromised personal safety in an organisation such as a library are clearly less to do with money, (increasing litigiousness notwithstanding!) than with reputation and status in the community.

Stage 2: Involve everyone

The second stage in devising a security management strategy is concerned with ownership of the problem. Library and information managers must recognise that the responsibility for effective security is collective, and not exclusive to any particular individual or group within the organisation. The role of management is an enabling one in which the right security environment is established. The aim is to achieve an ethos of security in which everybody feels involved, and while each of the techniques enumerated below does not constitute on its own a solution, each nevertheless contributes to the security ethos which is the responsibility of managers to promote.

The working group

A Standing Committee, Working Group or similar aggregation of involved parties should be established with a brief to monitor all security concerns of the library or information service. This committee should be formally constituted, and should meet regularly under the chairmanship of a senior manager. The frequency of meetings will obviously depend on individual needs and circumstances, but, for example, a meeting every second Monday of the month would be a reasonable schedule to adopt. More frequent meetings would be even better. Membership of the committee should not be restricted to staff alone, but should include other appropriate representatives, either on an *ex officio* or on a consultative basis, such as local government officers, councillors, and professionals working in the field – security consultants, local crime prevention officers and other sources of expertise. (Regular liaison with security professionals is, in any case, a pre-requisite in the establishment of a working security strategy.) Users should also be encouraged to participate where possible. It is vital that meetings are fully minuted and that members are actioned.

These measures will guarantee that the committee achieves the required degree of status and authority without which it cannot hope to operate in an effective manner.

The establishment of a security committee for the library or information service embodies commitment by management to the issue of security, and it makes an unequivocal statement of the determination of all involved in that organisation to make security work.

The survey

One of the first tasks of a newly established committee should be to commission a thorough security survey of the library or information service by the local Crime Prevention Officer. This is a free service offered by the local police force, and it will prove invaluable in the initial establishment of security priorities for that organisation.

The Group should also initiate an audit of the library's existing crime problem. It is vital to know the nature and extent of the problems involved before taking the appropriate measures to deal with them.

Contingency plan

Another early objective for the security committee should be to draw up a written disaster contingency plan. Accidental disasters are outside the scope of this book, but adequate planning for any kind of disaster, whether it be accidental in the form of fire or flood, or as a result of criminal activity, will mitigate the effects of that disaster. The contingency plan should also encompass the organisation's policy in the event of real or hoax bomb warnings.

Prompt repairs and maintenance

The appearance of an organisation is a valuable psychological weapon in the armoury of management against crime. It is most important for libraries and information services not to give the appearance of neglect or slovenliness, but that damage and dilapidation are reported and remedied quickly. The role of library management in establishing the right ethos by encouraging awareness of this priority among all involved in the organisation, and by supporting it financially, cannot be over-stated.

Accounting

Good record-keeping and up-to-date inventories are another ownership issue which library and information managers should utilise in their security strategies. It is very much more difficult to redress the effects of criminal activity in a library which has failed to maintain adequate records of its property and assets.

Security discipline

The last area of concern in this aspect of security planning is the question of good security discipline. This encompasses a wide range of little matters which, if taken together, do more than anything to promote the air of calm, efficiency and confidence in an organisation which criminals find very unsettling. These are some examples:

- badges (permanent for staff, temporary for visitors)
- notices, produced and displayed professionally
- smart dress
- good key discipline
- unobtrusive bag searches, and removal of unattended bags; use of transparent deposit bags perhaps
- challenging strangers and unauthorised entrants in a non-provocative manner; may require assertiveness training
- digital locks in restricted/closed areas
- internally secure fire exits
- curtains/blinds for night-time working
- equipment responsibility; individual staff members responsible for their machines
- zoning of the library/information service
- high level of staff presence

Stage 3: Decide and do – physical considerations

The third stage in the security management strategy after making an appreciation of the risk and ensuring ownership of the problem, is to make decisions and to act upon them. The matters of interest under this heading are many and varied, but a *sine qua non* of a successful physical security strategy is the survey of the library or information service by the local Police Crime Prevention Officer mentioned in Stage 2 above.

The library or information manager conscious of expenditure in lean times should bear in mind that this service is free.

Perimeter and grounds

It is useful to begin outside the library building itself and to envisage the process as a peeling off of the layers of an onion: consider the outer layer first – the vulnerability of the perimeter and grounds; look at the fences (generally token barriers), gates, pathways, gardens etc., and in particular at concealed areas in the vicinity adjacent to the building.

Exterior lighting is of particular importance as a deterrent against intruder crime, since it increases the likelihood of observation of illicit activity, and helps in the recognition of offenders. Good lighting deters intruders, and is generally inexpensive to install. However, the form of lighting installed is crucial, and aesthetics must not prevail over practical usefulness: globe lights, for example, are of little use other than as ornaments, since they create shadows and localised pools of brilliance which actually assist intruders. An overall, low level of lighting is the preferred method.

Consideration may also need to be given to the more costly option of regular security patrolling of the exterior of buildings. Crime Prevention Officers will advise on the best solution for individual circumstances.

Building shell

The shell of the building is the next area of concern. Managers must be aware of the weak points in the fabric of their libraries, particularly where the visibility is poor and the opportunities for concealment high. Basic lighting, again, should be a cost-effective deterrent. Special attention should be paid to:

- walls: are they easily scaled; position of drainpipes etc.
- doors: use strong doorframes; reinforce/replace exposed hinges; use only British Standard locks; consult locksmiths
- windows: fit window locks on accessible windows as a minimum measure, more substantial measures if circumstances demand
- roofs: are they easy to access via drainpipes, fire escapes, low walls, fences etc.; consider the positioning of flat roofs near-by, rooflights etc.

– refuse bins, building skips etc.: do they facilitate illicit entry by being located out of sight; are they a fire risk – secure covers prevent deliberate and accidental fires

Professional advice is easily procured for all of these areas of concern, and this should be done wherever possible.

Interior

The last element in this physical category is the interior of the library or information service.

Alarms are a necessary part of any practical defence against crime, and it is essential that intruder alarms fitted to any library or information service should signal simultaneously at a central station away from the building itself. Personal alarms are another useful option, whether fixed or portable, but it is vital that they remain operative all the time. A public address system is expensive to install, but may be a necessary investment in certain circumstances in order that appropriate warnings to staff and/or users can be conveyed in a quick and clear manner.

Potential criminal activity in libraries and information services can be largely forestalled by a judicious approach to the organisation of internal space. The aim of managers in this is to maximise the ability of staff to supervise public areas in an unobtrusive, natural manner, and even if those staff do not actually notice much, it is the fact that he or she may be being observed which will have the desired unsettling effect on the criminal.

The initial planning of the building is a crucial factor in this process, since it is often impractical to relocate offices and bookstacks after they have been installed. Offices and staffrooms should therefore be sited adjacent to public areas in a discreet arrangement, and bookstacks should be planned to render maximum supervisory potential for staff: a circular arrangement with stacks radiating outwards from a central service point is a desirable, if not always achievable, arrangement. At the very least the exit – and ideally there should be just the one – should be covered.

The organisation of space should also try to bring together as much valuable equipment in one secure area as possible, although in an information technology oriented organisation such as a library or information service, this may not be a practical option. There are now, however, various security devices available on the market which offer, if not total security, then at least a cost-effective deterrent. All equipment should, of course, be security coded as visibly and as indelibly as possible, and secure stores and cabinets should be used for portable items.

Libraries and information services maintain substantial records, both manual and in machine-readable form. Where possible, duplicate copies should be generated and kept in safe, remote locations.

Most large organisations are involved with cash dealings of one sort or another, and libraries and information services are no exception. A basic and self-evident rule is that cash on premises should be kept to the absolute minimum, and that cash-handling is as unobtrusive as possible. All cash handling procedures should be kept secret, and routines varied regularly. Cash tills should be used, since they reduce the opportunity for snatch-theft, and these tills should be cleared regularly.

Staff supervision of public areas can be considerably enhanced, particularly at times of minimal staffing, by investment in the various surveillance devices that are available, such as mirrors and closed-circuit television. However, CCTV in particular is expensive and carries with it significant staffing implications; dummy cameras have an initial deterrent value, but are not a long-term option.

The security needs of the library staff themselves should not be left out of the process, and suitable lockers and cloakrooms should be provided.

On the topic of keys, it is a truism that the best lock is only as safe as its most available key, and the complex arrangement of master keys and key suites in organisations today raises the profile of this important security issue. Key copying needs to be eliminated, and staff to whom keys are allocated should be fully accountable for them; they should sign for them in a central register when accepting them and maintain responsibility for them until required to sign for their safe return. Secure areas and safes should not be suited under any circumstances, and keys allocated to staff for specific jobs should be returned and not taken home.

Fire exits are important in safety terms, but may also be seen as something of a security risk. They must be secure from the inside, and alarms should be fitted.

The last point concerning internal security is access. There should be only one access point in the library or information service. Multiple entry and exit points increase the likelihood of through routes in buildings, which can encourage criminal activity of the kind commonly referred to as 'steaming'.

Stage 3: Decide and do – procedural considerations

The second element of the Decide and Do component is concerned with procedural aspects. This is the area of security management which entails least expenditure, but which at the same time can have the greatest effect. However, library and information managers should be aware that the successful operation of a security strategy on a daily basis must be predicated on trust, not suspicion. There is a danger that too high a security profile may create a challenge in the eyes of users, and otherwise perfectly upright library users – students in academic libraries, for example – may well find the temptation to pick up the gauntlet irresistible.

The main issues of security procedure which managers need to address in their security strategies are discussed below:

Cash-handling

The necessity for regular clearing of cash-tills, and for cash transactions to be conducted in as private a fashion as possible, was mentioned under the Physical heading above, but it bears repeating here. There are also other good practices to follow: cash should be cleared from library premises regularly, and this job should be conducted by internal security or, preferably, if funds allow, professional security firms. The use of library staff for this job is not advised. If the use of library staff for cash transfer is absolutely unavoidable, then the following procedures should be adopted: routes and transfer times should be varied; if transport is required, a well-maintained vehicle should be used, with a separate driver so as to obviate any parking problems; one person should carry the cash, and a second person should accompany him/her as 'minder'; they should both be fit and able-bodied, and should walk facing the oncoming traffic in the middle of the pavement. Consideration should also be given to the type of container used to carry the cash: there are a number of options, ranging from locked briefcases with chains for attaching to the carrier, to fully alarmed containers which discharge smoke or indelible dyes when activated. The advice of the local Crime Prevention Officer should be sought in the first instance.

Equipment

The need for equipment inventories to be comprehensive and kept fully up-to-date is very important. Details of serial numbers should be recorded, and for particularly valuable items it might be advisable for photographic records to be kept on file. Staff should be encouraged to supervise the security of their own items of equipment.

Records

If feasible, duplicates should be retained in a safe place.

Personal property

While stressing the need for library and information service users to maintain constant vigilance for the safety of their own belongings, it is equally important to encourage staff to be alert to the vulnerability of their personal property while at work.

Keys

The potential problems involving keys have been dealt with in the Physical section above. It is, however, vital for managers to instill good key practice among staff key holders at all times.

Locking up

In connection with key practice, correct procedures for clearing and locking up buildings at closing time need to be established. This is especially important if an alarm system is fitted: false alarms must be avoided at all costs since these antagonise local residents and the police thereby drastically reducing the effectiveness of these costly devices. Buildings should be cleared systematically and thoroughly by personnel working in pairs.

Access

Access to any area within a library or information service should be clearly defined, and staff must enforce restrictions by challenging, in a non-confrontational manner, any unauthorised user found to be outside the designated public areas. If digital locks are fitted, managers should insist that they are used consistently and correctly.

Alarms (buildings and personal)

The procedures to be adopted in the event of any alarm being activated should be clearly defined and publicised. Those responsible for contacting the appropriate authorities – usually the police – must be quickly ascertainable and a written model call available for immediate guidance for staff. It is important for library managers to be able to justify calling the police to an incident, and suitable instructions for staff will make the task that much more straightforward. When to call the police, who calls, and how the call is made are questions which must be addressed by managers.

Police

On the subject of the police, it is advisable for managers to maintain regular contact with their local officers, particularly the local Crime Prevention Officer. If a good relationship is established all parties will benefit. The occasional presence of a uniformed police officer on the premises is a useful procedural tactic.

Staff presence

Library and information staff should make their presence known as much as possible by walking the floors of the building at reasonably regular intervals. While it is important that this should not be done in an over-obtrusive fashion, it should be encouraged in order that awareness of activity in the building is increased. Staff should also be prepared to interfere if their suspicions are aroused, and they should remove any unattended baggage. Users will soon get the message – with luck, it will be the right one!

Membership

The establishment of suitable procedures for verifying membership of a particular library or information service assists in the creation of a good security ethos. Borrower or ID cards should be checked for bona fide presence in buildings, and in certain types of organisation (e.g. academic libraries) entry should be refused if proof of identity cannot be shown. Spot checks at acceptable intervals are worthwhile, and in restricted entry organisations users should be encouraged to wear or display at reading tables their membership or ID cards. A useful tactic is to implement an arrangement whereby newly registering users are not allowed to borrow books until their authenticity has been established by the posting of membership documents to the address given. Determined miscreants can find ways around the identification issue, but it is nevertheless an important element in security management.

Security notices

Warning and advisory notices should be installed at suitable locations so that the message of the organisation regarding security is clear to all. The sum total of that message is that theft and damage are not tolerated. (Honest users will be appalled to learn what the small minority of criminals is capable of doing.) While most notices should be presented in a professional manner, the urgency and attention-grabbing value of occasional handwritten notices should not be underestimated. These should, however, be used sparingly and changed very frequently.

Checking and searching

Guidelines which conform with the legal constraints of consent and reasonable grounds for action should be established in written form for the correct procedure to adopt in these situations, and tact and sensitivity are pre-requisites in such circumstances.

Cloakrooms

Manned cloakrooms are effective methods of reducing crime in libraries, but they are costly in terms of staffing and space. Automatic cloakrooms are expensive in capital outlay and also occupy valuable space, but once installed they benefit everyone. A compulsory deposit paid on bags and coats left in these secure surroundings removes the opportunity for two types of theft, namely users' and institutional property. Where cloakrooms are not a viable option, a useful tactic may be to restrict the size of bags allowed to be carried into the building, as happens at the Public Record Office.

Late night opening

This constitutes a special area of vulnerability for library and information managers, and a number of procedures should be adopted to reduce risk. With minimal staffing resources, consideration should be given to reducing access to certain, clearly defined areas of the building in order to maximise staff surveillance. Staffing levels should never require that individuals, particularly females, should work alone at night; there should be at least two staff members working in any establishment at this time. Curtains or blinds may need to be installed, and then used. Managers should also give thought to the arrangements for the safety of their staff after late night duties. It may be necessary for suitable transport to be at the disposal of staff.

Lavatories

These are havens for criminal activity of even less charm than theft or criminal damage, such as importuning and drug abuse. Regular security patrols may be necessary in the worst circumstances. The installation of ultra-violet lighting is a useful device against drug takers, since this prevents clear sight of veins.

Self defence

The value of this as a security device can be easily over valued. Physical violence is a very remote possibility in any situation, and the threat of self defence or martial arts techniques may well exacerbate a tense situation. Self defence also needs regular practice in order to be of any real use. Staff should be made aware that the exploitation of these techniques is an entirely personal decision.

Training

In all of these procedural matters, properly planned and regular training is of the utmost importance.

CONCLUSION

The foregoing is an attempt at developing a security strategy for libraries and information services by a practising Crime Prevention Officer. Some of the observations and recommendations may be viewed by library managers as being inappropriate or even excessive in the context of their types of organisation. Libraries are, however, an integral and significant part of the fabric of the community, and they cannot afford to see themselves as being in some charmed way outside the purview of some of the more baleful manifestations of that community. Crime and criminals percolate through all sections of society, and the position deteriorates day by day.

The question of security in libraries generates some intractable problems for the crime prevention expert, and it is apparent that book theft is not the only issue which gives cause for concern. Nevertheless, the security of the book collections remains the principal worry and is the concern least amenable to straightforward, physical solutions.

The premeditated criminal will always exist, but, thankfully, he or she represents the least significant threat to libraries. Of much more importance are the various types of opportunist criminal. These, however, can be deterred by strong, effective management, and it falls to the library manager to devise a security strategy which will create the atmosphere of calm efficiency in which the genuine library user is at his or her ease, while the wrongdoer feels vulnerable, anxious and wary.

REFERENCE

Quinsee, A. G. & McDonald, A. C. (1991), *Security in academic and research libraries*, proceedings on three seminars organised by SCONUL and the British Library, held at the British Library 1989/ 1990. Newcastle upon Tyne: University Library.

APPENDIX: MANAGING SECURITY CHECKLIST

Appreciate the risk

The Crimes
The Criminals
The Consequences

Involve Everyone

Working Group
Survey
Priorities
Security Discipline
Prompt Repairs and Maintenance
Accounting
Contingency Plan

Decide and Do

	Physical	*Procedural*
Perimeter and grounds	Fences	Cash
	Gates	Equipment
	Lighting	Records
	Patrols	Personal property
Shell	Walls	Keys
	Doors	Access
	Windows	Locking up
	Roof	Public address
Interior	Intruder Alarm, incl. PA	Police
	Organising space	Staff presence
	Secure stores	Membership
	Equipment and records	Reader passes
	Safe	Security notices
	Surveillance	Checking/searching
	Staff room & facilities	Cloakrooms
	Keys	
	Fire exits	

5

The role of architecture and design in a security strategy

HARRY FAULKNER-BROWN

Anyone who borrows a book
must be a crook
Anyone with a book to lend
must be round more than one bend
Persian Proverbs

An architect generally suffers the disadvantages of never having had to run or manage a library. In his or her professional activity he or she really has to ascertain the clients needs and types of library problems. Then by a process of questioning, not unlike a medical diagnostic approach, an understanding of the library process and type of service begins to emerge. When the architect fully understands the library functions he or she can then attempt to solve, while creating the design of the whole, a series of important problems to assist the satisfactory use of the library building by both staff and users. This process of assimilation varies depending on the skill and experience of both the librarian and the architect.

Too often reports of the relationship between the librarian, who is acting as the client, and the architect, who is commissioned to design the building, are far from cooperative and respectful, even though initially they might have been so. Inevitably, this is reflected in the final result and either the librarian or the architect or both express dissatisfaction with one or several aspects of the design of the building. Close cooperation between the two contributors is essential and it can be furthered by each party taking pains to understand the other's problems and points of view. This can be made easier and the result can be stronger if the principles of library planning are explored by each party together and fully understood before beginning the design of the library building.

There are complicating factors which need to be considered. Is the building for a small branch or a large public library, an academic or a Parliamentary Library, a National Library or one of the many special libraries that exist? The differing requirements can be quite bewildering to the architect. But then again, what sort of architect might the librarian have to work with? Will the problem be a theoretical one being studied by an inexperienced student at the beginning of his learning career, or a keen new practice of architects trying desperately to make its mark by strong design statements to attract the press and public, and perhaps being insistent on its solutions? Will the architect be so busy that the amount of contact time between librarian and architect is so small that ideas and understanding cannot be fully developed? Will the architect be one of what Keyes Metcalfe used to call 'prima donna architects', the highly successful architect who is top of the professional tree, who perhaps has made a reputation on city centre tower blocks and other building types, is in great demand by clients who want a fashionable great name as an architect, but who might not have designed a library? These are only some of the problems which can face a librarian acting as client, in his relationship with a person or a design unit which is going to determine the conditions in which the library staff will work for many decades.

FAULKNER-BROWN'S TEN COMMANDMENTS

With the amalgamation of all these factors and with the great variety of types of libraries and architects, the problem of how best to cope with them seems formidable especially since librarians themselves vary a great deal in outlook and experience.

Library planning requirements and qualities have changed during this century, slowly at first but more rapidly with the changing needs of libraries and library users. Although internal arrangements and library services vary from place to place, and from one type of library to another, recent library buildings of all sizes have many common factors, which have crystalised into ten desirable qualities, Faulkner-Brown's Ten Commandments as some European librarians have referred to them.

A library should be:

1.	flexible	with a layout, structure and services which are easy to adapt
2.	compact	for ease of movement of readers, staff and books
3.	accessible	from the exterior into the building and from the entrance to all parts of the building, with an easy comprehensible plan needing minimum supplementary directions
4.	extendible	to permit future growth with minimum disruption
5.	varied	in its provision of book accommodation and of reader services to give wide freedom of choice
6.	organised	to impose appropriate confrontation between books and readers
7.	comfortable	to promote efficiency of use
8.	constant in environment	for the preservation of library materials
9.	secure	to control user behaviour and loss of books
10.	economic	to be built and maintained with minimum resources both in finance and staff

These are the broad outlines of ten important qualities. Irrespective of size, from the most humble branch library to the largest national or city central library, these qualities can be applied in varying degrees.

PROBLEMS OF SECURITY

Here our concern is for quality number 9 – the library building should be secure, to control the behaviour of all users (including staff) and to control the loss of books. Another is the considerations which are important in the library building, planning and design process, especially in its initial stages.

So often there is a conflict between these ten qualities and it is important, because of the differences in library types and services, for the librarian to attempt to ascribe weight to each of them so that the predominant qualities are not diluted by those of lesser value.

Between the librarian and the architect these conflicting qualities should be brought into a comfortable and acceptable balance, at the same time recognising the vital importance of making the library appealing to the users and a comfortable and attractive place in which to work both for staff and users.

Preserving the collection is a problem as old as libraries themselves. Five hundred years ago books were chained, night watchmen were used and the users were so few in number that they were all well known. Now with such a large quantity of books on open access and readers in vast numbers, the problem of security does not change but methods of achieving it do.

A medium sized central public library, or an academic library of similar size, can have different patterns of use but have similar problems of security. Where possible, in most libraries, there is great merit in limiting the access to the building to a maximum of two entrances – one service entrance for goods and staff and one for the public. The service entrance does not constitute a problem if it is locked, and is accessible for deliveries when a doorbell is answered by a member of staff. Staff access should also be here so that the front door is clearly shown to be locked during non-opening times.

There are two principal conflicts, both lying at the main entrance. One is the balance to be achieved between the necessary level of security by supervision and checking, the other is making the entrance attractive and inviting to users.

Different approaches to this problem are needed in different types of library. The extremes of security can vary between, at the lowest, a small branch library with very few members of staff, where the value of the collection is not significant and where supervision can be merely the siting of the issue desk near the main entrance. In earlier times this was placed at the entrance door with a narrow restricted exit which required all exiting users to pass a control point. Latterly this has become more relaxed and a more open and inviting entrance/exit is being used.

College libraries quite often require a similar level of security – the users are part of a community and a great deal of trust is encouraged and usually found. Part-time staff, and either postgraduate informal supervision, or sometimes no supervision at all especially at night, is not uncommon. The level of security is therefore extremely low but it is a reflection of both the community trust and the low value of the collection. Some colleges have two types of collection – that described above and a special, perhaps ancient and very valuable collection. The security in the latter is of a very high order – it is usually locked with access allowed in the company of a staff member, who is present at all times of use and is a reference collection only. There is an exception – Fellows of the College are usually admitted unaccompanied, where the level of trust is supreme.

The other extreme of security is in a special collection or rare book library. This can be a collection of very valuable books within a university or national library – an enclave of maximum security within an already secure library. The contents of such a library can be so scarce and valuable that unusual measures might be necessary. In the new National and University Library of Iceland in Reykjavik the priceless and unique collection of national books and manuscripts are within a secure library building, two-thirds of which is devoted to undergraduate and postgraduate use in the University. One third is given over to the National Collection. It is on a floor of its own, the approach to which is a well supervised glass enclosed staircase. Admittance is controlled by a member of staff responding to an entry bell. Inside the National Department security is determined by a closed access system controlled by a specialist librarian invigilator. Below the Department is a closed access bookstore within which is a vault secure against burglary, fire and flood, and protected by a fire detection system and a gas flooding fire prevention system. The whole building is sprinklered.

The above two extremes, while quite common, can be seen to be peripheral only to the general problems of library crime and security. There are many other factors to consider and many of them conflict with each other.

Obviously exit supervision is the critical element in considering this subject. How best to achieve this again depends upon the weight of importance which is ascribed to the problem. Certain procedures can tighten security, others can, for different reasons, compromise security. To decide which takes priority is not always easy to determine. Probably the factor about which most discussion has ensued is whether or not bags and coats are allowed inside the library or whether they are left outside the control point in manned or unmanned cloakrooms. Uniformity either in a single institution or between independent institutions is not always forthcoming.

QUESTIONS OF SECURITY

The following questions affecting security need to be answered at the outset, to enable the architect to begin to conceive a solution to all the library needs.

Will brief cases and bags be allowed inside the library?

Depending upon the type of library, users might place great value on being able to have brief cases and bags with them when working in the library. If security is only needed at a modest level, such as in some types of public library, permitting outdoor clothes, shopping bags and brief cases in the library are usually acceptable risks. A manual cloak room is extravagant in staff costs, and any cloakroom is expensive in floor space and therefore initial capital costs.

In a library requiring a higher degree of protection two basic solutions are available. One system is to set aside space for a cloakroom, with or without lockers, which will require users books to be examined by a member of staff on exiting. The other is to invest in an electronic book detection system which is dealt with in chapter 16. Both have pros and cons, should be determined by the type of function and philosophy of the library service and should be balanced against other factors such as having an inviting and in some cases unrestricted entry.

Another factor which needs to be considered at the same time is the ease of exiting safely in case of fire. It is not intended to deal with this important aspect here other than to point out that when the building is large enough, it is usually preferable to deal with the fire exit routes and sizes of openings quite separately from the entrance. This means that fire exits, which are usually unsupervised, can be provided without the need for special emergency arrangements at the main entry/exit point. The security of the fire exit is usually dealt with by break-glass locks which are alarmed. It might seem rather precarious and less than satisfactory in a high security building, but it can be seen to be quite acceptable in many library buildings throughout the world.

What steps are appropriate to prevent mutilation?

The architect will need to know the steps the librarian is considering to avoid books being damaged or pages removed. Again the type of library service and content is highly significant. Most plates worth removing are usually (but not universally) to be found in rare book or special collections. Supervision is expensive, but for the really rare items it is inevitable and overseeing by library staff invigilators is probably the only answer. Elsewhere, informal overseeing by other users can be helped by having an open layout without cul-de-sacs. Perhaps one factor which has created some controversy is the provision of users toilets throughout the library space. Convenient as this undoubtedly is for readers, it does provide a private sanctuary where mutilation has been known to take place. Some librarians insist on all user toilets being planned on the public side of the control point or library exit. Although this reduces convenience it increases security. Sometimes this thinking results in toilets, lockers and cloakrooms being in a preferred location outside the control point. The University of Reading Library illustrates this method.

What considerations should be given to planning the building to ensure the necessary protection of the collection, the occupants and the building in the event of arson?

Under the present requirements of the Building Regulations buildings are classified into certain categories of fire risk. When a library building achieves a certain floor area or volume, a number of precautions need to be taken to protect the users and allow them to evacuate the building quickly and safely. This generally has the benefit of protecting the building and its contents. Buildings are therefore designed using materials and physical conditions which will prevent fires starting. In the event of combustion taking place, protection of exiting users is assured for a certain period. However, if a fire is started by a deliberate act of arson it might take a slightly different form, in that an incendiary device is likely to be more difficult to extinguish than a waste paper fire or an electrical short circuit. The librarian and the design team need to consider the risk of arson taking place. If the risk is high, then despite the inbuilt prejudice librarians have about the use of sprinklers, they really are the only effective way of dealing quickly with a fire caused by an incendiary device. They are expensive and vary in degrees of sophistication. They have a series of heads disposed at regular centres throughout the building. The best type has a head which will only operate when the temperature reaches a predetermined level. By spraying the area immediately below with water, the temperature is reduced and when it returns to a certain acceptable temperature (which means the fire is out) the head shuts itself off. This gives immediate response, prevents the spread of fire and minimises water damage. Most libraries rate the risk of arson (and fire) below the level necessitating fire suppression and use fire detection only.

The Los Angeles Central Library fire in April 1986 was started by an arsonist who set fire to bound periodicals. Nearly half a million volumes were destroyed and half a million damaged. The building was designed on old fashioned out-of-date principles in 1926 with self supporting bookstacks virtually open from top to bottom through seven tiers.

Today arson is recognised as the leading fire threat to libraries and in the United States accounts for more than 80% of reported fires. This fire was reported by Morris (1986), a consultant in loss control and risk management. The conclusions are worth repeating:

> 'Bookstacks in libraries are not a 'light hazard' occupancy; the fuel load is extremely heavy.
>
> Bookstacks should be compartmented horizontally (i.e. with solid floors and not more than two stack tiers between floors, so as to limit the spread of any fire) and stairways enclosed.
>
> Automatic suppression systems should be installed for optimum protection against fire; automatic detection is valuable and useful as an adjunct system.
>
> Consider the futility of depending on a fire brigade for rescuing your collections once a fire is established; this fire and the Philadelphia fire of 1972 (Klein Law Library) kept two of the greatest fire organisations in the US occupied for hours and they were unequal to the challenge in spite of heroic efforts. A sprinkler system would improve the odds nearly 100%.
>
> Include arson in your thinking about new construction, detection systems, fire protection systems, day-to-day operations.
>
> Consider getting the advice of a fire protection engineer.'

CASE STUDIES

The chapter is concluded by giving eight varying examples which indicate the result of careful cooperation between the architect and the librarian and show the relationship between the entrances, supervision and the considerations given to cloaks and toilets. They are deliberately included to indicate the variety of possible solutions that could be considered.

Close cooperation between the librarian and architect bearing in mind the features and facets outlined above and in the examples will go a long way towards the successful resolution of the increasingly difficult problems presented by crime in modern society.

Jesmond Library, Newcastle upon Tyne, 1963

The problem offered by the Libraries Committee to design a district library on an existing site in Jesmond at first appeared straightforward. From the outset both the client and the architect were in agreement that the site was fortunately in a residential shopping area in Jesmond, and that the building should be a supermarket-for-books, without any outmoded striving at misplaced dignity, but with some deference to civic ownership.

The brief schedule of accommodation required storage for about 18,000 books, staff rooms and a study room, and a maximum use of glass on at least one front – for self advertisement as well as to give an impression of spaciousness. It made the valid point that complete visual control was necessary with minimum staff supervision.

The demand of a set-back at the main entrance to cope with the outspill of users indicated a corner entrance, suggesting a plan roughly square with a corner missing. The traditional circular library plan to give the obvious advantage of panopticon supervision from a central desk at once suggested itself as a solution and was proposed with some misgivings. But the librarian seized on it with enthusiasm and encouraged its development. It worked well, allowed a deep wedge to the core to be used as a vestibule/queuing/display area on the entrance route – but was too small.

The two entrances at opposite ends of the building with a broad inviting corner entry for users and a staff/service entrance from the rear lane is simple and direct. Excellent supervision at the entry and in all parts is evident.

There is no book detection system and neither fire detection nor fire suppression systems.

Nottingham University Library, 1972

Prime requirements of the University

The University required a new library building to serve staff, research students and undergraduates in the Faculties of Arts and Social Sciences and to provide accommodation for the sub-department of manuscripts and the library photographic unit. Separate library facilities for the Pure and Applied Sciences, the Departments of Law, Music, and Medicine are provided elsewhere.

There was a requirement for future expansion of the building to anticipate increases in undergraduate members, book stocks and muniments.

The University expected the majority of the book collections and bound periodicals to be grouped into two divisions – Arts and Social Sciences, each served by subject librarians located in the divisional areas. There was to be a central reference collection shelved in one sequence adjacent to the catalogue. The loan and return of books were to be at one central issue desk, and there was to be a separate short loan collection of the books most in demand by undergraduate readers.

The University required users to find the main library services without aid, and quickly to learn the layout of the building as a whole. The library was to be operated largely on an open stack system with defined closed stack areas.

There was also a requirement to allow maximum flexibility of usage with air conditioning for the protection of books and manuscripts and for the comfort of readers and staff. Appropriate acoustic privacy was required, to permit most areas to be delineated by furniture rather than walls.

The building

The main floor is at Level 2 with the users' entrance at the east, from which the principal elements can be seen – the catalogue, reference and bibliography area, issue desk and separate exit control, the main stairs, the short loan collection for undergraduate reserved books and the coffee and smoking area. This floor also accommodates the technical processes area, with the cataloguing and acquisitions departments backing up the issue counter, and a machine room and staff rest and refreshment room adjacent.

Above the main floor there are two floors, Levels 3 and 4, of open access bookstacks and reading spaces: one for Arts and one for Social Sciences and Government Publications, both similar in layout. They each have space for about 187,000 books and 480 readers.

Below the main floor there is one floor, Level 1, housing the manuscripts sub-department, special collections, closed access bookstacks, muniments store, non-book materials room and conference room. Also at this level is the service entrance with the receipt and dispatch areas, binding preparation and general storage, the photographic unit, and the mechanical services and ventilation plant rooms.

The main entrance on Level 2 is unambiguous. The adjacent exit has a book detection system, and is quite remote from the issue desk to accommodate a heavy user traffic, which tends to peak, although in subsequent library designs this distance has been reduced.

The service entrance is at ground floor at the opposite side. There is fire detection but no fire suppression.

University College Cardiff, University Library (Arts and Social Sciences), 1975

Requirements of the College

The main requirements for the new library were for as flexible a building as possible, on not more than four floors each with uniform levels and adequate load-bearing ability, and for full air conditioning. With a view to catering for the library needs for the College's planned expansion to 10,000 students by the late 1990s a site was made available which could provide for extensions to the building, the first stage of which needed to allow for such extension.

The internal layout envisaged the main reading and open bookstack areas to be located on the three floors, on a subject divisional basis, each to be serviced by divisional staff who would be engaged in all relevant library processes. Other facilities to be provided included library administrative offices, technical services, a central bibliographical and reference collection, a reserve or short loan collection, closed access shelving for special collections, a closed access stack, and for a library bindery, this latter to be a completely new development.

The building

The building is on four floors, with a large structural grid of 13.5m x 9m. There are only six internal columns at each level so providing a very flexible space. At Stage I, the main entrance, which is at Level 2, is on the south west corner, and the main staircase is positioned centrally on the west side of the building close to the entrance. Both are in their final position, and, at later stages, will naturally assume a central location. The main floor is also at Level 2 with the users' entrance at the south, from which the main elements can be seen – the general reading area, divided from an open reference and reading area by an openwork timber screen (part of which is folded back by day but which can shut off the remainder of the library when the library closes at the normal evening closing time, to form an after hours reading room controlled only by the library attendant at the exit control), the main staircase to the lower and upper levels, the catalogues and counter area, containing the issue system, the short loan collection, interlibrary loans and an Assistant Librarian Readers' Adviser.

Opening off this are offices for the Librarian, Deputy Librarian and Secretary and a combined special collection/committee room. Beyond the counter is an open plan area for book accessions and cataloguing with a separate machine room for telex, tape typewriter and some elements of the computerised issue system.

The two main subject divisional floors containing the main book and periodical collections and readers' seats, together with work space and enquiry counters for the divisional library staff, are on Levels 3 and 4. Level 3 houses the Economic & Social Studies Division which includes national and international official publications collections and the University College Law Library, while Level 4 contains the Arts Division, including Theology, and the Salisbury (Welsh and Celtic) Library. Provision for two areas of closed access stack has been made to give protection to parts of the special collections and books on Fine Arts and, separately, for the early printed and some later material belonging to the Salisbury Library.

The south part of Level 1 is occupied by the University Institute's (UWIST) Law Library, thus bringing under one roof the Law Library resources of the two institutions while the Institute remains in Cardiff; the physical arrangements are similar to Levels 3 and 4.

The north end of Level 1 is given over to a small closed stack, a loading bay with adjacent receipt and despatch, porters' rooms, a reprography room, storerooms, a library staff common room and kitchen, and a readers' coffee bar.

Again the main entrance at Level 2 is at the opposite end of the building to the secure service entrance at Level 1.

There is fire detection but no fire suppression.

Newcastle upon Tyne University Library, 1980

The building is a deep plan structure on four floors. The main approach, across the bridge to the main entrance at the north west side of the building, is at the same level as the main entrance (Level 2), with one floor below and two above.

The building has four stairs and two lifts in four permanent vertical cores. The remaining floor area is open flexible space, the use of which can be changed merely by the re-arrangement of furniture. It is colourful, comfortable, inviting and aiming to strike a balance between visual liveliness and the repose appropriate to a modern academic library.

The structure is reinforced concrete with regularly spaced columns to carry heavy library loads. The building, although air conditioned, has high thermal performance construction, is designed for energy conservation and will be relatively inexpensive to run and maintain. The even artificial illumination is suitable for bookstacks and reading.

The building has four permanent, inflexible cores containing stairs, lifts, toilets and ducts. Two lifts are provided to facilitate the movement of stock, staff and readers, which is essential for a library supported by reserve stock held in outlying library stores and a constantly changing collection. The library is planned to provide good horizontal communication and book movement, and the vertical communication and book movement are equally as good. The two lifts are disposed singly in each of the two east cores. The north one is to be used by readers and the south by staff. In the event of either being out of use the service entrance at Level 1 is arranged so that either lift can be used.

The entrance floor provides for the immediate needs of the user. Here is located the principal interface between the users and library staff providing reader services, at the main counter where the issue desk functions and all forms of enquiry take place. On the user side there are the reference and bibliography collections and the main catalogue, a controlled area for the use of special collections, and an area for an undergraduate collection. There is immediate access to a lift, two stairs, several small seminar rooms and an enclosed coffee area. On the staff side there are areas for accessions, cataloguing, processing, library administration and all reader services backing-up the counter. Not too far removed is the staff room. The reader services area is provided with two stairs and a lift.

Below the entrance floor is Level 1 to which access by users is limited to a seminar room to seat 60, the bindery and conservation areas and the photographic department. About half of this floor is given over to book accommodation and the remainder to the service areas for loading, receipt and despatch, porters, staff lockers and various storage rooms.

Here the main entrance on the north east corner has an exit control point using a book detection system which is manned by a porter. The main issue and enquiry desk also serves the undergraduate collection, has good supervision over the entry/exit point and the foyer which gives immediate access to the stairs and lift.

There is fire detection but no fire suppression. The four fire exiting stairs leading directly to the open air are clearly defined.

University of Strathclyde Andersonian Library, 1981

The library is designed within the eastern part of the Curran Building on four floors of equal area, on Levels 2, 3, 4 and 5. The main entrance is on the west elevation with the ground level raised to Level 2 to allow pedestrian access to the building from Cathedral Street. Access to the library is via a staircase to the library entrance which is on Level 3. This reduces the maximum travel distance from the entrance to two floors. Vehicular access to the library is provided in the north east corner from St James' Road into Level 2. Access for the disabled is either by means of the lift from the car park at Level 1 or via the north east entrance from St James' Road next to the loading bay at Level 2.

Within the library there are three principal service cores running vertically through the building containing stairs and ductwork enclosures. Two of the cores have toilet facilities with the main user toilets in the south core.

A passenger/goods lift serves all library floors and gives direct access to the technical services area on Level 3 and the loading bay and receipt and despatch area on Level 2. It also extends to Level 1 car park.

Most of the library is designed as an open plan with carpeted floors which together with a controlled ambient noise level provide an appropriate level of acoustic comfort.

Two previously existing departmental libraries have been centralised within the new library, which houses the main administration for all University Library services, including a section for rare books and special collections. On Level 3 there is an out-of-hours reading area which can be closed off from the remainder of the library.

The entrance arrangements are similar to previous examples with a book detection system in operation at the exit control point.

There is fire detection but no fire suppression. The original building was a publishing warehouse fully sprinklered. The sprinkler system was removed.

Durham University Central Library, 1981

The building

The new building is essentially an extension to the existing Science Library creating one complete Central Library which functions and is expressed as one building. It is planned on four floors to coincide with the floor levels of the Science Library.

The main approach is from the south side across a ramp to the main entrance floor at Level 2, keeping vertical circulation to a minimum with two floors up and one floor down. Existing services are maximised so that the new building needs only one stair and one lift creating two service cores with toilets and service ducts.

The development of the design has resulted in a deep planned building, basically square with the corners cut off. It is linked to the existing library through the two large glazed areas existing on the south wall of the Science Library, ensuring the maximum interface between old and new.

The building consists of the entrance floor at Level 2, and three similar floors containing central book stacks, together with perimeter reader accommodation offering a choice of seating i.e. open carrels, large and small reading tables, and easy chairs. The areas are to be open plan and the arrangement easily adjustable. All levels are air conditioned, illuminated artificially to a uniform level, with carpeted floors and an absorbent ceiling for good acoustic privacy.

The entrance floor provides for the immediate needs of the user. The main counter, the principal interface between staff and users, is immediately visible on entering.

On the user side are the catalogues leading into the reference/ bibliography section and the short loan collection designed to be either open or closed access. The main stair and the coffee area are easily accessible from the entrance.

On the staff side behind the counter are areas for accessions, cataloguing and administration linked to senior staff rooms which are also accessible from the user side.

Technical and back-up facilities (processing, binding, receipt and despatch, machines, porter, etc.) as well as staff areas are accommodated in the single storey section of the Science Library, and the existing service road and entrance have been retained to serve these facilities. The original lift in the Science Library readily serves this technical section and also means that there is good vertical movement of books in the event of either being out of use.

Entrance arrangements again follow the general pattern, with a book detection system at the exit control point.

There is fire detection but no fire suppression.

Dundee University Library, 1985

The library is a simple rectangular three storey building with a regular reinforced concrete structure, 4330m², founded with the ground floor at a level midway between the car park level and the ground floor of the New Dines Building.

Level 1 is the entrance floor which provides for the immediate needs of the user. Here is located the principal interface between the users and library staff providing reader services at the main counter where the issue desk functions and all forms of enquiry take place.

On the users' side there are reference, bibliography, catalogue and periodicals display areas. On the staff side there are reader and bibliography services for accessions, cataloguing, processing, library administration and the receipt/despatch and porterage accommodation.

Above the entrance level are two floors for similar functions containing, generally, bookstacks in the centre and reading places around the perimeter, offering a choice of seating between open carrels, large and small reading tables and easy chairs, with 10 lockable study carrels on each floor with good acoustic privacy.

The building is designed so that the disabled have easy access to and within the library, and special toilets are provided at Level 2.

Both the secure service entrance and the well controlled main entrance with book detection system, are on the ground floor at some distance from each other. The counter arrangement gives good supervision of the entrance/exit.

There is fire detection but no fire suppression.

Reading University Library, 1982

An existing university library was inadequate for the developing university needs. With the emphasis on flexibility rather than fixed function planning in new academic libraries, the aim was to try to counteract the inflexibilities of the old library building and produce a more efficient integrated library, both in layout and in services.

The new building is a five storey extension attached to the whole of the north face of the existing stack area, the exhibition hall and the east face of the reading rooms, giving maximum confrontation with the old library.

By positioning the extension as proposed, the impact on the site is minimised, the existing strong visual feature of the reading room block is retained and the junction at the east end of the existing is simply expressed.

The development of the design results in an elongated extension. The existing building features are maximised so that only one new stair is needed and no additional lifts, with the result that only one new service core is needed to service the whole extension.

The library consists of an entrance floor at Level 1, and above it four similar floors principally containing open stacks with perimeter reader accommodation.

The entrance floor provides for the immediate needs of the user. The main counter, the principal interface between staff and users, is immediately visible upon entering.

On the user side is the short loan collection to the left. To the right are catalogues, quick reference, generalia and photocopying. The main stair and lifts to upper floors are part of this central user area, situated in the existing library.

Behind the counter are the two main staff areas, reader services and technical services, situated to make best use of the extension, where an improved environment and external views can be provided whilst still giving access to the lifts and reference collection.

Technical and back-up facilities, i.e. unloading, packing and porters together with staff areas, are situated at the east end of the extension where a new service area is created by continuing the existing service road.

On the upper floors the areas are open plan and the arrangement easily adjustable. At Levels 3 and 5, it has been possible to remove the screens between the stack areas and reading rooms and exhibition hall, thus allowing the Librarian more flexible planning arrangements and a better book/reader confrontation.

At the entrance level, it has been necessary to replan the existing facilities in order to make the best use of space available. The major part of this involves closing the two main entrances and the public concourse, together with the siting of a new entrance in the west elevation and the expansion of the bindery.

Cloaks and toilets are clearly shown on Level 1 to be outside the library control point to improve security and reduce the risk of mutilation.

There is fire detection but no fire suppression.

REFERENCE

Morris, J. (1986), The Los Angeles Central Library fire. *Library Association Record*, vol. 88, no. 9, (September), pp. 441–443.

6

Copyright and managements

Raymond A Wall

What should managers in libraries and information services be told about observing copyright? The communicator would say 'As much as possible', but the unpopularity of this subject could cause receivers of the necessarily complex details to reverse that answer in no uncertain terms. So what can be done here without tempting receivers to become switched off and without expanding a chapter into a complete book?

Those seeking more than this chapter are referred to various items in the literature, as represented by the Bibliography at the end. However, the uninitiated – taken as those entering the information professions, since existing professionals should already know something of copyright – may like to start with a concise paper on the basics (Wall, 1989a). Unfortunately, it is quite impossible to be concise about the various details of copyright which information workers and their managements need to know. Attempts at concise statements are often found to be dangerously misleading.

The complexities arise from the vast range of kinds of material and circumstances of use, plus the ramifications of the law itself. Most people have heard of the sale of film rights in a novel, yet the possibility of multiple copyrights in the same item is little understood. Even the simplest pamphlet carries an author's copyright for his life plus 50 years together with the publisher's copyright in the printed page for 25 years and, if there are illustrations, their originator and/or photographer will also have copyright in them for life plus 50 years.

This author was seconded, initially on a part-time basis, as Copyright Officer during November 1985 to March 1989 in order to spearhead a campaign on behalf of all Joint Consultative Committee organisations: the Library Association; Aslib: The Association for Information Management; Institute of Information Scientists; Standing Conference of National and University Libraries (SCONUL); Council of Polytechnic Librarians (COPOL); and the Society of Archivists. The campaign involved focusing user opinion and needs in respect of new law, preparing briefing documents and lobbying Parliament. Via Aslib's own working group, chaired for many years by this author, liaison was maintained with other bodies such as the Confederation of British Industry (CBI), the Royal Society, Association of County Councils, Association of Metropolitan Authorities, and the Council for Educational Technology (CET).

1956 AND ALL THAT

A certain amount of background is desirable here. Many of those who have lived with the Copyright Act 1956 during the long interval before the Copyright, Designs and Patents Act 1988 will be aware of the photocopying controversy between copyright owners – especially commercial publishers – and the users of copyright materials, as championed by representative library and information professionals.

Cheap and easy photocopying of high quality by the Xerox process began in the 1950s, and some American periodical publishers blamed the post-Second World War fall-off in individual subscribers on the increasing ease of photocopying rather than on their own pricing policies. Thus differential pricing of periodicals for multiple use situations like libraries started in the US and spread to the UK. This was obviously intended to compensate the publishers concerned for the replacement of individual subscriptions by the use of library copies, including the taking of photocopies whether legally permitted or not.

Now, however, it has been pointed out on behalf of several publishers that, because the number of individual subscribers has become negligible, the multiple use rate is considered the standard rate whilst any separate individual rate is a special discount arrangement. A possible parallel means of covering multiple use in respect of books is the often very considerable differential between hard and soft cover copies when both become available at the same time, since library preference is usually for hard covers.

Some UK publishers were vociferous in claiming that the 1956 Act's legal permissions did not override a publisher's right in the layout of a printed page, except in the case of that Act's 'scheduled' (the non profit-based) library services. This was totally wrong from the user viewpoint and, since much of the early part of the licensing movement was based on it, the claim fed controversy.

The 1956 Act became recognised as ambiguous on this and other matters, so much so that no case law relevant to this chapter ensued. Some case law would have been helpful in establishing such details as will always be impossible to include in statute without creating a legal morass. The 1956 Act was also out of date as soon as it was passed. Sound and video recordings, and then computer programs and other electronic media, raised problems. Rights owners tried to compensate by specifying their own restrictions on each item or in respect of each service sold, and uncertainties for the users still ensue from doubts as to the legal status of rights owner claims when no full contract has been entered into in advance of purchase.

Copyright law tries to be even-handed both to rights owners and users, allowing the former to benefit from their work and the latter to make appropriate use of it, especially for the good of society. A 'balancing act' may not be found witty by commercial publishers but describes the result. The route from authors to publishers, booksellers, librarians, researchers, educators and back round to authors constitutes a communication loop. It is essential to all progress that the loop be maintained, whilst ensuring that the economic incentive to participate suffers minimal damage. Therein lies one of the root causes of copyright law complexity. Others are the large range of kinds of copyright material, modes of utilisation, and available methods of copying without paying more than the cost of producing the copy. The protection of copyrights requires some flexibility in rights owners but ultimately depends on honesty in users.

This chapter is organised under the following main headings:

- key concepts: infringement; fair dealing; library copying service
- licensing
- the new Act of 1988
- guides for users

- recommendations
- bibliography (incorporating references)
- appendix: outline of contents of 1988 Act

The details of 'do's' and 'don'ts' will be found in the references in the section on guides for users, for otherwise the entire substantive content of the published guides would need to be repeated here. The purpose of the section outlining key concepts is to try to remove some common misconceptions of long standing which could interfere with the correct interpretation of the new Act.

KEY CONCEPTS

Infringement

The law gives exclusive rights to the first owners of copyright in respect of particular actions. These are known as the 'restricted acts': to copy the work; issue copies to the public; perform, show or play the work in public; broadcast the work or include it in a cable programme; or to make an adaptation of the work or do any of the foregoing in relation to an adaptation (which includes translation). Anyone doing any of these acts in respect of an item which is still within its copyright period without some form of permission will infringe copyright if the whole or any substantial part of the work is involved.

There has been much discussion of 'substantial part', which statute leaves to the courts to define in particular cases. Case law of 1916 however established that 'substantial' means significance of content and not only extent of an extract. During the House of Lords Committee stage on the 1988 Act, it was remarked that a single note of a song could be deemed substantial if it called to mind the entire piece, especially if used deliberately in a television advertisement for that purpose. Copying the more important parts of a book, beyond library copying service extents, could be judged infringement.

There are also several forms of 'secondary infringement' by a person if he 'knows or has reason to believe' that infringement is involved:

a) importing an infringing copy
b) possessing or dealing with an infringing copy
c) providing means for making infringing copies

    d) permitting use of premises for infringing performance

    e) provision of equipment for infringing performance

Because the phrase 'in the course of a business' appears in several of those, some people believe that b) holds possible dangers for an industrial or other profit-based service. This might occur if a copy produced with permission for one purpose were misapplied for another, infringing, purpose – for example, if a single copy produced against a declaration by an individual solely for his research or private study were to be added to stock or, worse still, used as a master for producing multiples for distribution to others.

Some librarians have over-reacted to c), thinking that it inhibits the use of self-service photocopiers. They should however look at the focus upon 'an article specifically designed or adapted for making copies of that work' in section 24 of the 1988 Act and be reassured. The phrase turns upon 'specifically designed', 'copies' in the plural, and 'that work'. What is meant here is, for example, a set of plates for pirating a particular book, or a DAT (digital audiotape) copy of a particular sound recording for replicating other copies. In any event, if a manager has taken all steps to discourage infringement on his machines with notices, conditions of service or access, etc. (see Library Association Guides, 1990), he can hardly be said to 'know or have reason to believe' that infringement will take place.

However, the law goes on then to specify a whole series of 'permitted acts', mainly: fair dealing; some education permissions; copying by librarians or archivists; and various public administration purposes.

Fair dealing

The law states that fair dealing does not infringe any copyright in a literary, dramatic, musical or artistic work, or in the case of a published edition, in the typographical arrangement for, principally:

    – purposes of research (of any kind) or private study

    – criticism, review and news reporting

Fair dealing is focused upon because it has been so misunderstood for years, apparently by the majority of librarians, on four counts:

    a) taking fair dealing to be a form of concrete allowance

    b) noting the absence of any specified extents of copying and assuming that 'anything goes' when an individual copies for research or private study

c) noting the list of kinds of copyright work in the law and assuming this to cover everything

d) confusing it with library copying service

On a) and b), it has to be emphasised that the fair dealing concept is only a form of permissible defence which may be employed in the event of a court case. In other words, anything done under fair dealing is open to question of fairness by a copyright owner. The fact that the fair dealing provision lays down no limits does not amount to *carte blanche*.

On c), care is needed over the use of the word 'work' in statute. When preceded by 'literary, dramatic, musical or artistic' it means *only* the original works. Physical media (published editions, films, recordings, etc.) are also copyright works. For research or private study, fair dealing includes only one physical medium: that of a published edition, and so applies to copyright in its typographical arrangement.

There is no such thing as fair dealing in respect of audiovisual or electronic media, with the possible exception of computer programs in electronic form. These remain 'literary works' regardless of format because an electronic copy carries no rights in itself but only in its content. The law does not specify the following but it appears common sense: that anyone wishing to take advantage of the apparent fair dealing in computer programs would have to very careful on two counts:

- another's program must not be used to create another work which is replicated, whether offered for sale or not
- adaptation of any kind is specifically forbidden without permission (section 21 of the 1988 Act)

A publicly accessible electronic database, defined as a 'cable programme service' in the 1988 Act, carries its own copyright in the service itself for 50 years from first availability of a given item in the database. Thus, although the content may be a literary work, such as an electronic journal or a compilation of abstracts, and therefore subject to fair dealing, downloading cannot legally occur until the first hurdle of copyright in the service itself is overcome by permission or licence or contract – the latter being the norm anyway (Wall, 1989b).

The 1988 Act has left many uncertainties, particularly in respect of audiovisual and electronic media, to be sorted out between users and rights owners (Wall, 1990b). The outcome of work on 'electrocopying' (*Report of the IFRO Working Group on Electrocopying*, 1989), a project on which is soon to be the subject of collaboration by the British Library, should prove interesting. Electrocopying is the term used to cover electronic storage, display, manipulation (including searching), dissemination (including downloading and networks), and reproduction or printout.

On d), misunderstanding of such key matters can interfere with the correct interpretation of other parts of the 1988 Act. The danger of confusing fair dealing and library copying service dates from the 1956 Act, and is described below.

Library copying service

Under the 1956 Act and now the 1988 Act, declarations must be signed by persons requesting photocopies from staffed services in 'prescribed' libraries. 1989 S.I. No. 1212 (Statutory Instrument, 1989a) makes all UK libraries 'prescribed' in one way or another, but in this context the word means non profit-based services. Such services are in fact only specifically authorised to copy written or printed material in response to requests and declarations by people wanting them for research or private study, or for certain interlibrary needs, or for archival preservation purposes where other materials may be involved.

'Research or private study' happens to be one of the fair dealing purposes as well as the authorised purpose of library copying. But library copying service by a non profit-based organisation constitutes a specific permission, as long as the conditions laid down in S.I.1989 No. 1212 are satisfied. Such library copying service is a legal permission and overrides any consideration of 'fairness'. Thus library copying service by non profit organisations is very special, and there is no wonder that librarians have been made more responsible in the conditions made under the 1988 Act. In any case, it is just as important to libraries that copyright should be upheld as that users should be assisted as far as possible, because without incentives the whole system of communication and information would fail.

However, any person or any library, including profit-based organisations which are, of course, not authorised under library copying service provision, may copy on behalf of someone under fair dealing for research or private study, as long as only one copy is made for a given need (section 29(3) of the 1988 Act). The Act thus clarifies the 'proxy copying' situation, at least in respect of research or private study as fair dealing.

Any library, like anyone else, can also copy on behalf of someone for any other fair dealing purpose than research or private study, though they could again be open to any accusations of unfairness by rights owners. Also, anyone and therefore any library can act in respect of any of the other permissions in the Act, such as copying for judicial proceedings. The latter is an example of a permission that can involve multiple copies which, except as so permitted, are always to be considered illegal.

Profit-based services are not required to obtain declarations and most did not do so after 1956, though it is now recommended that they should adopt the practice to cover themselves.

Librarians began using the phrase 'fair dealing declaration' when the law said nothing of the kind – nor does the 1988 Act. Who among us has not slipped into using this phrase at some time or another? The links between the fair dealing concept and non profit-based library provisions actually consist only of the research or private study purpose held in common, plus the ability of any library to copy under fair dealing.

Whereas, because anyone copying under fair dealing provisions could be challenged as to fairness on a specific item, profit-based services are theoretically at risk, one should feel 'safe' from challenge in respect of research or private study as long as the copiable extents and other conditions for non profit-based services are not exceeded. Rights owner representatives have not demurred from this interpretation, except that the British Copyright Council does not at present agree that copying periodical articles is fair when done by anyone other than a non profit-based service (Library Association Guides, 1990). However, it seems most unlikely that any copying done by an individual or by a profit-based library would be judged as infringement when a similar copy could be obtained in any event from a non profit-based library.

In the latter regard, special note should be taken of the inclusion under fair dealing of 'artistic works' which are in fact excluded from library copying provisions. Hence, unless a copyright owner (such as

Ordnance Survey for maps) has indicated a copying extent as fair dealing, extra care must be taken when attempting to assess the fairness of a copying need.

Lastly, another kind of misunderstanding has arisen in some academic libraries about interlibrary copying for an industrial or commercial enquirer. Any library can act as an intermediary in respect of a research or private study application from an individual. That individual may apply through a non profit-based or a profit-based library. There is nothing against any non profit-based library sending a research or private study copy to a library acting for an individual in industry or commerce. Nor of course is there anything against a non profit-based service supplying a copy directly to such an individual. However, although profit-based libraries can copy for transmission to an individual, whether through another profit-based library or directly, they do so under fair dealing and thus could be open to a claim of unfairness with a specific item. But profit-based services cannot have copies for stock without permission or licence (see the section on copyright-cleared photocopies below).

LICENSING

Non-collective licensing of copying is no stranger to the information and publishing scenes. The Ordnance Survey has long licensed copying of OS-based maps for such purposes as planning applications, and a number of public libraries hold such a licence. OS also has its own licences for multiple copying for classes, for digital mapping, and for business use (*Crown copyright*, 1990; *Copyright – publishing*, 1989). The British Standards Institution brought out its own licence for class copying in advance of more general action about such multiple copying. Specific licences for re-publication of parts of individual works have long been provided by their publishers. The leasing of large computer software packages, the producers' only answer in the absence of relevant law before 1988, is effectively licensing. Electronic databases have similarly acted in advance of new law by entering into service contracts with users which lay down copyright requirements of varying clarity and extent.

That reprographic copying, especially in multiple, for educational purposes is not permissible should have been clear from the 1956 Act. But according to surveys of copying in UK schools, Xeroxing combined with cash-limited budgeting and inflation led teachers regularly to infringe copyright by producing multiple copies for classes, even of whole books. The Whitford Report (*Copyright and designs law*, 1977) recommended the legal imposition of blanket licensing, and by 'blanket' was meant the coverage of all needs of particular user groups. Subsequently, Government stated that this was possible via the existing legal framework: that is, the law of contract. It would indeed have been inappropriate to impose licensing since compulsory licensing would have contravened the Berne Convention and could have exposed UK works to individual national approaches elsewhere. After all, copyright is not only important to individual rights owners, but also to the national exchequer, since publishing amounts to a significant proportion of income from exports, though such income is reduced by piracy overseas.

The Copyright Licensing Agency (CLA) had developed out of support from the Publishers Association, the Periodical Publishers Association, and the Society of Authors via their collecting bodies: the Publishers Licensing Society and the Authors Licensing and Collecting Society. CLA pressure, together with a serious court case in respect of an individual local authority, led to CLA licensing in respect of schools and colleges. Most photocopying outside education is of periodical articles whose authors care little for royalties and are more interested in kudos and the ability to copy the work of others with as little formality as possible, so it must be assumed that most of the support and pressure has come from the more commercially based publishers, of which the CLA has not published a list.

Licensing progress

However, the licensing of local authorities for copying in schools and colleges led onwards to university and polytechnic licensing, and the CLA is currently in discussion with the Confederation of British Industry (CBI) on possible means of licensing certain kinds of copying in industry and commerce.

In industry, commerce and professional group practices, the vast majority of photocopies are individual copies made from periodical articles. These are mostly written by people who have no particular desire for benefit other than the dissemination of their work and the ability to share the work of others on a flexible basis. Licensing proposals which seek to absorb fair dealing copies by counting them in and fixing prices accordingly should be resisted, for the legal provision of fair dealing for any kind of research, even if for commercial ends, was hard-won in the 1988 Act and should always be defended (Wall, 1988).

The fact that publishers must be the main beneficiaries of licensing, when so often they have already benefited by obtaining authors' work freely or cheaply for commercial publication at high prices, has been one reason for opposition to licensing proposals. It is nevertheless quite inappropriate for anyone to copy from a periodical to such an extent as to make a subscription (or further subscriptions) unnecessary. Nor should firms send copies of selected articles outside the immediate subscriber location, for effectively they would be milking their subscriptions. This causes all subscribers to bear the loss as subscription rates continually increase, and damages research and education when cash-limited establishments have to trim back subscriptions annually in order to survive. How can excessive copying be covered in industry, where the incidence of copying is extremely difficult to monitor, except by some administratively cheap form of licensing against the contingency of infringement by individuals?

The CLA operates in response to positive mandating and enlarges the 'positives' by negative mandating – in other words, if a publisher fails to respond to a circular it is assumed that he does not object to the CLA acting for him until further notice. Such further notice occurs when relevant royalties are collected and offered to the publisher, who is thereupon asked to mandate the CLA positively. The CLA now commands a significant proportion of support from UK publishers, and has arrangements with several overseas agencies such as the Copyright Clearance Center in the USA.

At present the CLA is concerned only with photocopying and, until agreement is reached with the CBI on possible forms of licence to offer to industry and commerce, the form of licence which has so far surfaced is that offered to educational establishments. The CLA is working on a copy-shop licence and another form for professional groups, possibly such as the Law Society.

Educational licensing turns on the illegality of using reprographic copying, whether single or multiple, for class purposes. Multiple copying is taken, broadly speaking, to be the production of more than one copy of the same item at more or less the same time for more or less the same purpose. When students have been referred to an item and each takes his own copy, that is claimed to be multiple copying of the 'related' or 'systematic' variety, in rights-owner parlance. The Government made it clear prior to the new Act that it was never intended that fair dealing should in any way encompass copying of this nature. A teacher may nevertheless copy for his own research or private study purposes as fair dealing, or get a library to do that for him, as long as the copies are not used in class.

The CLA educational licence, for example for a university, covers copying for any internal purpose whatsoever for staff and students, within specified limits. The principal limits are: from periodicals, one complete article per issue – thus loan duplicates of high-use articles can now be stocked – and, from books, a maximum of 5% or one complete chapter. The number of copies must not exceed the number of students in relevant classes in a given year. Although the licence forbids sale of copies, this does not apply to cost-recovery from an establishment's own students and staff. Information on what is copied, to assist distribution of royalty monies by the CLA, depends on periodic sampling, and institutions should ensure that fair dealing copying is excluded as far as possible when sampling takes place.

A feature of a CLA licence is its accompaniment by a list of exclusions – whether of categories such as (not surprisingly) workbooks, or publishers, or individual works. The licence complies with the 1988 Act in offering an indemnity against litigation for infringement which might be claimed by an individual publisher, provided the terms of the licence are followed. Since following the terms must include taking note of the list of exclusions, an unlikely event in the hubbub of daily practice, the applicability of the indemnity may be limited. Until the licence can be issued without exclusions other than categories such as workbooks and other ethically uncopiable items, it cannot be said to be a blanket licence along the lines conceived by the Whitford Committee (*Copyright and designs law*, 1977). It is however the best that can be done at present. Even though the reliability of the sampling basis of licensing schemes is regarded by many as open to considerable doubt, at least some rights owners are now getting something in return for photocopying in educational establishments. Also, licensed users are said to feel more secure from litigation due to the indemnity.

Nevertheless, some publishers, for example of a number of scholarly journals, still readily give free photocopying permission for small quantities and reasonable extents. Since licensing took no account of this, it formed one of the reasons for objection. A more important objection arose from the failure to provide a truly blanket licence. It is still not possible, nor will be for the foreseeable future, to obtain a licence which removes all need for care about copyright and adherence to a detailed set of terms. But despite objections, CLA licensing should be regarded as fully established as a means of covering a regular copying need. Irregular copying needs, such as those of individual consultants or organisations which copy sporadically and on a small scale, have yet to be addressed by the CLA and hence can still be covered only by permission seeking. Permission seeking must in any event be the practice whenever the law, or a permissive phrase printed on an item, or licence terms, fail to cover a user need. This applies generally, not just in photocopying. An important point about permission seeking is the design of a concise standard form which makes it as easy as possible for a publisher or producer to reply, preferably simply by photocopying the completed form.

Copyright-cleared photocopies

A recent agreement between the British Library Document Supply Centre (BLDSC) and the CLA allows the supply of copyright-cleared photocopies of periodical articles to requesters. This can overcome problems such as additional copying needs from the same journal issue – whether single or multiple – and copies for addition to the stock of a profit-based library (*Copyright cleared*, 1990). Each BLDSC fee will incorporate a standard royalty charge per article per copy. The establishment of such a service may perhaps prepare the way towards getting publishers at last to agree to print per article per copy charges in every journal issue like titles associated with the Copyright Clearance Center in the USA, long suggested in the UK as one way of dealing with irregular copying needs (Wall, 1990c).

Some libraries with staffed photocopying services find the keeping of files of photocopy declaration forms for the necessary six year minimum most inconvenient. A feature of CLA licensing is the overriding of the need for statutory declaration forms and other conditions. If the price were right, certain kinds of library might be tempted to take out a licence to override the legal formalities, especially if it also covered more than one journal article per issue and thus caused fewer permission seeking delays. But there will always be limits of some kind and therefore a need either to contact rights owners on users' behalf or get them to do this for themselves and bring a written permission to the library. It could be more fruitful for managements to investigate other means of completing and keeping declarations, such as a ledger with declaration text overlay for each page of signatures as a person signs. And all are recommended to bear in mind the need, already referred to earlier, to preserve legal permissions, especially library copying and the concept of fair dealing for users, otherwise future law might drop them altogether.

Off-air recording

Because the 1988 Act allows off-air educational recording by educational establishments of any broadcast in the absence of a licence, the Educational Recording Agency (ERA) (Heathcote, 1989) has been set up and, along with the Open University's own licensing, all educational off-air needs are now licensed.

Off-air recording is permitted for 'private and domestic use', the word 'and' being important, so time-shift recording within the family is now legal.

In an educational establishment, the Act allows the performance or reading or showing of books, plays, music etc., as part of the establishment's activities, provided the audience contains no members of the public. Likewise, for instructional purposes, an educational establishment may play or show sound recordings, films, videotapes, broadcasts, and cable programmes before an audience containing no members of the public.

With regard to videotapes, even those tapes bearing a phrase such as 'licensed for home use only' can be shown in schools, since the British Videogram Association (BVA) regards that environment as domestic (see also notes about rental below).

It has been ascertained that the Department of Science interprets S.I. 1989 No. 1068 (Statutory Instrument, 1989b) as encompassing not only local authority-controlled establishments, and universities and polytechnics, which are clearly covered by the wording, but also *any* educational organisation, however funded. Thus the Act's educational permissions cover a state-funded body like a nursing college and even a privately funded educational or training establishment. Thus such

101

bodies can claim CLA, ERA and Open University licences on the same basis as other establishments.

Licensing of rental

The BVA has no wish at present to set up licensing alongside the commercial hire industry, where the price covers royalties up front. However, nor does the BVA discriminate against sell-through copies which may be acquired by libraries from stores or supermarkets. There is therefore nothing against anyone, and any library, setting up a videotape loan or rental service without a licence, as far as the BVA is concerned, for domestic use. This should not however be taken as precluding a risk of an individual producer raising his own objections. And it should be made clear that a public performance by or in a library always requires permission. When films are hired, the hire company takes care of the royalty question.

The British Phonographic Industry Limited is to allow public libraries to run rental services for sound recordings free of royalty, subject to certain limitations on acquisition rate and actions to discourage illegal home copying. It is possible that the arrangement may in future also apply to other non profit services such as those in universities and polytechnics, who should consult the Library Association if they wish to run services. Profit-based organisations, including commercial hire shops, are most unlikely to be granted a form of licence for rental of sound recordings, especially in compact disc form. The different approach from that on videotapes should be noted – it comes about from the fears raised by the advent of DAT or digital audiotaping which could be used to make perfect copies of compact discs or other recordings at great loss to producers.

As yet, computer programs in electronic form, also entitled to the new rental right, are not covered by licensing. This is because it has not yet proved possible to identify and communicate with a body which represents the majority of software houses and which might be prepared to agree to licensing of rental at least by public sector libraries. The LA now has the problem in hand, but it would seem fruitless to seek licensing of rental of complete utility items such as small packages of statistical software, which rights owners will expect to be purchased by every user. Nor should one seek to rent educational programs except for a specific clientele such as via a school library service. And the big business packages are excluded because they are subject to revision indefinitely and are in any event on lease and not purchased.

What remains is entertainment programs – but computer games, along with educational software claimed to be copied by schools, are said by the software houses to be the areas of maximum economic damage. Cases are known of worldwide exchange of illegal copies of games by juvenile users of the networks. Without anticipating too much the outcome of discussion, it would seem conceivable that public libraries might be allowed to lend or rent out demonstration or sampler discs of utility and entertainment software, and provide on-the-spot use of a reference set when microcomputers are made publicly available by the library. By those means it should be possible to imitate the shop-window effect of sound recording loans by public libraries, to the benefit of rights owners as well as the users.

Discussion is under way between the National Council for Educational Technology and a body called the Educational Software Publishers Association on the copying of programs for school use. But it seems improbable that anyone else will be allowed any general or collective form of licence, whether of copying or of rental, in respect of complete items of computer software.

There is however nothing in the 1988 Act to prevent the *free loan* of *any* copyright material by anyone or any kind of library other than public libraries. These, with their liability for royalties if so required even when loans are free, must seek licences from rights-owner organisations in respect of sound recordings and computer programs in electronic form. Some computer program discs carry such phrases as 'No loan permitted', but this has doubtful validity unless also covered by full contract or conditions of sale known in advance.

Licensing of performance

A library which lends from its collection of multiple copies of plays or orchestral music sets should remind borrowers that public performance requires permission to be sought. Showing or playing of audiovisual or electronic media to the public also requires permission, for example from the producing company in respect of videotapes. However, showing or playing of such media in an educational establishment for educational purposes to a non-public audience (students and staff, for example) is permitted by the 1988 Act.

The public performance, or performance in an educational establishment for non-educational purposes, of music and of sound recordings is the concern of two bodies: Phonographic Performance Limited (PPL) and the Performing Right Society (PRS). PPL licences, for example, the playing of tranquillising music in lifts or recreational areas, acting in respect of rights in the recordings. The PRS acts on behalf of composers and music publishers. Thus organisations using recorded music in public should approach PPL and PRS. Those putting on live performances need only approach PRS.

Yet another body, the Mechanical Copyright Protection Society, must be approached if music is to be re-recorded, for example, the incorporation of a portion of a sound recording as background to an audiovisual item such as a tape-slide programme or videotape.

THE NEW ACT OF 1988

On 1 August 1989 the Copyright, Designs and Patents Act, 1988 came into force. As well as introducing a new unregistered design right, the Act covers trade marks and performing rights in consolidating and revising the law, and is the first all-in-one act coverage of intellectual property by any nation. The Appendix outlines the contents of Part I.

Main features

The main features of the Act, for librarians (Wall, 1990a), are:

- the Act clarifies that copying for research or private study as 'fair dealing', even if done by an individual for himself or a profit-based library on his behalf, *does* override publishers' rights in the printed page
- library copying service is confirmed from earlier law for 'prescribed libraries'
- loopholes for multiple copying have apparently been closed successfully throughout the Act, including the 'related' or 'systematic' copying which can result in multiple copies of an item being found among the same group of people. Librarians have been made considerably more responsible for controlling copying service, though they can rely upon user declaration forms unless there is reason to believe they may

be false. There is no mention of self-service machines, but see the subsection 'Notices on limits' on page 111

- 'research' means any kind of research, even that done towards commercial ends, despite an early attempt in the Bill to exclude commercial research from fair dealing
- a new 'rental right' is established for sound and video recordings and films, and computer programs in electronic form. The right is owned by the producing company in the first instance and lasts for 50 years. However, public libraries must pay royalties on loans of such media, if so required by rights owners, whether or not rental charges are made
- photographers are now authors and are therefore the first owners of copyright in their work for life plus 50 years – unless done by an employee in the course of employment, when the employer is first owner
- care is needed with definitions, and some are conspicuous by their absence whilst others form a hinterland of exploration. For example, microforms are not mentioned anywhere in the Act but may be considered covered via the definitions of 'facsimile' and 'reprography'
- computer programs are now 'literary works' and, unlike other works put into another physical medium such as music in a sound recording, carry copyright only as literary works for the usual life of programmer as author plus 50 years regardless of physical form
- videotapes are 'films'. Audiovisual media carry copyright for 50 years from the end of year of first issue. Broadcasts are also copyright for 50 years from first use of the items concerned and belong to the person responsible for arranging the broadcast. Non-interactive electronic databases, publicly accessible via a telecommunications system, may carry copyright for the database producer not only in respect of the individual works included but also as a 'cable programme service' for 50 years from first use of an item, and as a compilation. ('Non-interactive' should be taken, unless case law shows otherwise, as the absence of ability to modify database content by the user.)
- compilations are now included in the definition of 'literary works'. In short, original works like books, music, plays,

computer programs, compilations, and so on carry copyright for the life of a personal author plus 50 years. If there is no personal author or the work is anonymous, the period is 50 years only. All physical media other than printed matter also carry copyright for 50 years only. A publisher's copyright in the typographical arrangement of a published edition (not a reprint) lasts for only 25 years after the year of first publication

- 'anything' is permissible for the purpose of judicial proceedings, but the Law Society has agreed to recommend its members to apply this only when proceedings are actually under way

- licensing of copying on a voluntary basis is encouraged without making it compulsory. By making certain procedures royalty-free unless a licence becomes available, the Act has also encouraged rights-owners to provide licensing schemes. A 'scheme' is by definition collective, covering more than one author or producer and more than one work, for example, the newly established Educational Recording Agency now provides licences for the off-air recording of broadcasts for educational purposes, except Open University material which has its own licence

- a Copyright Tribunal has been formed, based on the former Performing Right Tribunal, but on copyright will only be concerned with problems arising in respect of licensing schemes. Much of the Act is taken up with the organisation and administration of licensing schemes

- moral rights appear for the first time in UK law: the right to be identified as author or director; to object to derogatory treatment of a work; the right of a person not to have a work falsely attributed to him; and the right to privacy on the part of a commissioner of photographs taken for private and domestic purposes. Moral rights cannot be assigned but can be waived

- a new category 'Parliamentary copyright' now accompanies Crown copyright

- some 20 sections concern 'Remedies for infringement' and 'criminal liability' is mentioned for the first time in UK law, although it was possible to suffer a prison sentence for certain infringements of the 1956 Act. Damages need not be limited to

an estimate of economic loss by a copyright owner and can be punitive
- two of the appended Schedules are particularly relevant: Schedule 1 covering 'transitional provisions and savings' and Schedule 7 containing 'consequential amendments'. It is via the latter that public libraries have been made liable for rental right royalties even if they do not charge for loans

During Committee stages, the Government made it clear that contract law can override any part of the Act. Licences, leases, and conditions of sale known before purchase are clearly contractual. Other attempts at restricting user actions, such as printing phrases in books, on recordings etc., have never been tested in court, but it seems unlikely that they could be judged contractual when they aim to restrict actions further than the Act itself. Rarely, phrases on items may give greater freedom, and should of course be followed.

The Act is incomplete without the various sets of Regulations made under it. The most relevant set to this chapter is that on libraries (Statutory Instrument, 1989a) where readers must be prepared for at least one difference from the Act as passed: the ability of non profit-based libraries to copy for archival purposes; where the Regulations now limit this to cases where an item is wholly or mainly for reference on the premises, as well as the Act's limit to items whose purchase is not reasonably practicable.

Some enquirers question why the Act contains nothing about international copyright: 'What can we copy of American publications?', they say. Independently of the Act, international agreements exist about copyright. Under the oldest, the Berne Convention, each signatory nation must give at least the same protection to foreign material as it does to home-produced copyright items. Few nations are not yet in the 'Berne Union'. Unless a national source is known not to be in Berne, UK law should be followed for all the relevant items.

Uncertainties

As regards working experience with the 1988 Act, not only should its ink be regarded as barely dry but also it leaves many points to be sorted by voluntary agreement or licensing or some form of contract law between rights owners and users. For example: public library managements still need to know where they stand regarding rental of sound recordings and computer programs; some basic standard downloading allowances to underpin widely varying terms in service contracts would help (Wall, 1989b; Wall, 1990b) and copying to build topic files is not covered by the Act (but should continue *pro tem*). Common Market moves on harmonisation of copyright law could further complicate matters, for Directives could override UK statutes. However, any enquiries on negotiation or licensing progress should be through library professional bodies – unilateral approaches, other than simple permission requests, to rights owners can cause confusion and have adverse effects.

GUIDES FOR USERS

Library Association and British Copyright Council guides

The LA guides (Library Association Guides, 1990) aim to replace the interim ones issued by the LA in March 1989, before the appearance of the principal Statutory Instrument (1989 S.I. No. 1212) in August 1989 produced several unexpected approaches. The first of the March 1989 series is however not replaced: this was an outline of the main changes represented in the 1988 Act.

The 1988 Act authorises 'prescribed libraries' to provide photocopies in response to requests for the purpose of research or private study. The Regulations in S.I. 1989 No. 1212 of August 1989 contain definitions of prescribed library or archive which differ from what was understood to be in plan at the time the first edition of the LA guides was issued in March 1989. As mentioned earlier, 'prescribed' for specified library copying service means non profit-based bodies, and a suggested definition of profit appears in the LA guides. But it should be emphasised here that *any* library, including that of a profit-based organisation, may copy on behalf of an individual for fair dealing purposes, including research or private study, and the British Copyright Council guide (Clark, 1990) acknowledges this fact.

There is considerable overlap among the LA guides, which are designed for particular kinds of library, because all non profit-based services on the one hand and all profit-based services on the other hand have a great deal in common. They are however the most authoritative statements published, and should in general be taken as overriding parts of other references, including some books which are otherwise helpful.

There was a useful exchange of drafts between the LA and the Copyright Licensing Agency on behalf of the British Copyright Council, and the latter's own guide (Clark, 1990) was issued very soon after the LA guides. The BCC guide covers *only* photocopying, and completely replaces *Photocopying and the law* (1965 and 1971) and *Reprographic copying of books and journals* (1985).

It cannot be over emphasised that both the relevant guides of the LA series and the BCC guide, along with the other references segregated at the end of this chapter as core material, are essential. That being said, some residual differences between the LA and BCC publications require comment.

Limits: non-periodical material

Since there is no limit in the Act on extents of photocopying which might be judged fair dealing in a court case, the BCC pamphlet gives guidance. This effectively indicates the acceptability of the same limits for individual copying as are licensed for multiple copying in educational establishments. This restricts an individual's copying from books to one copy of a maximum of a complete single chapter regardless of percentage of total, or otherwise of a maximum of 5%. The LA guides, on the other hand, whilst stating the latter for books in general, express the view that 'up to 10% of a work should be permissible for *short works* provided that the extract does not amount to more than 20 pages. This view has not been accepted by the BCC.'

The latter is primarily to cope with the frequent absence of chapters *per se* in short books and in reports and pamphlets, and, since the Act's 'reasonable proportion' is decided by the librarian of a non profit-based service, the LA view can be generally followed. On copying by individuals and profit-based libraries, readers are reminded that fair dealing lays down no specific limits to copying, leaving it to the courts to decide what is fair in infringement cases. It is nevertheless in the interests of both rights owners and user managements to adopt limits. For rights owners, the aims are to reduce what is seen as unfair exploitation and copying to replace purchase. For user managements, the aims are not only to guide individual users and staff but also to avoid as far as possible sharing blame for infringement on the premises by those operating self-service equipment.

However, in respect of library copying service by non profit-based services, the BCC guide itself gives, as an aid to deciding what might be a 'reasonable proportion' of non-periodical material, 'a rule of thumb maximum figure of 10%'. Circumstances should be taken into account by the librarian. If a book were known to be out of print and unobtainable, for example, this should not deter a librarian from authorising the copying of a larger proportion. Again a reminder seems necessary: that the Act's provisions on copying service by non profit-based libraries override any consideration of fairness, subject to the conditions governing such copying.

Limits: slides

Then, in respect of slides or transparencies 'for instructional purposes which do not involve publication', the BCC states its view that one of either may be made of 'an illustration in a published edition of a work provided that the source is duly acknowledged'. This is less restrictive in some ways than the LA guide, though the BCC does add the requirement for acknowledgement of source, a long overdue piece of advice for those slide producers who habitually omit any details of source, a bad practice from the information point of view as well as copyright.

Limits: periodical articles

The BCC must perforce acknowledge that a library service can produce a copy of an article in a periodical in response to a request, since that is a clear legal permission. But the BCC specifically states this to be unacceptable as fair dealing. The LA guide however takes the opposite view. Periodical publishers have never recognised the copying of periodical articles as fair, and a new reason – the electronic journal – has affirmed their stance. In this context, users should bear in mind that the Act specifically authorises non profit-based libraries to copy an article 'in a periodical' and that in a court case this is most unlikely to be extended to an article appearing in any other form, which should be regarded, like a book or pamphlet or report, as a complete work in itself.

It is, however, unlikely that a court case would ensue from an individual's copying of one article from an issue for research or private study and, if litigation did ensue, it would seem even more unlikely that a judge would rule against an individual – or indeed a profit-based library – copying to the same extent that a non profit-based library could do on his behalf. Furthermore, the Association of Learned and Professional Society Publishers (ALPSP) has recently published a statement which leaves the BCC exposed on this point (St. Aubyn, 1990), for the ALPSP recommends succinctly that 'the limit of photocopying under fair dealing should not exceed the library photocopying limits' in the Act, meaning of course prescribed or non profit-based libraries.

An important agreement reached in December 1990 between the BLDSC and the Copyright Licensing Agency just as the LA and BCC guides were issued provides a means of purchasing copyright-cleared photocopies of periodical articles (refer to the section on copyright-cleared photocopies earlier in this chapter). The BLDSC can now provide more than one article per issue for any purpose, short of further replication or re-publication.

Notice on limits

The LA states exactly the same extents as probably acceptable under fair dealing as those which are legally permitted under library copying service provisions, with the addition of the above recommendation on reasonable proportion of non-periodical material and notes on British Standards, Ordnance Survey maps, and HMSO publications. Thus the LA notice for display beside all photocopying machines, offered for sale in conjunction with the guides, states extents which are applicable both to fair dealing and to library copying service permissions. This was decided not only to reduce confusion to users but in the hope of minimising excesses on self-service copiers due to over optimistic individual assessments of what might be fair.

Precautions against sharing infringement blame for excessive self-service copying is given by agreement in the same terms in both the LA and the BCC guides. Unlike the LA notice, the CLA licensing notices are wordy and seem unlikely to be read before copying.

Advice

A useful feature of the LA guides is their inclusion of advice on commonly occurring problems such as the legality or otherwise of current awareness bulletins with copying service as an adjunct. The content of all guides, or statements in correspondence from bodies like the British Videogram Association and the British Standards Institution, are of course subject to revision in the light of further developments, such as any case law which might ensue from the new Act. However, they should be followed with confidence in the interim. In addition to the LA guides, one on special libraries in the public sector is in preparation, although those can be covered *pro tem* by studying the public library guide plus any relevant parts of the educational ones.

A helpful incidental point about the BCC guide is its use on the title page of a novel modification of the phrase which has caused so many questions from individual users – the forbidding of any copying at all without permission. The new BCC phrase starts with 'Except as permitted under the ... Act, 1988...' and includes a reference to the CLA licence as an alternative to permission seeking in respect of photocopying. Hence libraries in the UK should continue to ignore the customary form of phrase.

The above guides, and those which follow, are all subject to revision in the light of experience of working with the new Act, possible case law, and additional questions from users which may need to be incorporated.

Other guides

The HMSO's *Dear Librarian* letter of several pages (*Dear Librarian*, 1989), the Ordnance Survey leaflets (*Crown Copyright*, 1990; *Copyright – publishing*, 1989), the British Photographers' Liaison Committee's guide (*Photographer's guide...*, 1989) should also be consulted if the LA and BCC guides do not apply to a problem. The CET's own concise notes on main points for educational establishments are now embodied in Crabb (1989). Some other items have been included as guides in Library Association Guide *Copyright in school and college libraries* (1989): these include the Music Publishers' Association code of fair practice in respect of sheet music (*Code of fair practice...*, 1992).

RECOMMENDATIONS

a) readers of this chapter should be prepared for differences in interpretation in the items in the bibliography, even between the authors of legal manuals on the 1988 Act. The latter are usually inadequate in detail in any event for librarians

b) the LA and BCC guides should be seen as essential reading as the most authoritative statements at present available, updated to some extent by this chapter

c) managers should also hold copies of the Copyright, Designs and Patents Act, 1988, Statutory Instrument 1989a, and Statutory Instrument 1989b, and study the law at first hand when in doubt, consulting when necessary on specific problems or points of difficulty of interpretation

d) note should be taken that various deterrents, not least expense, exist against a rights owner bringing a case in respect of an individual unless he sells or re-publishes the copy or runs off multiple copies for distribution. The organisation owning the equipment could however share blame if infringement occurs in more than isolated instances, and no-one wishes to suffer the time-waste and expense of a court case, not to speak of the risk of punitive damages greatly exceeding any estimated loss to a rights owner. Therefore it is very important to display notices beside self-service photocopying equipment plus other precautions recommended in the LA guides, plus any licensing notices which may apply to the organisation

e) apart from the increased responsibility of librarians and the complexity of the law, librarians are often expected to advise other departments on their own problems. For these reasons as well as the uncertainties (see page 107), it is recommended that at least one staff member should make a special study of copyright and keep up to date

f) rather than tell requesters of copying above norms to get permission and bring it in writing, it is safer to provide such copyright clearance as part of the library service

g) staff and readers should be asked simply to follow the notices beside machines, raising questions when in doubt with the specialist member of staff

h) questions which could affect the whole profession, like progress on the licensing of sound recording or computer program rental services, should be raised via the professional bodies

BIBLIOGRAPHY

Clark, C. (1990), *Photocopying from books and journals: a guide for all users of copyright literary works*. British Copyright Council. (This completely supersedes the withdrawn *Photocopying and the law* of 1965 and 1970, and *Reprographic copying of books and journals* of 1985. It should also be assumed to supersede the more liberal *Photocopying from periodicals: a code of fair practice* by the Periodical Publishers Association Limited (1980) which, though never officially withdrawn, is no longer distributed by the PPA.)

Code of fair practice agreed between composers, publishers and users of printed music, revised edition (1992). Music Publishers Association.

Copyright and designs law (1977), Report of the committee to consider the law on copyright and designs. Chairman: the Honourable Mr. Justice Whitford. HMS0. (CMND. 6732)

Copyright cleared! (1990), *Document Supply News*, no. 28, (December). British Library Document Supply Centre. (Plus brochure issued Spring 1991.)

Copyright, Designs and Patents Act 1988. HMSO.

Copyright – publishing (1989), Ordnance Survey. (Despite its title this also includes a note inviting enquiries about licensing of OS material use in digital mapping.)

Cornish, G. (1990), *Copyright: interpreting the law for librarians*. LA Publishing.

Cornish, W. R. (1989), *Intellectual property: patents, copyright, trade marks and allied rights, 2nd. edition*. Sweet and Maxwell.

Crabb, G. (1989), *Copyright clearance: a practical guide, 3rd. edition*. National Council for Educational Technology.

Crown copyright (1990), Ordnance Survey, Copyright Branch. (Brief notes include copying for: local authorities; the general public; exceptions regarded as fair dealing; business copyright licence holders; photocopying machines; (and a form of notice about OS for display beside self-service machines); and supply of map extracts by local authorities for planning applications.)

De Freitas, R. (1990), *The law of copyright and rights in performances*. British Copyright Council.

Dear Librarian: photocopying Crown and Parliamentary copyright publications. (1989). HMSO (enquire Norwich). (Companion to *Dear Publisher...* of same date)

Dworkin, G. and Taylor, R. D. (1989), *Blackstone's guide to the Copyright, Designs and Patents Act, 1988: the law of copyright and related rights*. Blackstone Press. (This includes a copy of the Act itself.)

Flint, M. F. (1990), *A user's guide to copyright, 3rd. edition*. Butterworth.

Heathcote, D. A. (1989), Copyright and offair recording: a new ERA. *Audiovisual Librarian*, vol. 15, no. 4, pp. 211–212.

Laddie, H. *et al.* (1990), *The modern law of copyright*. Butterworth.

Library Association Guides (1990), 2nd edition.
   Copyright in public libraries.
   Copyright in industrial and commercial libraries.
   Copyright in polytechnic and university libraries.
   Copyright in school and college libraries.
   Copyright in National Health Service libraries.

Merkin, R. (1989), *Richards Butler on copyright, designs and patents: the new law*. Longman.

Penn, C. (1990), Photocopying Crown and Parliamentary copyright publications. *Library Association Record*, vol. 92, no. 2, (February), pp. 117–118. (This expansion of the previous item by the Director of the Publications Division, HMSO, gives useful explanation and contact addresses.)

Photographers' guide to the 1988 Copyright Act (1989), British Photographers' Liaison Committee.

Report of the IFFRO Working Group on Electrocopying (1989), Chairman: Charles Clark. International Federation of Reproduction Rights Organisations.

St. Aubyn, J. (1990), Notes on learned journal copyright. *Learned Publishing*, vol. 3, no. 4, (October), pp. 203–212.

Shuter, J. (ed.) (1988), *Copyright licensing*. MCB Publishing. (Contains both publisher and librarian views.)

Statutory Instrument (1989a), The copyright (librarians and archivists copying of copyright material) regulations. S.I. 1989 No. 1212. HMS0.

Statutory Instrument (1989b), The copyright (educational establishments) (no. 2) order 1989. S.I. No. 1068. HMS0.

Wall, R. A. (1988), The case for research as fair dealing. *Library Association Record*, vol. 90, no. 8, (August), p. 438.

Wall, R. A. (1989a), The nature of copyright. *Library Association Record*, vol. 91, no. 3, (March), pp. 130.

Wall, R. A. (1989b) Copyright and online. *Aslib Information*, vol. 17, no. 11/12, (November/December), pp. 264, 266–267.

Wall, R. A. (1990a), Copyright: the new Act of 1988. *The Law Librarian*, vol. 21, no. 1, (April), pp. 18–25. (Based on paper to September 1989, Oxford, Conference of the British and Irish Association of Law Librarians.)

Wall, R. A. (1990b), Libraries and copyright in non-print media. *European Intellectual Property Review*, vol. 12, no. 9, (September), pp. 311–314.

Wall, R. A. (1990c), Copyright and photocopying: status report on industry, commerce and professional groups. *Aslib Information*, vol. 18, no. 11, (November), pp. 345–348.

Note: the list above includes sources which have been heavily drawn upon, and may be useful to the reader but which do not necessarily receive a specific reference in the text.

APPENDIX: COPYRIGHT, DESIGNS AND PATENTS ACT, 1988

Coverage of part I, Copyright

There are ten chapters:

I   *Materials which are copyright* (subsistence, ss. 1–2); descriptions of kinds of work (ss. 3–8); who is entitled to copyright (ownership, ss. 9–11); and how long it lasts (duration, ss. 12–15) for the various kinds of material.

II   *Actions which infringe copyright* if done without the copyright owner's permission (restricted acts, ss. 16–27). Establishment of rental right in sound recordings, films and computer programs (s. 18). Forms of secondary infringement, such as importing or dealing with infringing copies or means of making them (ss. 22–26).

III   *Exceptions to copyright*, (ss. 28–76). The fair dealing concept (ss. 29–30). Copying or recording for educational purposes (ss.

32–36). Library copying (ss. 37–43). Copying for proceedings: Parliamentary or judicial (s. 45); Royal Commission or statutory inquiry (s. 46). Material open to public inspection or on official register (s. 47). Public Records (s. 49). Design documents and models (s. 51). Anonymous or pseudonymous works (s. 57). Abstracts published with journal articles (s. 60). Rental of sound recordings, films and computer programs (s. 66). Broadcasts and cable programmes (ss. 68–75), including: time-shifting (s. 70); photographing TV or cable programmes; free public showing/playing (s. 72); modifying or subtitling for handicapped (s. 74); archives (s. 75).

IV   *Moral rights* (ss. 77–89), newly introduced into British law. Examples are: the right to be identified as author; and an author's right to avoid the consequences of false attribution of a work to him, or of unjustified modification of his own work.

V   *Dealings with rights* – the basic processes of transfer such as assigning, bequeathing, or licensing (ss. 90–95).

VI   *Possible consequences of infringement* (remedies, ss. 96–115). Court actions for damages. Criminal liability in respect of infringing copies, and search of premises.

VII   *Collective licensing*, though the word collective is not used (ss. 116–144). How licensing schemes may be set up and controlled. The powers of the intended Copyright Tribunal which will arbitrate on collective schemes.

VIII   *Copyright Tribunal*: authorisation, jurisdiction and procedures of a new body to replace the existing Performing Right Tribunal (ss. 145–152).

IX   *Qualification for copyright protection*: geographical and citizenship factors (ss. 153–162).

X   *Miscellaneous and general* (ss. 163–179). Crown copyright and a new Parliamentary copyright (ss. 163–165). International organisations (s. 168). Folklore: anonymous unpublished works (s. 169). Meaning of educational establishment (s. 174); of publication and commercial publication (s. 175). List of minor definitions (s. 178). Index of defined terms or expressions (s. 179).

7

Information technology, the law, and the library manager: an introduction

J Eric Davies

Information technology (IT) represents the result of mankind's application of a range of scientific phenomena, coupled with social, economic and even political factors. Like any technology it does not exist in a vacuum but in a social context wherein it is sometimes nurtured, often tolerated, periodically suspected and even occasionally resisted. It is frequently applied (and sometimes even misapplied!). There are then often tensions – at times creative, at times destructive – between technology and society. These tensions may be resolved by disseminating information and education about the technology or perhaps more negatively by occasionally regulating or legislating about and against it. That special legislation is sometimes demanded and deemed necessary is itself symptomatic of the often ambivalent attitude towards technology. Moreover, modern high cost and highly powerful technologies attract the criminal mind. The criminals' current awareness is often as good as anything that the library and information science profession can provide!

As with many other techniques the view through the looking glass of law, crime and information technology has interrelated perspectives. The library and information science manager needs to be aware of these and their relationship to library and information science activity if the challenges of applying such technology successfully are to be overcome. Figure 7.1 outlines these.

Firstly, there is the perspective which somehow regards the technology as something special, unusual, and even dangerous which needs to be

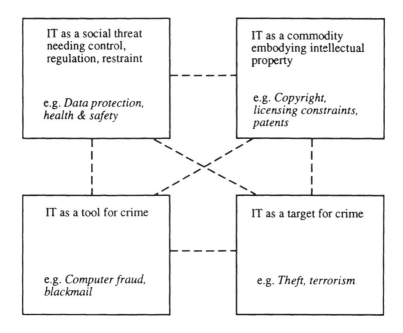

Figure 7.1: Information technology legal scenarios

restrained and controlled. Information technology in this context follows in a long line of developments which have provoked such tentative reactions from society, ranging from steam rail travel, through to bioengineering. The manager must be aware therefore of the constraints placed upon his or her application of the technology by society as exemplified in some law, regulation or contract, in order to avoid falling foul of their provisions. It is worth remembering that ignorance of the requirements does not provide a defence for the transgressor.

Secondly, information technology systems and products representing, as they do, the distillation of a vast input of creative and entrepreneurial energy have a very high commercial value, much of it represented by the intellectual property embodied in the novel design of hardware, or logic and structure of software. The manager must, when acquiring such commodities, be aware of and respect rights of intellectual property owners. Again ignorance of these factors provides no protection.

Thirdly, there is the perspective from which, put crudely, the technology itself becomes a tool (and sometimes a highly refined and efficient tool) for lawbreaking. Here again there is a long history, even tradition, of the lawbreaker adopting the latest technology be it sixgun or thermal lance to pursue an anti-social goal. The manager in this context has to maintain an awareness of the various methods, and their countermeasures, which lawbreakers misemploying information technology are wont to apply. Allied to this aspect is yet another misuse of IT. The value, utility, vulnerability and in some instances portability of information technology equipment and systems attracts the criminal and provides the fourth perspective from which to view the legal aspects of the topic. It is imperative that the manager pay serious regard to security in order to remain one step if not more ahead of the criminal and even the terrorist.

The issues and practicalities of various components of the legal dimensions of information technology in library and information science will be discussed within this framework in more detail in chapters 8–10.

It cannot be too heavily stressed that the full texts of any Acts and other documents referred to should be consulted before any decisions or actions are taken, since the descriptions of legislation here are necessarily summarised and generalised.

THE EUROPEAN DIMENSION

The substance of chapters 8–10 on IT and legal issues is centred around UK legislation and practice. However, a number of Draft Directives are emerging from the European Communities which, if enacted, promise to have a considerable influence on the IT scene and on the manager's priorities and procedures. There are proposals on data protection, software intellectual property and IT health and safety for example. Account has not been taken here of these because at the time of writing they have yet to reach the status of completed legislation. The proposals may be rejected, or they may be considerably modified. (In the case of the data protection Directive it is earnestly hoped by many data users that this will be so!) Those who seek to follow the proposals and associated arguments may do so by consulting the appropriate Draft Directives together with relevant press and journal reports. The introduction of European legislation will not in any case invalidate much, if any, of the general advice to the manager contained in this section. It beholds the manager to keep alert regarding developments, however.

8

The social regulatory perspective: data protection

J ERIC DAVIES

The foremost example in this area must be data protection legislation. The aspects of health and safety legislation should not however be overlooked but fall outside the purview of this volume.

The primary source for current practice is the Data Protection Act 1984 and its associated Statutory Instruments. Much has been written and disseminated about the Act and some sources are noted in the bibliography at the end of the chapter. But the most authoritative guidance originates from the Data Protection Registrar's Office, not least in the very informative Guidelines series issued by the Office.

It should be appreciated that data protection as characterised by the British legislation does not simply revolve around the issue of privacy. It is a far more complex subject involving a combination of confidentially, reliability and what may be described as fair dealing when handling or processing personal information by information technology.

The need for an individual's affairs to be accorded a reasonable degree of confidentiality is certainly catered for, but the legislation also imposes a requirement for reliability of personal information used, together with an obligation to collect and use that information fairly. Arguably, a person's absolute privacy, which might be regarded as a right not to be included in any legitimately created and operated database, is not assured.

Briefly, the Act is designed to specify acceptable activity and to allow for the establishment of a system for monitoring and regulating the use of personal data in computers in order to protect the interests of the individual. With its introduction Britain was able to ratify a Council of Europe Convention on data protection and thus safeguard commercial and technical interests in trans-border data use also.

Certain terms are used very precisely in the Act and it is as well in the beginning to establish their scope. They are fully defined in the Act, mainly in Section 1, but Figure 8.1 provides an outline.

Acceptable activity with regard to data is specified through a series of general Data Protection Principles which are enumerated and interpreted in a Schedule attached to the Act (Schedule 1 Part I and Schedule 1 Part II). To summarise, they require personal data in a computer to be:

a) obtained fairly and lawfully
b) held only for one or more lawful purpose declared by the data user
c) used or disclosed only in accordance with the data user's declaration
d) adequate, relevant and not excessive for performing the declared purposes
e) accurate, and where necessary up-to-date
f) not kept longer than necessary for the declared purposes
g) made available to data subjects on request
h) properly protected against loss or disclosure

There is also a further condition regarding the indefinite retention and use of personal data for historical, statistical or research purposes without breaching the first and sixth Principles subject to adequate safeguards for a data subject's interests (Schedule 1 Part 2, Sect. 7.). This 'ninth principle' is an important and useful provision for any archival approach to computerised personal information.

The monitoring and regulatory system surrounding data protection is based upon the Office of the Data Protection Registrar which has powers to identify, record, examine, approve, direct, operate sanctions and even undertake litigation in appropriate circumstances regarding the activities of data users with reference to the Principles and the law. The Registrar is also obliged to receive and investigate complaints from data subjects, and to disseminate information about data protection. Anxiety regarding these extensive powers and responsibilities should be allayed because there is also a Data Protection Tribunal which has been established to

Data

Information recorded in a form in which it can be processed automatically.

Personal Data

Information or opinions relating to a living, identifiable individual, but not a data user's intentions towards them.

Data Subject

An individual about whom personal data relates.

Data User

A person or an organisation holding data that is processed or to be processed, or who controls the contents and use of a collection of data.

Disclosing Information

Making available information, or extracts of information, of data held. The medium of disclosure may be oral, handwritten, printed or screen display, or otherwise.

Computer Bureau

A person or an organisation who processes data for data users, or allows data users the use of equipment for such processing. (Not confined to Computer Bureau Businesses.)

Processing

Amending, augmenting, deleting or re-arranging data, or extracting the information constituting the data, but excluding simple word processing.

Data Equipment

Equipment for automatic processing of data or for recording information to enable it to be so processed.

Figure 8.1: Definition of data protection terminology

hear appeals from data users (but not from data subjects) against the decisions of the Registrar.

Central to the operation of the system is the requirement that data user's activities have to be formally recorded in the Data Protection Register, except for examples of data use or types of data user covered by exemption. Operating without being registered unless exempted is a punishable offence. In practice the majority, if not all personal data processing within a library or information service will require registration as there are few exemptions appropriate. An outline of exemptions appears in Appendix A.

The Register thus presents a record of ongoing activity – it's nature and purpose and by whom – which is freely consultable by the general public.

The individual data subject's interests are reinforced by a right of access to data. An individual has, with some exceptions covered by exemption provisions, the right to establish what data is held about him or her, and further to see a copy of any such material. A fee may be charged for this but a maximum (currently £10) is prescribed. Other provisions allow for the correction, or even deletion of inaccurate information. Normally, a request for access must be met within forty days though the time limit for access to examination marks differs significantly to allow for delay between determining, and announcing results.

DATA PROTECTION IN THE LIBRARY

Information technology has pervaded operations to an extent that within the typical modern library and information service there are many and varied examples of the use of personal information in computers and related systems. These may include such internally created examples as records of users and their interests, material circulation records, details of services provided and to be provided to users, specialist information files on people, organisations and related material, local catalogues of material (which include personal names of authors and others), staffing records, payroll systems and accounts systems.

Examples applying information generally acquired from outside a library and information service may include commercial electronic databases (bibliographic and factual), centralised cataloguing records, other library and information centres' catalogues, booksellers' and publishers' databanks, expert systems, and electronic messaging systems.

Appropriate action regarding the data protection legislation must be applied in these situations. In most, if not all instances factors such as the exemption provisions will not significantly reduce the burden.

Managing for data protection

The range of steps which need to be taken by and within an organisation concerning data protection is wide and a variety of people are involved.

At a corporate level there are several things which must be done, but there are initiatives and actions relevant to the individual context also. These are discussed in turn below. Everyone bears a responsibility within an organisation to maintain good data protection attitudes and practices. A governing body or board, if one exists, bears ultimate responsibility for an organisation's conduct, operations and reputation. Senior management is accountable and has authority to make the appropriate policy and strategy decisions. Most large organisations will have a specially designated Data Protection Officer to ensure the overall implementation and coordination of policies and strategies. Others in an organisation need to ensure that the factors within their ambit are properly under control in relation to data protection. The individual has a responsibility to himself or herself, the organisation, and the wider community to make data protection work. It is important that nothing significant is overlooked by leaving it to someone else – someone else may be leaving it to you! Data protection integrity can so easily be compromised by the weakest link in the organisation whether it be the inexperienced new recruit with insufficient supervision or the senior manager too preoccupied to grasp the detail of the subject.

Policy implications

Even at the policy making level it is wise for an organisation to demonstrate its commitment to good data protection. Thus, a governing body and even its subordinate components might usefully adopt a policy statement or resolution affirming the importance of good practice and endorsing the Principles of data protection as a basis for activity. A plan to review the working of this policy is also desirable and may be introduced as must also, of course, a mechanism for implementing the data protection policy.

The library managers role

The library and information service manager's response will be conditioned by the nature and size of the organisation in which operations take place. For example, a large multi-national company or even a large local authority undertaking may have specially designated personnel to deal with the detail of the matter and the library manager's role is to work with such people to maintain an awareness of data protection requirements and good practice throughout his or her area of responsibility.

In other instances far more executive responsibility may devolve onto the individual library and information service manager, particularly in the medium sized or small organisation. The extreme example may be regarded as that of the one person-operated information centre for perhaps a voluntary organisation with few resources where possibly all data protection matters, including registration of activity, may have to be undertaken by the information centre manager.

In whatever context they find themselves, library and information service managers will need to maintain a full awareness of the data protection implications of their activities and those for whom they are responsible. Some common strands for managing data protection emerge whether they are recommended, directed or implemented by the library and information service manager.

A checklist for the manager is provided in Appendix B which should assist in determining action and establishing procedures.

Implementation

In general terms implementing good data protection requires that:

a) a system for communicating important information about data protection requirements should be installed

b) complementary to the above, a system for training about data protection (and thus ensuring that communications are understood) should be introduced

c) identification (and where appropriate subsequent registration) of personal data processing activity must be undertaken, together with continuous monitoring of proposals for new systems, applications and developments and data use to ensure lawful operation before they are enabled; similar action is required for accurate renewal of registration

d) activity must be conducted in accordance with the Principles of Data Protection and the law. Thus, appropriate methods and practices for so doing have to be devised and implemented. These encompass activity from collection/acquisition of data to final disposal/discarding/destruction, together with arrangements for dealing with the authorities and, very importantly, a routine for complying with enquiries, and requests for access from data subjects

e) a sound and comprehensible managerial structure to establish and identify responsibility to maintain good and lawful practice, and to accommodate data protection issues and problems should be developed

f) appropriate and adequate security arrangements are in place

PRINCIPAL ISSUES OF DATA PROTECTION

In the author's opinion, some aspects of data protection require particular attention either because of their general importance to good practice, their complexity or their criticality to the whole issue. These are:

- practices in fair obtaining of data
- the registration process
- practices for data subject access
- training

These are discussed more fully below.

Fair obtaining of data

The Data Protection Registrar has paid particular attention to the issue of fair obtaining of personal data in recent times. Perhaps as the pressures of initially registering so many data users have subsided time has been found to explore this and other issues. The matter has caused some data users to rethink their approach. What might have been safely regarded as an area of little ambiguity and controversy may have become a little more uncertain in some instances and certainly exacting in others. Briefings, notes and statements from the Registrar's Office have certainly emphasised the need for data users to pay particular attention to the way in which information is obtained, and methods and training need to take account of this.

In short, the Registrar's office has re-emphasised that not only must data be generally obtained and be seen to be generally obtained fairly and lawfully, but each and every specific instance of obtaining data must be capable of withstanding rigorous scrutiny regarding fairness within its own context. Thus, those who adopt a too generalised approach to obtaining data may have to revise methods and practices. (It may be argued that much of the advantages of using computers may be eroded if a highly generalised approach to handling very similar data is unavailable to a data user.) This is all the more unfortunate as the vast majority of data users operate with the highest motives and the best possible methods.

Some points are worth making in order to reinforce the need for care and consideration in assessing the fairness of collecting data.

Firstly, the data user's dealings with individuals should be characterised by candour, and policies and methods applied to collecting information should be as clear and transparent as possible. In addition, the circumstances of collection as well as the methods used are important and should be assessed carefully for fairness. Furthermore, the concept of fairness is applicable to each piece of data collected, and to each person from whom data has been acquired. The data user cannot therefore safely assume that what will be fair to one person will necessarily be fair to another whose circumstances and awareness are quite different. Thus, to reinforce an earlier point, the over-generalised approach in which individual circumstances are not fully taken into account are very much to be guarded against.

A data user should not make the error of assuming too high a level of familiarity with data protection legislation or indeed methods of data processing on the part of data subjects from whom information is being collected. It is generally safe to take the yardstick of knowledge as that of the average person in the street. It may be unsafe to regard data subjects as having a detailed knowledge of the Data Protection Act, the existence of a Register, the Office of the Data Protection Registrar, or even an awareness of their rights. This implies that statements that go a little beyond, 'Your data is being processed by a computer in accordance with the Data Protection Act' are desirable in documents issued to individuals.

It follows that documentation used to collect data, and certainly that which is available to the data subject, should be clear and unambiguous. It is recommended that such material should describe briefly what information is needed, for what purpose it is to be used and how it is to be handled, to whom it will be disclosed, together with an outline of the data subject's right to access and correction or erasure of data.

The registration process

It was noted earlier how the registration process operated by the Data Protection Registrar is central to the implementation of the legislation. As such it must be given due priority by any data user. By this time most organisations may have registered activity, but maintaining registration is an ongoing process because of amendments and renewals. Though the act of applying for registration may strictly involve the Chief Executive or Secretary of an organisation, in practice several people may be involved in collecting, collating, and presenting the information needed for applying for registration. Ideally, in an organisation with any sizeable activity, a Data Protection Officer, possibly with support staff, will coordinate and execute the work. Briefly, the information needed for each usage and purpose comprises:

- name of the data user
- address of the data user
- purpose for which data is held or used
- sources of data
- types of data subject (that is, what kind of people are described)
- types of personal data (that is, what kind of information about people)
- disclosures of data
- overseas transfers of data

It should be appreciated that the basis of data protection registration is that purpose to which data is being applied together with the nature (including its sources) of that data and the use (especially disclosures) to which it is put. Many are misled into regarding it as purely concerned with the files being kept and their identification and description. It takes but a little thought to realise that the contents of one file of data might be applied to several functions and would need to be described in a registration under several purposes. For example, a list of library users might need to be entered under many headings.

A necessary preliminary to making an application for registration is determining exactly what activity is undertaken and thus what needs to be registered. In anything but the smallest organisations this will entail a survey, either formal or informal, of ongoing and proposed activity. It is important that the latter be included in order that appropriate declarations can be made on an application for registration. Even if surveying activity is someone else's responsibility, the library and information service manager will certainly be called upon to identify and describe what operations are underway or planned within his or her ambit of responsibility. An example of a survey sheet is shown in Appendix C.

Following the thorough survey of activity the information gathered has to be collated and analysed to eliminate exempted categories which need not be registered and to group together like activity which may be taking place within an organisation and for which one registration may usually be appropriate.

Formal application for registration as a data user is undertaken on an official form obtainable from and returnable to the Registrar of Data Protection together with a fee. The form provides for details about a data user and the particular use of data to be specified and thus registered. To simplify the process, standard codes have been devised to specify the more common elements needed to describe activity. In Appendix D a list of standard purpose codes is reproduced to illustrate the approach adopted. The existence of these codes does not preclude the use of text to describe activity or data (and in some circumstances a standard code must be amplified by a short statement in further description). However, if the codes are adequate for an accurate description then it seems perverse (and time consuming) not to do so. Moreover, not using them must surely delay matters at the receiving end too!

Registration may be requested for a duration of one, two or a maximum of three years. Unless the activity and data use described is especially short term then it does not seem appropriate to opt for a shorter period than the maximum. Registrations may be renewed for a further period (on payment of another fee), amended (for no fee) or cancelled. A renewal reminder is sent by the Registrar.

The completed application form describing the user's activities is submitted with an accompanying fee (currently £56) to the Office of the Data Protection Registrar which acknowledges its receipt and later issues an acceptance if the application is satisfactory, or, far less frequently, a refusal if it is not. The Office may also seek further information to clarify the details of an application before coming to a decision. Once a correct application has been submitted, holding and processing data may continue pending the result of the application, except where a user has had a previous application refused or been de-registered in the previous two years.

Notification of approval from the Office of the Data Protection Registrar is accompanied by a copy of the Data Protection Register entry. This should be kept on file to provide a ready reference regarding the declaration made to the Registrar and thus the scope and limits of working, especially when any amendments are deemed necessary, and when renewal is imminent. The library and information service manager may play only an indirect part in the registration process as a provider of details of his or her activities. Regardless of who has responsibility for the registration process, it is most important that the library and information service manager establish that activities within his or her remit are accurately and properly registered and acquire a copy of the appropriate Register entry for reference, as noted earlier.

Data subject access

The right accorded individuals under the Act to establish whether data about them is held, and if so, to examine it, is an important development in personal information handling which places very firm and specific obligations upon data users. Arrangements, in terms of methods and personnel to meet these obligations without delay and error must therefore be devised.

Even if overall responsibility for these matters resides elsewhere in an organisation, the library and information manager will need to respond regarding those systems and data under his or her control. To the library and information manager this means that computer systems must be capable of providing the appropriate output in the required timescale; and further that a workable system of receiving, checking and acting upon requests for data subject access are in place. Data may not be withheld or its disclosure delayed simply because it is inconvenient or too costly for the data user to provide it.

To ensure consistency and swiftness of treatment it is advisable that specific personnel are delegated to make the detailed response to requests. Deputies for such personnel will be needed to cater for absences because the process will not wait in such circumstances. Documentation regarding data subject access is also important, if only to provide a record in case of queries and disputes about the treatment of requests and the reliability of data. It is highly recommended that a log of data subject access requests and fulfilment be maintained, together with a file of associated correspondence. A typical procedure is outlined in Figure 8.2.

RECEIPT
- – send acknowledgement/reply
- – send Standard Form for requesting access
- – request a fee of up to £10
- – check requestor's identity
- – ask requestor for further information to help find data (if this is considered reasonable)
- – log details of request

PROCESSING
- – check systems for data
- – check against exemptions
- – if request is in order, then within 40 days – except for exam. marks – send appropriate intelligible unmodified information or, if no disclosable information available, inform requestor of no data
- – log details of fulfilment
- – ask recipient of data for a receipt

QUERIES AND COMPLAINTS
- – accept and document any complaints about access or quality/reliability of data provided
- – if complaints appear reasonable then provide further access, or undertake correction or erasure of data
- – if complaint appears unjustified seek professional advice before entering into disputes and possible litigation

Figure 8.2: Procedure for treating data subject access requests

Receiving requests

When a request is received, at the very least an acknowledgement has to be sent in reply. This reply may also specify a fee for providing access if it is the organisation's policy to levy one. Currently up to £10 may be requested for access to each registration. Some organisations have introduced a standard form for data subject access requests and this may also be included. The data subject is not however obliged to use the form even if it does make the process more convenient for the data user. It is most important that the identity of the person making a request is properly ascertained and verified before any information is provided in response. Clearly, providing information to an imposter compromises data protection.

It is in order, however, for a data subject to authorise another as his agent to receive data on his behalf. Here again, appropriate safeguards regarding authorisation and identity must be in place. Steps taken to verify identities will vary, particularly with the sensitivity of the information being handled. An item such as a driving licence, a membership card of an organisation, or possession of papers addressed to the requester may generally suffice.

The data user is permitted to seek information from the requester to help find data if such a course of action is reasonable and the data user is not merely being obstructive or delaying the process. For example, a library and information service manager might reasonably ask of a requester whether and when he had been a client, member of, or supplier to a library and information service and of which branch, thus allowing a more focused and precise (and possibly less costly) search of systems to be undertaken.

It should also be noted that a data user is to some degree protected from the frivolous or the time waster insofar as according to s. 21(8) of the Act a court will not insist on an access to data if'it would in all the circumstances be unreasonable to do so, whether because of the frequency with which the applicant has made requests to the data user ... or for any other reason'.

This is however, unsteady ground, because what is too frequent and what is unreasonable are subjective matters open to interpretation. Someone who asked for information twice a day surely is being unreasonable whereas twice a year could arguably be acceptable.

Processing requests

The validity of a request for data having been established, there follows the need both to check appropriate systems for relevant data and to determine whether all or part of the data available is exempted from the need to provide data subject access by the provisions of the Act.

Where appropriate information is found, output should be produced in a format and presentation suitable for distribution to the data subject. It must be readily intelligible by the recipient and any codes or symbols used in a text must be deciphered or rendered decipherable by a key or legend, also supplied. Intelligibility does not, however, extend to having to explain the meaning of technical terms, or say, Latin names.

A very dim view is taken of any attempt to doctor any unreliable information discovered in the course of processing a request for access. The data so retrieved should not be modified or corrected before it is given to the data subject. However routine amendments to data such as those that occur daily (or even hourly) in a library circulation system can, and indeed should, proceed otherwise the accuracy of the data in the system is jeopardised. What is required therefore is not a standstill on processing subsequent to a request, but that a user refrain from interference with data.

Where some of the data held is covered by exemption from the access provisions, only the remainder has to be provided to the data subject. Even if no information is held about a person, or that which is held is wholly exempted from the access provisions, then the requester has still to be notified that no data is available.

A data user is not obliged to inform the requester that an exemption provision is being applied when either no data or partial data is provided. Equally, when all available data is being provided there is no obligation to indicate this either. To accommodate such situations, the form of words used in responding to or fulfilling a data subject access request may be as follows:

NO DATA AVAILABLE
In response to your request I do not hold any personal data which I am required to reveal to you under the terms of the Data Protection Act 1984.

DATA AVAILABLE
In response to your request the following/accompanying information represents personal data which I am required to reveal to you under the terms of the Data Protection Act 1984.

A valid request for data subject access must normally be complied with within 40 days of receipt of the request. A different time limit may apply for examination marks where the data user has five months from the date of the request, or 40 days from the announcement of results, whichever is the earlier, to respond. The data user may on the other hand choose to make no distinction in dealing with requests for examination information and decide to follow the normal 40 day rule.

Given modern data processing techniques and practices, the time allowed is, in most circumstances, quite reasonable and should present no problem to data users.

It is prudent practice to obtain a receipt from the data subject for any statement or information provided in response to a request for data. The importance of maintaining a log of responses has been noted earlier. Disputes about what was, and was not provided may then be more easily resolved subsequently if such documentation is available.

Handling queries and complaints

By definition this area lends itself less readily to routine methods because the number and nature of queries and complaints received will inevitably be both variable and unpredictable. In the ideal, well-ordered, data protection environment they should be minimal. A performance measure of an organisation's management of data protection might well relate to the number of queries and complaints received and resolved amicably.

The primary consideration is to treat queries and complaints courteously and seriously. Once again recording and documentation are important to establish what was claimed by whom and when. Where a straightforward complaint about an error in data which can be easily verified and has caused no damage or distress to a data subject is received then the sensible approach is to rectify the problem immediately and thank the data subject for his or her diligence.

Queries may arise about the operation of the legislation or about the methods of the organisation. Data subjects may not be fully aware of exemptions influencing what they may and may not receive for example. It may be good public relations to have a leaflet available describing what data is collected, how it is used and the provisions of data subject access as was discussed under the fair obtaining issue.

In situations where complaints are more forcefully made and/or their implications more serious, or their substance is disputed by the data user, then it is wise to seek legal professional advice as confrontation and litigation should not be contemplated lightly. Moreover, even where a case is resolved in favour of a data user, confidence in an organisation's approach to personal data processing may have been eroded at least in the eyes of one individual. The public relations of the situation should not be overlooked.

An easier way – routine (free) access

Some organisations have found it convenient and economical (as well as good public relations) to provide, at intervals, a brief standard form of output to data subjects as a matter of routine rather than wait for an access request. Whilst not pre-empting the data subject's rights this is a sensible practice which is mutually beneficial to both data user and data subject. There are many advantages to this approach:

- the data can be provided off-peak when processing load best allows and may avoid costly special runs and checks for a small number of requests
- it provides a means of checking for accuracy and up-to-dateness of data with the cooperation of the data subject and it reinforces confidence in the organisation's attitudes and methods towards personal data handling
- it can be used to test the system's capacity to respond and provide appropriate data, but without placing the operation under extreme pressure

This strategy may not be suitable for all applications in all organisations. It may be feasible to undertake it for the members of a library or information service, for example, but prohibitively expensive to perform a similar exercise for all the suppliers and customers of a multi-national company.

Training

Adequate and timely training in data protection principles and practice is an important factor in establishing and managing good data protection practice in an organisation. The philosophy and methods of such training have been given detailed treatment by this author (Davies, 1987/88) but some general points regarding the management of training are rehearsed here.

Firstly, the justification for training is not too hard to defend. Good data protection relies on people and the way they perform as much as it does on systems and equipment. Training, properly organised and executed, enhances human performance in this as in any other sphere of operation. Everyone responsible for, or operating with, personal data needs to receive appropriate training since each in some way has a bearing upon the quality of treatment given to personal data. Training should not be viewed as a once and for all affair; although initial training for new personnel or for people who are moving to new roles is very important, regular updating and renewing of knowledge and skills is equally vital to preserve a high standard of attention to data protection. The choice of trainer and venue for training are frequently dictated by circumstances within an organisation. For example, an organisation with a well appointed training suite and knowledgeable local trainers may have little cause to seek further. Conversely, a small organisation with few available resources for training may have to send staff for specialist training elsewhere. The advantages of a local trainer with a knowledge of the local context and problems for data protection may be balanced by the broader experience and perspective of an external speaker. There is also the opportunity for meeting and discussing problems and comparing methods with others when attending extra-mural training. In an ideal situation the best of both worlds might be utilised with a combination of in-house and distant training. The final arbiter will inevitably be the cost, both direct and hidden (e.g. absences from the job, travel), of training.

Both the content of training and the methods by which it is accomplished will vary considerably from one organisation to another and even within organisations. A range of information and skills need to be imparted through a variety of training techniques. Factors which influence choices include: the organisation's size, systems, methods; the amount, and nature of personal information used; and the range and number of people to be trained. Nevertheless, it is feasible to identify workable target statements – aims (a general description of what should be achieved) and objectives (a specification of measurable outcome) – for data protection in any context. An example of such aims and objectives is included in Appendix E.

FUTURES

Not surprisingly for an issue related to such dynamic and far reaching technologies, data protection has followed an evolutionary path since the introduction of legislation in 1984. And the Office of the Data Protection Registrar has not been content simply to administer the operation either. Responding to its obligations it has disseminated information and consulted widely about data protection matters.

The Data Protection Act broke new ground by introducing controls and constraints into an activity which had previously relied on voluntary good practice to maintain standards. Moreover, the activity was, and is, complex and fast moving. Not surprisingly, people (and systems) took time to adjust, and some problems with its operation and effectiveness have been identified. A major review and consultative exercise was undertaken by the Data Protection Registrar in 1988 and the results and conclusions were fully reported in the Registrar's 5th Annual Report in 1989. Briefly the main findings were:

a) concern about privacy and computers is widespread
b) the Data Protection Principles are generally satisfactory and work well in practice, though some changes in their interpretation may be desirable; they should apply to all data users regardless of exemptions
c) the conditions for and methods of registration are too complex – many users are unsure of whether they have to register or not, and have difficulty in specifying their activity accurately and completely; specified exemptions are not always clear; the registration form causes some confusion
d) the process might be simplified by either:
   universal registration – where all data users might have to provide minimal details of activity, or:
   highly selective registration – where either i) only data users processing for a relatively limited range of specific purposes would have to register; or ii) only certain categories of organisations would have to register (libraries, information centres and educational institutions would very probably be included in any scheme for restricted registration)
e) data subject access has generally proved useful for individuals and not too burdensome for users and should continue
f) a right for data subjects to seek information about a data user's activities – nature of use and purpose – should be introduced (under a scheme of universal registration this might, together with the existing access right, become the main mechanism through which any real monitoring of data use could be accomplished)

Parliament is not typically speedy in revising legislation especially to meet new technical circumstances and it is unlikely therefore that any rapid changes to principles and practices requiring a new Act of Parliament will emerge in response to the Registrar's findings. Nevertheless the information gathered by the Registrar provides useful input to decision makers and may herald what eventually will emerge on the statute book.

TECHNICAL DEVELOPMENTS

New technical dimensions to data protection are periodically emerging which will ultimately demand the attention of legislators, regulators, and managers. Two examples, not too distant from the library and information services manager's realm of operations, and demonstrating the dynamic nature of the issue, are briefly instanced.

Expert systems

Expert systems, or knowledge based systems of varying degrees of complexity and sophistication or refinement have been developed to support work in situations ranging from controlling the operations in a chemical process plant, or advising physicians on medical diagnosis, treatment and prescribing, to charting a way through a maze of social welfare regulations for benefits claimants and advisers. Typically, they comprise a data base or knowledge base, a set of rules that operate on the facts, an inference system which chooses which rules to use, and an explanation system that describes and even justifies why a particular course of action is recommended, or in automatic systems even implemented.

Expert systems may conceivably contain in their knowledge base personal information about living people though this need not necessarily give cause for concern or raise problems. The information will be subject to normal regulation for data protection purposes. It is when these systems encroach upon providing support for decisions about very sensitive issues relating to living persons that anxieties may understandably arise.

As things stand at present, though personal data use and the data elements involved have to be registered for data protection purposes, the criteria (rules and inferences) which an expert system applies to such data to reach critical decisions or recommendations need not feature in registration. How can they? They are not personal data! Even a requirement to register the purpose of an expert system does not adequately overcome the problem. The purpose describes what a system does, or is aimed to do – not how it does it.

Concern about this issue has been expressed by a Working Party of the Council for Science and Society in which a vivid example is presented of how unfair and inaccurate conclusions can be drawn if rules and inferences are insufficiently objective:

> IF subject address is in postal district Brixton
> AND subject age is less than 25
> AND subject race is non-Caucasian
> THEN subject credit rating is poor

As the report states 'it (the knowledge based system) may provide as apparent fact information that is actually derived from accurate data using dubious rules' (Working Party on Benefits and Risks of Knowledge Based Systems, 1989).

Lest this be thought to be too distant from the library and information services manager's world, it can readily be envisaged that expert systems could be applied to analysing scenarios and supporting decisions regarding selected clients' borrowing and reading habits, and in personnel recruitment. Some care is therefore needed in the design and construction of expert systems, and even more in their application to the real world.

Digital image coding

The techniques to digitise and store photographic images is now readily available. One department within an organisation known to the author employs such technologies in order to maintain records of persons concerned with its activities, whether as employees or people receiving its services. Though not posing insurmountable problems for management, the employment of such digital imaging and storage systems should make the manager pause for thought.

The information so electronically processed is clearly personal data about an identifiable individual (identification being the main point of the exercise!) and thus falls within the ambit of data protection legislation and practice. Whilst the purpose of such systems may be easy to identify and describe, the data elements may not fit so neatly within the customary concepts of data protection.

Some additional narrative description of the function and process of the system will therefore be necessary when a registration application is being submitted to the Data Protection Registrar. In addition, questions of accuracy and up-to-dateness of the information (the images) will have to be addressed. If they are employed for security purposes then clearly the data user will be more than willing to update regularly, though some circumstances affecting accuracy may be difficult to anticipate and control. What if the data subject purposely changes his or her appearance? A beard may be grown, and then removed a little later; or hair may be dyed and the style changed! Further complications may arise if an image is accurate but not very flattering to its subject. The issue wanders into the realms of subjective determination of factors which impinge on data protection.

Data subject access must not be overlooked either and appropriate routines and technology are necessary to enable an individual to receive a copy of the image. Merely producing a digital printout of the stored image as a series of zeros and ones is clearly insufficient!

Within the library and information services manager's ambit/context it can be readily envisaged that digital imaging systems could contribute to identity cards and membership documents for certain categories of service and especially those in academic, research and industrial organisations. The British Library Reading Room at Bloomsbury, for example, already requires of users that they be photographed. The growing need for security in library and information services may increase the extent to which photographic identification is required and digital systems may provide an efficient, flexible and reliable way to store and process such information.

BIBLIOGRAPHY

Chalton, S. and Gaskill, S. (1988), *Data protection law*. London: Sweet and Maxwell.

Davies, J. E. (1986), *Data protection.: a guide for library and information management revised edition*. Oxford: Elsevier.

Davies, J. E. (1987/88), The importance of spreading the word: the Data Protection Act and staff training. *Training and Education: a Journal for Library and Information Workers*, vol. 5, no. 1, pp. 3–22.

Evans, A. and Korn, A. (1986), *How to comply with the Data Protection Act: policies, practice procedures*. Aldershot: Gower.

Gulleford, K. (1986), *Data Protection in practice*. London: Butterworths.

National Computing Centre (1990), *Data Protection codes of practice*. Oxford: NCC Blackwell Ltd.

National Computing Centre and Department of Trade and Industry (1987), *Security and the 1984 Data Protection Act: guidance for computer users*. Manchester: NCC.

Pounder, C. N. M. *et al.* (1991), *Managing data protection second edition*. London: Butterworth-Heinemann.

Savage, N., and Edwards, C. (1985), *A Guide to the Data Protection Act: implementing the Act*. London: Financial Training Publications.

Sizer, R. and Newman, P. (1984), *The Data Protection Act: A practical guide*. Aldershot: Gower.

Working Party on Benefits and Risks of Knowledge Based Systems (1989), *Benefits & risks of knowledge based systems*. Oxford: Oxford University Press.

APPENDIX A: OUTLINE OF DATA PROTECTION EXEMPTIONS

Exemption from registration and supervision/data subject access/non-disclosure provisions

Categories of data use or circumstances:

1   Held only for payroll and accounting purposes – subject to certain limitations on disclosure.
2   Domestic, personal, family or related household affairs information or for recreational purposes.
3   Clubs, societies members' data – subject to consent of members.
4   Distribution Lists – disclosure limited by consent of subjects.
5   Held where the person holding the data has a statutory duty to make the information available to the public.
6   For safeguarding National Security.

Exemption from data subject access/non-disclosure provisions

Categories of data use or circumstances:
1 Prevention and detection of crime.
2 Apprehension and prosecution of offenders.
3 Assessment or collection of any tax or duty.

Exemption from data subject access provisions

Categories of data use or circumstances
1 Relevant to making judicial appointments.
2 Covered by legal professional privilege.
3 Preparing statistics.
4 Carrying out research.
5 Where providing subject access would expose the person complying with subject access provisions to proceedings for an offence, other than one under the Act.
6 Data kept only for the purpose of replacing other data in the event of the latter being lost, destroyed or impaired.
7 Consumer credit data (but this is accessible through the Consumer Credit Act 1974).

Exemption from data subject access provisions and subject to an appropriate Order issued by the Secretary of State

1 Physical or mental health information.
2 Social work information (from local authorities etc. or voluntary bodies).
3 Information for the purpose of discharging statutory functions regarding the regulation of financial services and activity and designed to protect members of the public against loss.
4 Other data, disclosure of which is prohibited or restricted by any law, if it is considered that such prohibition or restriction should prevail.

Exemption from Non-Disclosure Provisions

Categories of data use or circumstances:
1 Where urgently necessary to prevent injury or damage to health.
2 Where disclosure is required by any law or by order of a court.
3 Where disclosure is made for the purpose of obtaining legal advice, or in legal proceedings.

4 Where disclosure is to the data subject or his representative, or by his consent.
5 Where disclosure of the data is for the purpose of safeguarding national security even if the data is not already exempted for such a purpose from the various provisions applicable.

By effectively being 'defined-out' of the scope of the Act the following may be regarded as exempt from all its provisions.

1 Information which is an indication of the intentions of the data user in respect of an individual. Sect. 1, Subsect. (3)
2 Operations performed only for the purpose of preparing the text of documents (word processing). Sect. 1, Subsect. (8)

As the scope of the Act is confined to 'automatically processed information', manually processed and organised records are not subject to any control under this legislation.

APPENDIX B: MANAGING FOR DATA PROTECTION CHECKLIST

1 Actions

a) Start being aware and informed and keep being aware and informed.
b) Establish contact with your Data Protection Officer.
c) Check existing activity regarding personal data which is under your control for data protection integrity.
d) Ensure that activities in c) above have been, and any innovations are properly registered.
e) Ensure that staff under your control are being properly trained and are receiving clear communication regarding data protection matters.
f) Establish and monitor an ongoing data protection management regime covering:
   – documentation
   – procedures
   – personnel
   – security

2. Management Regime

In establishing and monitoring an ongoing data protection management regime it is important to remember that general advice or even direction may be emanating from a Data Protection Officer or similar executive. Determining the fine detail will need the expert input of the manager, who knows his or her system and working situation best. Factors include:

Documentation

> Material which identifies responsibilities and describes procedure to be followed and operations undertaken by personnel.
> Material which describes operations and performance parameters of equipment.
> Material which logs, identifies and labels in detail files and associated material.
> Material which logs and identifies any instances of data disclosure, transfer and access. (A general and abbreviated description of routine instances may suffice.)

Procedures

> The design and implementation of methods which cover all aspects of personal data handling from collection to disposal and which comprehensively and continually assure data protection integrity in all operations. In particular, methods devised to ensure correct disclosure, transfer and access to information.
> The design of supervision systems for such methods.
> The design of easily activated response procedures to Data Subject Access Requests.

Personnel

> Sustained quality and quantity of staff to accomplish methods without compromising data protection.
> Structures which do not inhibit and compromise data protection through service breakdown by staff absences, transfers and the like.
> Specifications of precisely determined roles, responsibilities and authority regarding personal data.
> Continuous training and appraisal practices

Security

> Adequate protection against accidental loss, destruction, damage or corruption of data through impairment of operations, hardware or systems.
>
> Adequate protection against wilful acts resulting in loss, destruction, and damage or corruption of data through impairment of operations, hardware or systems.
>
> Adequate and effective security failure contingency and recovery planning (Disaster Planning), extending possibly to insurance cover for damage and litigation.

APPENDIX C: DATA PROTECTION ACTIVITY SURVEY SHEET

Data protection – census of files   Department:

1   FILE NAME

2   FILE REFERENCE NUMBER

3   FILE DESCRIPTION

4   PURPOSE (what is the data used for?)

5   TYPE OF DATA HELD (what kind of information is held about persons?)

6   DESCRIPTION OF DATA SUBJECTS

7   SOURCE (origin of data)

8   DISCLOSURE (specify persons, organisations to which data is authorised to be disclosed)

9   TRANSFERS OUTSIDE UK (specify countries to which data is authorised to be transferred)

10   DURATION FOR WHICH FILE NEEDED (if known)

11   OWNER'S DETAILS (Name/Department Telephone number)

12   MACHINE ON WHICH FILE PROCESSED/KEPT

13   SECURITY ARRANGEMENTS

For file

For machine

For output

For discard

14   EXAMINATION MARKS (give full details if file is concerned with generation or storage of examination marks or the results of course assessments, including the starting date of any processing)

15   ANY OTHER RELEVANT INFORMATION

16   NAME OF PERSON RESPONSIBLE FOR DATA PROTECTION IN DEPARTMENT

APPENDIX D: LIST OF STANDARD PURPOSE TITLES AND CODES (produced by the Data Protection Registrar)

P001	Personnel/Employee Administration
P002	Work Planning and Management
P003	Marketing and Selling (excluding direct marketing to individuals)
P004	Marketing and Selling (including direct marketing to individuals)
P005	Fund Raising
P006	Public Relations and External Affairs
P007	Management of Agents and Intermediaries
P008	Purchase/Supplier Administration
P009	Business and Technical Intelligence
P010	Membership Administration
P011	Share and Stock-Holding Registration
P012	Ancillary and Support Functions*
P013	Customer/Client Administration
P014	Lending and Hire Services Administration
P015	Reservations, Bookings and Ticket Issue
P016	Research and Statistical Analysis*
P017	Information and Data Bank Administration
P018	Trading in Personal Information
P019	Charity and Voluntary Organisation Objectives*
P020	Property Management
P021	Housing Management
P022	Education or training Administration
P023	Borrower Account/Credit Facilities Administration
P024	Investment/Deposit Account Administration
P025	Combined Borrower/Saver Account Administration
P026	Personal Banking
P027	Credit Card and Charge Card Administration
P028	Corporate Banking
P029	Corporate Finance
P030	Investment Management
P031	Life and Health Insurance Administration
P032	General Insurance Administration
P033	Pensions Administration
P034	Factoring and Discounting of Trade Debts

P035	Credit Reference
P036	Accounting and related Services
P037	Statutory Auditing
P038	Other Financial Services Including Broking and Dealing*
P039	Legal Services
P040	Other Consultancy and Advisory Services*
P041	Government Benefits Administration*
P042	Assessment and Collection of Taxes & Other Revenue*
P043	Collection of Rates
P044	Valuation of Real Property (- in Scotland, Valuation of Lands & Heritages)
P045	Licensing & Registration*
P046	Grant and Loan Administration
P047	Consumer Protection and Trading Standards
P048	Environmental Health
P049	Electoral Registration
P050	Fire Prevention and Control
P051	Highways and Transport Planning
P052	Passenger Transport Operations
P053	Planning and Development Control
P054	Social Services/Social Work*
P055	Waste Collection & Disposal
P056	Water and Drainage Services
P057	Policing*
P058	Crime Prevention & Prosecution of Offenders*
P059	Courts Administration
P060	Discharge of Court Business
P061	Other Administration of Justice*
P062	Provision of Health Care*
P063	Ambulance Services
P064	Blood Transfusion Services
P065	Occupational Health Services
P066	Public Health
P067	Health Care Administration
P068	Other Central Government*
P069	Other Local Government*
P070	Other Public Sector*

* Use of these Standard Purposes requires further information to be given on the registration form.

APPENDIX E: TRAINING AIMS AND OBJECTIVES

Aims

1 To establish awareness of data protection requirements (especially the legislation) and practices throughout the institution.
2 To establish an atmosphere within the institution in which respect for personal data and its integrity and security is accepted and practised.
3 To establish a situation in which both within and outside an institution confidence in the efficient and secure treatment of personal data is high.
4 To establish a situation in which the probability of any compromising of personal data by accident or design is negligible, or ideally zero.
5 To establish a situation where all due requirements of the legislation are carried out correctly, swiftly and efficiently.
6 To establish a situation where all mandatory and desirable data protection requirements and practices are accomplished as cost-effectively as possible.
7 To establish an awareness amongst those undertaking training of their rights and obligations as data subjects.

Objectives

1 Being able to summarise the Data Protection Principles and other major features and requirements of the Data Protection Act.
2 Being able to summarise the main points pertaining to the rights and obligations of data subjects.
3 Being able to identify the limits and extent of security necessary for different kinds of data and situations.
4 Being able to describe, and show understanding and appreciation of, the importance of systems and mechanisms for communicating with individuals on data protection matters.

5 Being able to demonstrate an ability to relate to and communicate with individuals in a manner which provides assurance about data protection.
6 Being able to demonstrate proficiency at operating systems, mechanisms and procedures correctly and without compromising data protection.
7 Being able to assess situations and identify problems regarding data protection which require reference to a higher authority.

9

Intellectual property

J Eric Davies

The notion of stealing ideas and inventions is not new, and neither is the concept of legislating to deter such behaviour and to protect the owners of such intellectual property. The advent of electronic information technology has introduced new complications into the issue, both in terms of the variety of forms in which ideas are now manifested and in their rapid rate of change.

The software, systems and equipment held and employed in the typical library and information service – software packages, library housekeeping integrated systems, electronic databases, and expert systems – have all been devised with considerable expertise and skill and this is generally reflected in their high commercial value. This input and its value needs protection.

The main mechanisms for so doing today are:

- copyright: in software and in databases and their contents
- contracts and licensing
- design protection for devices
- patent protection for equipment and components

The primary source for intellectual property considerations is the Copyright, Designs and Patents Act 1988 and its associated Statutory Instruments. Other relevant legislation includes; the Patents Act 1977, and the Registered Designs Act 1949 and associated secondary legislation. A sizeable literature of comment and interpretation has grown up around

152

the subject and some examples particularly favoured by the author are Cornish (1990), Dworkin and Taylor (1989), Flint *et al.* (1989), and Lester and Mitchell (1989).

It is copyright and licensing which will probably need to preoccupy the library and information service manager. If hardware and equipment is acquired from reputable suppliers disputes over design or patent matters related to such items are not likely to arise. Any in-house development or adaption of equipment and systems, say as part of a research project, may well impinge upon design and patents issues, however, as well as matters of copyright in software and documentation. Material held in library stock will normally only need to be considered from the viewpoint of copyright also.

COPYRIGHT, CONTRACTS AND LICENCES

Copyright

This subject has been treated at length by Wall in chapter 6. In contrast, the present chapter confines its attention to those issues relevant to the management of information technology systems and library stock. Earlier copyright legislation was, to say the least, ambiguous regarding certain aspects of information technology as a means of storing, transmitting and replicating ideas. The Copyright Act 1956 reached the statute book at a time when computers and software were in their relative infancy and had not become the ubiquitous office tool or home plaything of today. The idea of a lay person – even a schoolchild – being able to copy software with a few simple keyboarding instructions would have met with derision!

History tends to suggest that legislation rarely moves swiftly to accommodate either technological or social advances. However, the intellectual property problems posed by the spread of information technology and its increasing sophistication were finally recognised by the introduction of an amendment to the 1956 Act in 1985 which firmly established copyright for software. The Copyright, Designs and Patents Act 1988 brought the whole issue properly into the computer age – at least for the time being!

Copyright may be summarised as the exclusive right conferred upon an owner of copyright in a work, who is usually its creator, to perform certain acts, which generally involve replicating and disseminating that work. The current British legislation embodies these principles and also describes certain generally permitted acts regarding copyright works. It also affords a further moral right to creators of works enabling them to be identified as such, to object to derogatory treatment including modification of their work, and protecting them against false attribution to work. There are provisions for dealings and transactions in copyright works. Provisions for remedies for infringement and mechanisms for approving licensing schemes for certain areas are also specified.

A modern statute catering for this area is inevitably lengthy and complex, but its fundamentals should be capable of being fairly readily grasped. There are very many precise definitions of material and other items in the Act, and special terminology is sometimes used. Several definitions are listed in s. 178 and an index pointing to the sections in which various definitions scattered throughout the text appear is also very helpfully provided in the main body of the Act (s. 179).

Section 1 of the 1988 Act specifies the following types of work as being covered by copyright:

a) original literary, dramatic, musical and artistic works
b) sound recordings, films, broadcasts or cable programmes
c) the typographical arrangement of published editions

Further parts define more closely what is meant by each of these. Literary, dramatic and musical works have to be recorded, in writing or otherwise, for copyright to subsist. Of particular significance to the theme of this chapter is the definition of literary work to include:

a) a table or compilation
b) a computer program (s. 3(1))

A cable programme service is described as (s. 7(1) (a), (b)): 'a service which consists wholly or mainly in sending visual images, sounds or other information by means of a telecommunications system, otherwise than by wireless telegraphy, for reception:

a) at two or more places (whether for simultaneous reception or at different times in response to requests by different users), or
b) for presentation to members of the public'.

Significantly it excludes amongst other things (s. 7(2) (a)): 'a service or part of a service of which it is an essential feature that while visual images, sounds or other information are being conveyed by the person providing the service there will or may be sent from each place of reception, by means of the same system or (as the case may be) the same part of it, information (other than signals sent for the operation or control of the service) for reception by the person providing the service or other persons receiving it...'.

By this definition it would appear that an online bibliographic or reference database service may be regarded as a cable programme service (though there has been some argument about this point). A service permitting recipients to add to and modify the contents of the database service (in the way that for example, members of the BLCMP consortium undertake with their shared cataloguing database) would not, however, be so viewed. Such fine distinctions have to be kept in view.

Sound recordings and moving images falling into the definition of films should not be ignored as relevant categories since they may feature, sometimes together, in some of the more sophisticated information technology applications involved in interactive learning systems.

Ownership of copyright is normally vested in the author who has created or written a work. In the case of sound recordings or films the author is taken to be the person undertaking the arrangements necessary for making them (s. 9(2) (a)) and in the case of a cable programme, the person providing the service (s. 9(2) (c)). Authorship can be jointly shared where more than one individual is involved in a work (s. 10). Computer generated works pose a particular conundrum since by definition (s. 178) they are generated by computer in circumstances such that there is no human author of the work. For the purposes of the Act the author is regarded as being the person by whom the arrangements necessary for the creation of the work are undertaken (s. 9(3)). Where the author of a literary, dramatic, musical or artistic work is an employee making the work in the course of employment it is most important to note that the ownership of any copyright resides with the employer unless there is an agreement between them to the contrary (s. 11(2)). Where the identity of an author or authors cannot be established then the work is deemed to be of 'unknown authorship' (ss. 9(4) and (5)).

Copyright does not last forever and its duration is normally related to the date on which a work was created or the author's lifetime (or more accurately death!). Appendix A summarises the duration of copyright in various circumstances for the different types of material relevant to this chapter. With the rapid pace of development of information technology and the concomitant obsolescence of material it may however be thought unnecessarily academic to be too worried about the duration of copyright at present. It is most unlikely that material of interest to the library and information service manager will be out of copyright because of its age!

Several rights are accorded to a copyright owner to undertake what are described as 'acts restricted by the copyright' (s. 16). These rights may be passed on to others either in full, or partially, by gift, bequest or through a commercial transaction. Undertaking any of the restricted acts without the proper permission infringes copyright and there are civil and criminal sanctions/remedies available. In another part of the legislation certain generally permitted acts are specified which do not infringe copyright when undertaken but these will be dealt with later. Acts restricted by the copyright are summarised in Appendix B.

Note that copying a literary, dramatic, musical and artistic work means reproducing it in any material form and includes storing it electronically (s. 17(2)). Also, making an adaption of a literary work is construed as including making a translation, and in relation to a computer program, a translation includes a version of the program in which it is converted into or out of a computer language or code into a different one, other than incidentally in the course of running the program (s. 21(4)).

In defining publishing as issuing copies to the public, this is taken to include, in the case of literary, dramatic, musical and artistic works, making them available to the public by means of an electronic retrieval system (s. 175).

In addition, the restriction on issuing copies of a work is extended to include, for sound recordings, films and computer programs, any rental of copies to the public (s. 18(2)). Even free loan of such material by public libraries is brought under these restrictions by a note in schedule 7 of the Act (page 227).

Were the copyright legislation to go no further then it may be argued that the communication, assembly and transmission of ideas, and scholarly and research activity in general would be severely curtailed through the general impracticability of tracing copyright owners and the prohibitive costs of acquiring permission for the most minor use of material.

The Act describes a series of generally permitted acts that include what is termed fair dealing which do not constitute infringement of copyright provided all conditions are met. To maintain a balance with copyright owners' interests, provisions for the creation and approval of licensing schemes for certain acts and categories of material are also included. In some cases permitted acts are conditional upon there being no licensing arrangements available for the activity prescribed, thereby encouraging copyright owners to form licensing arrangements. Appendix C summarises some of the various permitted acts enumerated in the legislation and notes where licensing is specifically mentioned. It is not an exhaustive table as some of the conditions and circumstances included in the Act are fairly specialist in nature. Those relating to libraries and information technology have been included, of course, and receive fuller discussion below.

As noted earlier, the Act confers certain moral rights to creators of works, about which it is very specific. Moral rights are not assignable. It provides for the right (sometimes described as paternity right) of a person to be identified as an author of a work, or director of a film. Conversely, the right not to have material falsely attributed to a person is specified. In addition there is the right to object to derogatory treatment of one's work, such being described as treatment which is 'distortion or mutilation of the work or is otherwise prejudicial to the honour and reputation' of the creator (ss. 80(2) and (6)). Exceptions are specified to these rights however, insofar as the right of identification (but not false attribution) and of objection to derogatory treatment do not extend to computer programs. Less surprisingly, neither do they extend to cover computer generated works. There is the presumption, perhaps, that the honour and reputation of a computer is not open to damage. This argument diminishes however when the reputation of computer manufacturers, software houses, and individual programmers are considered, and especially when it is considered how vulnerable are programs to adjustment and amendment (derogatory or otherwise).

Insofar as copyright is a property right then it is transferable by a variety of means, legal and commercial. The Act contains detail regarding dealings in these rights in chapter V. It is worth noting that a right may be wholly, partially, or conditionally transmitted especially in commercial transactions. This is notwithstanding the licensing schemes that may also be operating regarding copyright material. With information technology products in particular, transactions involving copyright and copyright material may incorporate special conditions. This area will be further explored later under licenses and contracts.

As was noted earlier, the Act contains provision for both civil remedies and criminal sanctions to uphold the law against infringements of copyright. The owner of copyright may take a civil action against an infringer to seek an injunction to stop whatever the infringer is doing, and may further sue for damages to compensate for any loss suffered as a result of the infringement. The loss may be calculated in terms of royalties or profits lost through the infringement. But damages may not necessarily be limited by such considerations and may be influenced according to ss. 97(2) (a) and (b) by 'the flagrancy of the infringement, and any benefit accruing to the defendant by reason of the infringement'.

Thus, a sufficiently foolish and reckless infringer places himself in some real financial jeopardy where exemplary damages may be awarded. There are also provisions in the Act for the forfeiture or destruction, in certain circumstances, of infringing works and the wherewithal for making them following an application to a court from the copyright owner.

Criminal sanctions which can involve fines and imprisonment are brought into play for copyright infringements of a more commercial nature. They may be invoked where infringing copies are made for sale or hire, or are being offered for sale or hire exhibited in public, or distributed, in the course of a business; or where someone makes or owns equipment knowing or suspecting that it will be used for creating infringing copies for sale or hire. Moreover, the Act extends liability to prosecution to officers, managers and others who consent or connive to such activity within an organisation.

There may be implications for the library and information services manager in these sanctions if it is interpreted that running a library and information service is a business. Lending or hiring illegally made copies could attract sanctions as could allowing equipment to be misused for creating infringing copies for sale, hire, or use in the course of business. This points to meticulous scrutiny of sources of material and close control over the deployment and use of equipment on the part of the manager.

Not a little emphasis is placed in the Act on the concept and mechanisms of copyright licensing. A whole chapter comprising over two dozen sections is devoted to the detail and elsewhere in the Act a stimulus of sorts, for creating licensing schemes is provided by specifying an extended range of permitted acts unless a licensing scheme is in operation. Thus the Act contrives to maintain a balance between the legitimate interests of copyright owners and the reasonable activities of users and exploiters of protected material. Licensing schemes and licenses are arrangements and devices through which copyright owners permit, usually for some recompense, individuals to undertake some of the acts generally restricted by copyright, in their use of material.

The balance of interests in licensing is overseen by the Copyright Tribunal which has power to approve schemes and can adjudicate in disputes about the granting of licences and the terms specified in them. Certain licensing arrangements can also be submitted to the Secretary of State for ratification.

For licensing to work successfully, however, there have to be copyright owners who are willing and sufficiently organised to offer a scheme on the one hand, and a body of users anxious to use material beyond the permitted acts and able to afford licences on the other.

An example of what may be regarded as a successfully established scheme is that contracted between the Copyright Licensing Agency (CLA) and authorities representing higher and further education institutions, which extends, for ease of preparation and dissemination of learning material, copying of many books and journals beyond the permitted acts.

Equivalents for all sectors of use and for all types of material are yet to be developed. For computer software and related material the problem would appear to be finding a suitable industry body with whom arrangements about using, copying and (importantly for libraries) lending and hire can be negotiated and established. Progress in other related fields such as educational broadcasting would appear to be further forward with licenses being available from the Educational Recording Agency (ERA) and Open University Enterprises for appropriate off-air recording and use (*Audiovisual Librarian*, 1991). Nevertheless this is an area of copyright where diligence in noting new developments is very necessary.

Contracts, licences and agreements

The special licensing arrangements legislated for in the Copyright, Designs and Patents Act 1988 will not be discussed here having been covered in the previous section.

There is a preponderance of contractual and related arrangements with regard to IT and intellectual property. The use of material – software, databases, or even equipment – may therefore be conditioned by whatever constraints have been imposed by the vendors as part of an agreement to supply or licence to use. Limitations may be placed regarding by whom, for whom, where and how material is used, and to whom (if anyone) it may be passed on.

Online database suppliers generally prescribe conditions (and costs) regarding system access, retrieval and downloading of records which are designed to protect their investment in the considerable value represented by intellectual property in the systems they operate.

In some circumstances, contrary to what one might imagine (and be forgiven for naively believing!) though a significant sum of money may have been handed over for some software or database product, one may not have bought ownership of the material, but, rather, only paid for the right to use it, and moreover, the right to use it solely according to the suppliers conditions!

In other situations, special conditions on use may be prescribed in return for the supplying of material or services at preferential rates to special groups such as academic or public sector institutions. The conditions may not be unduly onerous, particularly in the light of what benefits or savings the recipient of the material or service may be enjoying, nevertheless their existence must be recognised and acted upon. With the increasing emphasis on, and adoption of, income generation, consultancy, and cost recovery schemes by public sector institutions in particular, the special conditions prescribed by vendors in return for generous price subsidies take on a new significance since they may prohibit any use of material for profit making purposes. Overlooking special conditions may result in litigation at worst, or even at best forfeiture of special supply arrangements and privileges.

Notice of such special conditions may be incorporated into order and purchase agreements, and indeed some contracts for supply of services and goods may be very lengthy and complex to accommodate all the conditions. In other circumstances such detail will not be so forthcoming. In any event the library and information services manager needs to be aware before acquiring and keeping material what limits apply.

Some of the material now commonly available and in use in library and information services – instructional software, software packages, CD-ROM databases, networked services – may be subject to special considerations with regard to their ownership and operation. These conditions will be specified on promotional material, sales literature and contracts and perhaps embodied in the screen text of products. Material can also be supplied subject to what has been colloquially termed a shrink-wrap agreement. Under such circumstances the packaging which surrounds material displays its special conditions of ownership and use. The act of breaking the seal and unwrapping the product signifies, on the part of the person acquiring it, acceptance of and an intention to comply with those conditions.

The library and information services manager has little choice but to accept and comply with these restrictive arrangements if the material is required in the form, or at the price at which is offered. Rarely are satisfactory alternative products or sources available and substitutes may not be entirely suitable either. However, once acquired, it has to be ensured that material subject to special conditions is properly utilised in accordance with those conditions and suitable managerial initiatives must be undertaken to ensure this.

Public domain software and shareware

In most cases, software copyright owners exploit and market their products commercially and users have to pay accordingly. Software costs may represent major expenditure for certain projects and applications, and software packages range in price from tens to several thousands of pounds. If there were not a thriving software industry sustained by such an approach, arguably the variety and quality of software available would be seriously diminished. However, some institutions especially in the public sector choose not to maximise income from software development but make products generally available without claiming royalties and similar payments. There is an increasing range of useful material developed by universities, colleges and public bodies available in this way. This software which is placed in the public domain and not claimed by a copyright owner is an inexpensive source of much use.

Shareware by contrast is not free (as the name might imply) but it is often distributed relatively inexpensively through the same channels as public domain software for reasons of economy, and so that its originator may maintain greater control over its development than might be feasible were it handed over to be marketed fully commercially. The user benefits from cheapness and simplicity of acquisition of software. The ramifications of public domain software and shareware have been succinctly described in a recent note by Thomas (1988).

Management implications of copyright and licensing

Clearly, the constraints of copyright and related legislation condition a great deal of the activity within a library and information service – not least with regard to IT systems. And as each technical innovation for replicating and disseminating material emerges, so it appears do new complexities and problems in intellectual property considerations, though the fundamentals remain. The current social and economic climate tends to have created a new awareness of, and placed a greater value than hitherto on, information as a tradeable commodity and on the materials and systems which convey it. Moreover the technology has, in many cases, allowed more reliable use measurement (and thus the price to be paid) and even enabled misuse to be monitored. Intellectual property owners, with a new piece of legislation behind them also appear to be more ready than ever to affirm their rights. Library services must therefore remain alert and responsive to intellectual property matters and issues not only to operate responsibly but to avoid litigation! They must similarly ensure awareness and responsiveness on the part of their users.

Appendices D and E illustrate, though not exhaustively, the range of activity in library an information services where IT and copyright have to be considered. Appendix F summarises some of the intellectual property factors which IT materials and systems involve. It is worth noting the convergence and intertwining of different factors in one medium, systems or service. For example, in a CD-ROM bibliographic database copyright will subsist in the retrieval and presentation software for use with the CD-ROM whether separately loaded on a machine or incorporated on the CD, it will also subsist in the graphics and design developed by the compiler for presenting and formatting the contents of the database, and further in the database content itself, which depending on its nature may be very complex. Moreover, any workstation used to exploit the CD will have appropriate device-driving software, in addition to, at least, operating system software and copyright will subsist in both these. Networked CD-ROM services will require yet further networking software in which again copyright will subsist. What is important is to realise that the terms, conditions, duration and ownership of the various copyrights involved may well be very different. Licensing arrangements for use of the various components of systems and services also impinge heavily on the way in which activity is managed in library and information services.

Key elements in the management of intellectual property issues and IT are communications, training, and supervision; and these relate to both staff within an organisation and its users far and wide even if they hardly ever visit a service point but use networks. To ensure that these elements are efficiently and effectively accomplished it may be desirable in all but the smallest organisations to establish the role of a Copyright

Officer. This function may by no means have to be full-time. It is worth the library and information services manager checking in a large organisation whether such a person, perhaps attached to the general administration, already exists, for such a source of advice and information is invaluable. Whoever undertakes the responsibility for management of copyright and related issues, some basic points remain to be made.

The first consideration is to ensure that everyone within an organisation who needs to be, is made properly aware of the limits, constraints and special features of working under copyright and related legislation, especially in relation to IT. This encompasses almost everyone in a modern library and information service and so copyright awareness should permeate the service. In one way or another, either as managers, supervisors, or operators of services, equipment and systems, or indeed part of the user community, a range of people become involved. Communications and training therefore play a significant part in the management of copyright matter in the electronic library.

Communication

Communication is very closely allied to training but for convenience it will be dealt with separately here. It is important to communicate facts and guidance regarding copyright to staff and users clearly and unambiguously though this is not easy given the complexity of the issue. Documentation and guidelines regarding the use of copyrighted material should be available to both staff and users of the service. The many useful textbooks now available on the new legislation are really too lengthy and involved to be considered for such an exercise. An exception might be Cornish (1990) which is arranged in a helpful question and answer format; the very helpful Library Association Guides (1990) are more appropriate especially for the professional's desk. It is perhaps also necessary to consider the creation of a brief leaflet to provide guidance in the local context of any service. This may be supplemented by appropriately located poster material after the style of the Library Association's general poster explaining copyright and photocopying. Such material can also take into account and describe any local arrangements and conditions pertaining through an institution's participation in licensing arrangements. With regard to licensing and related arrangements, a file of licences and similar contracts should be securely maintained within the library and information service. How can the operations which are subject to restrictions and limitations be properly undertaken and managed if the documentation prescribing them is not adequately organised and disseminated?

A less sophisticated, yet nevertheless important aspect of communication relates to the use of notices and labels at the point of use on material or equipment. Such notices can even appear on workstation screens. The notices can draw attention to the copyright protection given to items such as software and databases, and indicate the restrictions which apply to their use. They may even contain a disclaimer removing liability from the organisation for any infringements performed by an individual.

A further contribution to initiatives in communication about copyright can be provided by ensuring that someone is given the task of acting as a referral point for queries from both staff and users about IT copyright and related matters – this person might be the Copyright Officer. No one should be unaware of what the copyright implications of a given situation are or at least where they may find advice. It is probably true that more breaches of copyright are perpetrated through ignorance than through any wilful desire to cheat or steal from a copyright owner! Some of these situations could well be avoided by the provision of timely help and advice.

Training

Training seeks to reinforce, supplement and sustain the communication initiatives undertaken by an organisation. Many of the considerations rehearsed about training for data protection (chapter 8), such as when, where, who and how to train are similarly applicable to copyright, and more especially in the ever changing context of IT. The implications for the management of training are therefore clear. It needs to be undertaken thoroughly and consistently throughout an organisation from senior manager to the newest assistant, and its delivery needs to be regular and consistent both to maintain a sharp awareness and to incorporate new updating material.

Training in this area may be regarded as having an extra dimension because the library user needs equally to know and respect the scope and limitations of copyright. A user instruction programme should incorporate appropriate detail regarding how to comply with copyright requirements and the importance of so doing.

Supervision

Supervision is taken to mean the exercise of some degree of direction or control over the activities of users of material, however tenuous. Indeed, its inclusion in this discussion may itself imply the need for a closer scrutiny of what users do with copyright material than has been the custom. Arguably, the library and information services manager has not always been too ready to assume an appropriate level of responsibility for ensuring that copyright is fully appreciated and respected within an organisation, though there are signs that attitudes are changing – precipitated, perhaps by a more vociferous and forceful attitude from the community of organised copyright owners.

One of the manager's prime responsibilities is to ensure that conduct within the organisation is legal. With regard to the staff of a library and information service, it is fundamental that proper supervision and control over their activities with copyright material is exercised. It is therefore imperative that the manager ensure that the conduct of subordinates (and himself or herself) is within the law and that they do not place themselves, or the organisation, under threat of legal or similar action through infringing copyright and related measures. The developments of an in-house code of working may be appropriate to define the limits of activities, and extent of responsibilities, and accountabilities. This may be reinforced by specifying the obligation to conform to such a code of working in staff conditions of employment.

Equally, mechanisms to ensure ease of compliance with copyright requirements should be part of the scenario. For example, a standard routine for obtaining permissions or licences to undertake activities which require going beyond the permitted acts should be available, and its operation should be subject to an appropriate level of supervision.

Adequate and suitable security arrangements and checks to discourage unauthorised and illegal activities – such as the duplication and distribution of protected software – should be in place, and working.

Another important point worth making is that subordinates should never be directed, or even requested, to perform any breach of copyright or related measures – even as a special case. This places the individual in a most invidious position, and also demonstrates the manager's lack of commitment to respecting copyright.

The users of a library and information service may be a more difficult group to supervise effectively where respect for intellectual property is concerned. They will constitute a varied and amorphous sample of interests, skills, knowledge and attitudes, over which the manager will have generally little real control unless they inhabit closed communities where special rules and sanctions may have been established. Moreover, tensions can arise between the initiatives undertaken to promote the acceptance and use of services on the one hand, and the application of measures to protect intellectual property on the other, with the library and information service appearing to be overly restrictive and bureaucratic. A firm and steady hand on the management tiller is called for with supervisory mechanisms being introduced and applied sensitively and sensibly, but introduced they must be!

Part of the supervisory arrangements can involve requiring users to sign declarations that they will act legally and properly in their dealings with intellectual property – in a way this is allied to the process which prevails to ensure the legality of library photocopying. Therefore, a part of any library and information services enrolment procedure may involve a general declaration of this kind from the user. Unfortunately, it is doubtful how much real attention the typical user pays at the point of enrolment to such small print and still more questionable is how indelibly the detail of the procedure is retained in the memory. Moreover, aspects of the service which have special arrangements and licences may preclude such a generalised approach. What may be preferable and sometimes necessary (but hazarding more bureaucracy) is a routine which seeks specific declarations for the use of particular services or systems.

Thus a declaration might be sought from users of a software lending service. This would include a statement that the intending borrower was aware of the copyright protection of software and that he or she would not copy or distribute copies of any software borrowed other than in the course of using it in a machine, or as otherwise permitted by any specific software licence.

End users of databases may also be required to provide undertakings regarding the use of systems and output from them. Depending on the system being accessed, these declarations may specify an undertaking not to misuse the database content and any enabling retrieval or communications and networking software. Special conditions prescribed by a database vendor or system operator may also need to be incorporated. Other user behaviour specifications not encompassing intellectual property matters (and thus outside the scope of this chapter) may also be introduced, particularly with networked systems. The recently introduced BIDS/ISI Citation Indexes Service made available on the Joint Academic Network (JANET) to individuals in many academic institutions presents a suitable illustration of what is involved. Here, clearly the database content and format is the intellectual property of the Institute for Scientific Information (ISI) and the conditions, which include amongst other things, restrictions on the commercial application of the information from the database have to be respected by subscribing institutions and end users.

Part of the local management of the service therefore includes obtaining an appropriate declaration from end users. An example of what is required, based on a standard form of words prescribed by the database owners and the systems operators, is shown in Appendix G. More will be said about the control of use of the system later.

It may also be thought necessary to obtain declarations from people to whom the results of database searches, performed by an intermediary, have been given, especially if the database vendor or systems provider have imposed special restrictions on the use of information or systems. Many educational and public sector library and information services for example, obtain access to online and similar services at special (discounted) rates but these arrangements may be conditional on there being no overtly commercial application of the output. In such a situation one must at least secure an undertaking from those to whom information is distributed that these conditions will be fulfilled.

Realism dictates that the mere obtaining of signed declarations, whilst giving the library and information service some degree of legal protection, is not enough to ensure respect for intellectual property and compliance with the law on the part of users. It is clearly not practical to stand over each user to ensure proper behaviour and practice. Therefore, further controls and even actions may be necessary. What form they can take without too greatly inhibiting the full and proper use of systems is a delicate balance alluded to earlier in this section.

Password controlled access to end users of systems provides a way of at least ensuring that only those who have indicated their willingness to accept conditions of use are allowed onto a system. Those who refuse or fail to comply with such conditions can be barred from access to a system through the withholding or withdrawal of passwords. For example, the local control of the BIDS/ISI Citation Indexes Service involves supplying each end user with a code representing the institution's user identifier and password upon registration as a system user.

Another partial solution to the wholesale misuse of systems and information retrieved from them by end users may lie in imposing a general limit on the nature and extent of information which may be copied, downloaded or printed from a database. The control may be in place at the provider's end of the system or locally. Software, itself protected by password from unauthorised tampering, and located in the end user workstation, may determine limits to output. Some CD-ROM database retrieval software, for instance, allows parameters to be set to regulate downloading, and to limit the number of references or units of data that can be printed from a search.

In any event the individual user should be left in doubt that the library, having obtained the necessary undertakings, and taken other appropriate precautions and measures will view seriously any misuse of intellectual property and will not regard itself in any way as an accessory authorising misuse should the user be the subject of litigation or related action.

PATENTS AND DESIGNS

These two aspects of intellectual property will be discussed only briefly here. Their direct impact on the library and information services manager is likely to be significantly less than that of copyright and related licensing arrangements. Situations may occasionally arise, however, where at least an outline knowledge of patent and design matters is important to the appreciation of managerial responsibilities and actions.

Primary sources relevant to these topics include the Patents Act 1977, the Registered Designs Act 1949 and the Copyright, Designs and Patents Act 1988 together with associated Statutory Instruments.

Patents

A patent represents a bargain between an individual and the state through which, in return for formally disclosing and publishing details of an invention, he or she is granted an exclusive right, for a fixed time, to exploit the invention (for example by making it, using it, or selling it) and furthermore to prevent others from exploiting it. Patents have a long and distinguished history and are regarded as having originated in Venice, with the first one in Britain being granted to a maker of coloured glass about 500 years ago.

Today, with the internationalisation of trade, particularly in IT products, it is not only British patent protection that is important. Major companies obtain patent protection in many countries (Japan and the USA, for example). There is also a facility through the European Patent Office to obtain protection for an invention in several European countries in one operation. For brevity and simplicity, remarks in this section will be chiefly confined to the British scene.

Unlike copyright, securing patent protection for an invention is a fairly lengthy, formal and sometimes costly process. Precise documentation regarding an invention has to be drafted and filed at the Patent Office. There it is scrutinised for novelty, legal and technical soundness and after due process, if successful, the patent is granted. Patent protection lasts for up to twenty years from the date on which the application was first filed.

Fees to secure and renew a patent right have to be paid to the Patent Office. It is not unusual for professional help from patent specialists such as Chartered Patent Agents to be enlisted to ensure adequate protection for an invention and the successful passage of an application through the system, but this necessarily adds to the expenses of the process.

The processing of a patent application is necessarily thorough involving legal and technical principles. Firstly, a patent is granted for a tangible physical item or a process and not for an intangible idea. Thus it must be possible to make the novel item or operate the new process. Secondly, (and fairly obviously) the invention must have novelty. That is, it clearly must be a new invention and importantly, it must not have been publicised, demonstrated, or used elsewhere in the world before. This has significant implications for the management of innovation as will be seen later. Thirdly, it must pass a notional test which does not invalidate it on the grounds that its function or operation is obvious to any person of ordinary skill or with knowledge of the particular technology involved. Obviousness should not be confused with simplicity, however (for example, a paper clip is a simple device, but not obvious as an office aid until you've seen and used your first one!).

The owner of a patent right has a monopoly to the exclusive use and exploitation of the invention and the right may be transferred by sale, hire or licence. The owner may also protect his or her interests by taking legal action against others who appear to be infringing patent rights.

Designs

The notion of industrial design is a complex one probably in terms of intellectual property issues. Clearly, every manufactured article has to be designed however rudimentarily, in one way or another but not every new article is capable of being accorded design protection. There are articles which may be regarded as having their entire shape and appearance virtually dictated by the function which they perform. Others, whilst needing to be the appropriate shape and appearance to work properly also embody a certain aesthetic quality in their make-up. This latter kind incorporates design in the intellectual property sense. Design intellectual property protection can take two forms whose mechanisms of operation are significantly different – design right, and registered designs.

Design right

Design right, much like copyright, applies automatically to an appropriate original design of an article. It accords the owner the exclusive right to reproduce the design for commercial purposes. The owner may also seek appropriate remedies in the case of infringement of the right through unauthorised copying or unauthorised commercial dealing in copies.

For design right purposes, design is defined in s. 213(2) of the Copyright, Designs and Patents Act 1988 as 'the design of any aspect of the shape or configuration (whether internal or external) of the whole or part of an article'. To qualify for design right a design must be original and not, in the words of s. 213(4) of the Act, 'commonplace in the design field in question at the time of creation'.

Surface decoration is excluded from design right, as also are what have been termed 'must fit' and 'must match' items where the design features enabling one article to be functionally fitted, or aesthetically matched with another, as is the case with many spare parts and renewable components.

Design right is limited in duration and by other constraints. It is limited to ten years from the end of the calendar year in which an item made to a design was first available for sale or hire. In the first five years the right is exclusive but thereafter it becomes subject to licence of right under which provision anyone is entitled to a licence to make and sell or hire articles to the design. An exception to the norm concerns design right for semiconductor chips where exclusive protection lasts the full ten years with no obligation to issue licences to copy. This provision arises as a result of the need to comply with a European Communities Directive on the topic. There is also an overall limit of fifteen years from the year of creation of the design. (The design is deemed to have been created when first recorded in a design document or when an article to the design was first made, whichever is earlier.)

Ownership of the design right is accorded in the first instance to the designer of an item. In the case of computer generated designs the ownership is accorded to the person making the necessary arrangements for its creation. In the case of commissioned work, the owner is regarded as the person commissioning the work, and similarly an employer holds the ownership of a design right if it has been created by an employee in the normal course of employment. As a property right, design right can be transferred by gift, sale or by licensing.

Registered designs

A registered design confers a monopoly right upon the owner to make, import, sell or hire any article conforming to or containing the design. In addition the owner also has the right to seek legal remedies against any infringer.

As the name implies a formal process of registration of a design has to be undertaken to acquire registered design protection. It is therefore more akin to patent protection than design right or copyright.

Formal application for a registered design has to be made to the Design Registry at the Patent Office. Details of the design have to be submitted and a fee is payable. If the design is appropriate for registration and has priority or is new, that is it has not been publicly disclosed in this country nor been registered in an earlier application and is materially different to any other published design, then a registered design can be granted. Further application to modify a registered design can also be made. Anytime after an application has been filed articles can be made and marketed without compromising the priority requirements for registration.

For the purposes of registered designs, a design is defined rather differently to that for design right. According to s. 265(1)(1) of the Copyright, Designs and Patents Act 1988 'design means features of a shape, configuration, pattern or ornament applied to an article by any industrial process, being features which in the finished article appeal to and are judged by the eye ...'

The Act goes on (ss. 265(1)(6) (i), 265(1)(3)) to exclude solely functional forms and the 'must match' type of items as well as items where the aesthetic appearance of the article is not significant Other limitations to what can be accepted as registered designs include sculpture, medals and printed material such as book jackets but these would normally receive protection through copyright anyway.

The period of protection for a registered design can last for up to twenty-five years. The duration of initial protection extends for five years from registration, but it is renewable or extendable upon payment of a fee for four further terms, each of five years.

The legislation refers to proprietorship of registered designs and the author of a design is generally treated as the original proprietor of the design. There are exceptions however and these parallel those found in the design right provisions. For commissioned designs the person commissioning the work is regarded as the original proprietor and employers are regarded as the proprietors of designs created by employees in the ordinary course of employment. In the case of computer generated designs, the person making arrangements for the creation of the design is viewed as the proprietor.

Management implications

As noted earlier, the library and information services manager may rarely have to become preoccupied with patent and designs issues in relation to IT systems in use in a particular organisation. (That is not to underestimate however, the way in which IT features very prominently and effectively in retrieving information about patents and designs, particularly in specialist scientific and technical institutions, but that is a topic far outside this chapter.) The picture might alter however, if as a result of a research project or general in-house development, possibly in collaboration with technical specialists, some novel systems were developed, or equipment and components created within the library and information services environment. It might well become advantageous (and profitable!) for the library and information services organisation to be able to secure, protect and exploit rights to such innovations through patents or designs. Similarly, if equipment is being adapted or modified, it will be important to be aware of and respect existing patent and design protection applying to it before contemplating any claim for innovation. A knowledge of the fundamentals of the topic, together with an awareness of possible pitfalls become of value and importance to the library and information services manager in all such cases.

Some basic points are worth noting if the manager is involved in activity which may lead to protection for innovations being sought. Firstly, and most importantly, is the need to preserve confidentiality regarding the innovation at every stage up to the point at which an application for protection is filed with the authorities. It has to be appreciated that protection is given by the state in return for disclosing new knowledge and such protection will not and cannot be granted for something which has already been disclosed however trivially.

Demonstrating prototypes, writing descriptions in articles in journals (however obscure), and telling people who are not under any legal obligation to maintain secrecy all constitute prior publication in this context and as such are a bar to the granting of a patent or registration of a design. Equally, of course, other organisations' and individuals' efforts to acquire protection may be thwarted and thus a monopoly situation prevented if the decision to disclose is made. Care must be taken regarding the security and confidentiality that surrounds a project, therefore.

A second point relates to the need to maintain adequate documentation about projects and innovations. This implies keeping detailed drawings, sketches and notes of what and how things were done, and significantly when each stage was undertaken. What is required represents good housekeeping practice in any case but its importance can be magnified should disputes arise from challenges to claims, or infringements of rights. It is particularly important in the case of design right, for which no formal registration procedure is required, that it can be fully established and properly demonstrated when a design was created and first marketed, for example.

Thirdly, an obvious point. The invention or design developed must fit the criteria rehearsed earlier regarding eligibility for protection. And the rules, though clearly enumerated, are not always easy to interpret.

Fourthly, some assessment of whether protection is worth the trouble – that is, the human effort and expense – needs to be established. Balanced against the apparent and hidden costs of acquiring and perhaps deterring infringement of protection are factors such as the duration for which protection, exclusive and otherwise, is available, and, far less easily calculated, the likely return (if any) from being able to exploit, or permit exploitation of the invention or design.

Insofar as they represent very specialist areas of knowledge and practice, it is worth reiterating that the library and information services manager would be very well advised to seek expert professional help in any decisions and dealings with patents and designs. Even the Patent Office publicity warns against the risks of a do-it-yourself approach to this area. Assistance and advice may be sought from a Chartered Patent Agent (the Chartered Institute of Patent Agents is a body of long standing having received its Royal Charter in 1891). Many firms, academic institutions and public authority bodies employ specialist staff to deal with intellectual property matters and the library and information services manager should ascertain whether his or her organisation has a Patents Officer or Intellectual Property Officer to which to turn for help. But that help should be sought earlier rather than later!

REFERENCES

Audiovisual Librarian (1991), vol. 17, no. 1, (February), pp. 8–9.

Cornish, G. (1990), *Copyright: interpreting the law for libraries and archives*. London: LA Publishing Ltd.

Dworkin, G. and Taylor, R. D. (1989), *Blackstone's guide to the Copyright, Designs and Patents Act 1988: the law of copyright and related rights*. London: Blackstone Press Ltd.

Flint, M., Thorne, C. D. and Williams, A. P. (1989), *Intellectual property – the new law: a guide to the Copyright, Designs and Patents Act 1988*. London: Butterworths.

Lester, D. and Mitchell, P. (1989), *Joynson-Hicks on UK copyright law*. London: Sweet and Maxwell.

Library Association Guides (1990), second edition.
Copyright in public libraries
Copyright in industrial and commercial libraries
Copyright in polytechnic and university libraries
Copyright in school and college libraries
Copyright in National Health Service libraries

Thomas, E. (1988). Shareware and public domain software, part 1. *IT Link*, no. 3, (July), pp. 7–8.

APPENDIX A: DURATION OF COPYRIGHT

Based on Sections 12–15 of Copyright, Designs and Patents Act 1988

Material	Authorship (if relevant)	Duration
Literary, dramatic, musical, artistic	One known author	50 years from year of author's death
Literary, dramatic, musical, artistic	More than one known author	50 years from year of death of last surviving author
Literary, dramatic, musical, artistic	Author unknown	50 years from year work was first made available to public
Literary, dramatic, musical, artistic	Computer generated	50 years from year work was made
Sound recording, film		50 years from year work was made, or if released before end of period 50 years from year of release
Cable programme		50 years from year of transmission
Typographical arrangement of published editions		25 years from year of first publication

APPENDIX B: ACTS RESTRICTED BY COPYRIGHT

Based on Section 16 of the Copyright, Designs and Patents Act 1988

The right to:
- copy the work
- issue copies of the work (including in the case of sound recordings, films, and computer programs any rental of copies to the public)
- perform, show or play the work in public
- broadcast it, or include it in a cable programme service
- make an adaptation, or do any of the above to an adaptation

APPENDIX C: PERMITTED ACTS SUMMARY

Type of material	*Action/Purpose*
General	
Literary, dramatic, musical, artistic	Fair dealing; research or private study
Typographical arrangement	Fair dealing; research or private study
All material	Fair dealing; criticism, review
All materials except photographs	Fair dealing; news reporting of current events
All material	Incidental inclusion in artistic work, sound recording, film, broadcast or cable programme
Education	
Literary, dramatic,	Copying in the course of, or preparation for instruction by person receiving or giving instruction, (but not by reprography)
Sound recording, film, broadcast, cable	Copying by making a film or sound track in the course of, or preparation for instruction in film making etc. by person receiving or giving instruction
All items	Anything done in setting or answering examination question
Literary, dramatic, published	Compiling anthologies (but with limits)
Literary, dramatic, musical	Performing or showing in the course of educational activities
Broadcast, Cable	Recording for educational purposes, unless there is a licensing scheme
Literary, dramatic, musical, published	Reprographic copying for educational instruction (but with limits – 1% per quarter of any work) Unless there is a licensing scheme

Libraries and archives

Making and supplying copies to people

Published literary, dramatic, musical (except periodical articles)	Making and supplying a copy for research or private study but subject to limitations:not more than one copy; not more than a 'reasonable proportion' copied; not related to similar copy requirements by another person; cost of copying (or more) must be paid
Periodical articles	Making and supplying a copy for research or private study but subject to limitations: not more than one copy; not more than one article per periodical issue; not related to a similar copy requirement by another person; cost of copying (or more) must be paid
Unpublished literary, dramatic musical (works unpublished before they were deposited in a library or archive)	Making and supplying a copy from a document in the library to a person for research or private study but subject to limitations: not more than one copy; cost of copying (or more) must be paid; copyright owner has not prohibited copying

Making a copy within a libray for another library

Literary dramatic, musical	Copying an item in a collection to preserve or replace it
Literary dramatic, musical	Copying an item in a collection to replace a lost, destroyed or damaged item in another library or archive
Published literary, dramatic, musical	Making and supplying a copy for another library, when the person entitled to authorise making a copy is unknown and cannot be traced
All items	Making a copy of an item of cultural or historical importance when it cannot be lawfully exported from the UK unless copy is made and deposited in a library or archive

Specialised areas

Public Records (as defined by Public Records Acts)	Copying material in Public Records
Type faces	Using typefaces in the ordinary course of making text
Electronic Works	Where an original purchaser is entitled to copy or adapt material, in the course of using it, transferring this entitlement unless there are expressed conditions of supply preventing/prohibiting this
Abstracts of scientific and technical articles	Copying and issuing copies to the public – unless there is a licensing scheme
Sound recordings, films, computer programs	Rental to the public of copies provided a reasonable royalty is paid unless there is a licensing scheme
Computer programs	Rental to the public of copies 50 years after the program was issued in electronic form

APPENDIX D: COPYRIGHT AND IT IN LIBRARIES AND INFORMATION SERVICES

User Oriented

- Lending p/c software
- Lending interactive teaching material
- Supervising use of p/c software
- Supervising use of interactive teaching material
- Supervising CD-ROM searching
- Supervising Online Database searching (commercial)
- Supervising networked database searching (non-commercial eg JANET access to library catalogues)
- Supervising local database searching (e.g. OPAC's)
- Supervising LAN computer access in general

APPENDIX E: COPYRIGHT AND IT IN LIBRARIES AND INFORMATION SERVICES

Staff oriented

- Operating p/c software: word processing, spreadsheets databases etc.
- Operating interactive teaching material (staff training, user education etc.)
- Performing CD-ROM searches
- Performing Online database searches
- Performing networked database searches
- Performing local database searches
- Operating on LANs
- Maintaining (bibliographic and technical) local databases
- Maintaining local housekeeping systems

APPENDIX F: IT IN LIBRARIES AND INFORMATION SERVICES

Material/system	Intellectual property in
Software	Programs
	Accompanying text/documentation
Interactive teaching material	Programs
	Screen text
	Sound – speech/music
	Images – moving/still
	Accompanying text/documentation
CD-ROMs	Retrieval programs
	Database structure/format
	Database content
	Accompanying text/documentation manuals

Online networks	Communications programs
	Retrieval programs
	File transfer programs
	Utility programs
	Networking software
	Database Structure/format
	Database service as a cable service
	Database content
	Accompanying text/documentation manuals
Local databases	Communication programs
	Retrieval programs
	File transfer programs
	Utility programs
	Maintenance/update programs
	Housekeeping programs
	Database structure/format
	Database content
	Accompanying text/documentation manuals
LANs	Communications programs
	File transfer programs
	Utility programs
	Any other on LAN
	Accompanying text/documentation, manuals
Housekeeping systems	Involve a whole range of programs and output which may be proprietary and locally tailored, and accompanying text, documentation manuals

APPENDIX G: END USER DECLARATION FOR NETWORKED DATABASE

Citation indexes networked service

The University is a subscriber to a new database service introduced under an agreement between ISI (The Institute for Scientific Information) and CHEST (The Combined Higher Education Software Team), and provided by Bath University Computing Services through the JANET Network.

The service provides campus wide access to the electronic equivalents of:

Arts & Humanities Citation Index (AHCI)

Science Citation Index (SCI)

Social Sciences Citation Index (SSCI)

other ISI databases are to be made available later.

The service is open to those current members of the University who have been given a username and password (updated by E-Mail) in exchange for signing the necessary undertakings (summarised below) regarding use prescribed by ISI as the copyright holder. The user declares that these conditions will be observed in all transactions.

Copyright Notice ISI/Licensee

This data is protected by copyright and is made available on the understanding that its use is subject to the Agreement made between CHEST and ISI. Details of this Agreement are held online and may be read once you have logged in. The following is a brief summary of the major points:

–   The Institute for Scientific Information Inc. is the sole and exclusive owner of all rights to the data and compilations in the ISI Databases.

–   Any copyright statement must be maintained on any copies of the data.

–   The ISI Databases may be used by any employee student or other persons authorised by your Institution subject to the signing of the appropriate declaration.

Such use includes:

–   Teaching, research personal educational development administration and management of the business of the Licensee's organisation.

It excludes:

–   Consultancy or Services where the ISI Database are commercially exploited;

–   Work of significant benefit to the employer of students on industrial placement or part-time courses;

–   Use of ISI Databases for performing scientometric or bibliometric studies.

The data may not be copied except that you may print or download full or partial results of searches. You may also distribute to others in your organisation, in print form, up to 25 copies of individual items but solely for research or scholarship purposes.

10

Computer misuse

J Eric Davies

Though not the only source of loss and disruption, the misuse of computers and related IT equipment is a growing problem for society in general costing a great deal of time and money. Moreover, it serves to inhibit the adoption of IT in society. The liberating effect of electronic networks and systems which have taken and linked work beyond the single office and factory risks being countermanded by the need for centralised control and tighter security now demanded in order to avoid the worst excesses of the wrongdoer. Perusal of the press yields headlines which encapsulate the problem vividly, albeit sometimes sensationally:

> 'Security doubled as hacking jitters spread'
> 'Five given bail on computer theft charge'
> 'Interpol investigates Friday 13th virus'
> 'IBM to get tough on virus'
> 'Computer information wide open to theft'
> 'University Computer virus wipes out studies'

The Working Paper on Computer Misuse published by the Law Commission (1988) put the point a little more sedately: 'Computers now play an important part in our everyday lives. This technological development, upon which society is becoming ever more dependent in hundreds of different ways, has without doubt produced substantial benefits for us all. However, alongside these benefits lies the disadvantage that computers and computer systems are vulnerable to all manner of misuse. The consequences of such misuse are very serious'.

Hearnden (1990) paints a stark picture of the growth in computer-related wrongdoing and correlates it with the spread of computer use nurtured by the introduction of the microprocessor. Drawing on published data he contrasts, for example, the 4 recorded instances of computer-linked fraud in the ten years 1960–69, with the 159 reported in the three year period 1985–1987. He also echoes the general belief among those concerned that for a variety of reasons many more instances go unreported and thus unrecorded. His book goes a long way to help combat the situation regarding computer misuse.

Sometimes even expert opinion is divided about the seriousness and prevalence of misuse. Some computer professionals regard the hyperbole in the press about computer viruses as being rather overdone, but a recently reported survey conducted by the National Computing Centre revealed a high level of virus infection within business computer systems (Survey..., 1991).

Undoubtedly as IT products and systems become more and more commonplace and accessible (sometimes too accessible!) they attract the unwelcome attentions of the thief, the vandal, even the terrorist, and many other miscreants. The library and information services manager need not feel immune from such threats either! Indeed, there is a very big danger in maintaining an attitude of 'it can't happen here', because it engenders too relaxed an attitude to security. Instances directly known to the author include: apparent wilful damage to a library housekeeping system; suspected theft in transit of CD-ROM equipment; burglary of new (and uninstalled) branch library circulation system hardware; unauthorised borrowing of instructional software programs; to say nothing of several losses of personal computers and associated machinery.

The introduction of IT systems has then spawned a whole new series of misdeeds, as well as adding a new sophistication and complexity to some traditional and ordinary crimes. Efforts must clearly be directed to combating such activities. The emphasis must be on prevention – through effective security (making the act difficult, if not impossible to perform), and through legal deterrents or disincentives (maximising the likelihood of being found out and punished). A necessary, though less agreeable aspect of the problem since it involves a deal of post-event stable door bolting, entails having effective mechanisms in place designed to recover situations quickly (disaster planning) and applying legal measures to punish wrongdoers and, if possible, secure redress from them through civil actions. Many types of IT misuse are covered by what may be regarded as general legislation where the computer is incidental to the affair. However, with the enactment of the Computer Misuse Act in 1990, there is now a specific piece of legislation concerned with the subject on the statute book.

TYPES OF COMPUTER MISUSE

The Law Commission (1988) Report enumerated a number of types of computer misuse. These comprised:

- computer fraud
- unauthorised obtaining of information from a computer
- unauthorised alteration or destruction of information stored on a computer
- denying access to an authorised user
- unauthorised removal of information stored on a computer

The ambit of misuse may be considerably broadened beyond these categories. For the purposes of this chapter they have been conveniently divided into those that rely on the computer as a device with which to perpetrate the crime and those in which the computer is the target of crime. Some blurring of the distinction becomes apparent in some instances as will be seen.

Computer fraud

Computer fraud was defined by the Law Commission (1988) as 'conduct which involves the manipulation of a computer, by whatever method, in order dishonestly to obtain money, property or some other advantage of value, or to cause loss'. In practice this usually amounts to falsifying some aspect of accounting or inventory control systems to the advantage of the wrongdoer. Adopting the Audit Commission's practice it further divided computer fraud into input fraud, output fraud and program fraud. Input fraud involves dishonestly entering false data or suppressing or amending correct data to be input to a system. It is the most commonly reported, probably since it is the most readily available route to fraud for the lay person with little or no computing expertise. Output fraud involves dishonestly altering or suppressing the data emerging from a system in order to gain some advantages. Other than discarding or destroying the tangible output from the computer it is probably more difficult for the lay person to perform since at least some minor modification of output instructions will usually be necessary.

Program fraud enters a new realm where interference with the program or programs which are in operation in a system is involved either by adding, amending or deleting instructions. It clearly demands a greater degree of computing expertise from the wrongdoer. It is consequently regarded as less prevalent because there are proportionally fewer fraudsters who are programming experts. A worrying corollary of such a situation however is that since it takes an expert to commit such misuse, it also takes an expert to detect it unless the fraud is so large that discrepancies become easily noticeable through more conventional checks. This points to an even greater need for effective preventative measures to be installed to counter attempts at computer fraud.

Unauthorised obtaining/removal of information

The Law Commission (1988) enumerated three facets of unauthorised obtaining of information from a computer, though some might be more easily regarded as obtaining unauthorised access to a computer system. These included computer hacking, eavesdropping on a computer and its related equipment, and making unauthorised use of a computer for personal benefit. Moreover, as was noted above, a distinction was made in the report between such practices and the unauthorised removal either physically or electronically through a network of information. Whatever fine distinctions are made between these, they relate to a common problem of unauthorised access being gained by wrongdoers for a variety of motives.

Hacking involves gaining unauthorised access and entry into computer systems through a network or networks, though it may sometimes go beyond that and stray into the realms of unauthorised destruction or alteration of information should the hacker decide to interfere with the content of the system if only to demonstrate that the hacking has been accomplished. The archetypal hacker is often regarded as an amateur nuisance and enthusiast and in some media presentations achieves the status of folk hero by at least harmlessly demonstrating the vulnerability of important systems. The reality may be far more sinister as hackers can inadvertently cause serious damage to systems and, flushed by their initial successes, may turn to profiting from their endeavours.

Eavesdropping on computer systems may take many forms but essentially in addition to gaining unauthorised access to a system or its peripherals including any networking devices, information is also gleaned which may or may not be put to wrong use. The further action of abstracting or removing information by making or stealing copies of information compounds the problem. Information acquired in this way may simply satisfy the wrongdoer's curiosity but it may also be used to gain a material advantage (details of a sensitive financial and commercial nature, for example) or even to blackmail individuals and organisations. There are severe implications for data protection in such situations also.

Unauthorised use of a computer for personal benefit

A person may misuse a computer system owned by someone else by employing it to perform unauthorised work from which he or she benefits either materially or financially. Minor incidents may involve an employee's misuse of an employer's computer to list and print cricket fixtures and league tables, for example. More seriously, computer time may be regularly borrowed or taken to perform private work for clients which might almost amount to a bureau or commercial operation. The data security and data protection implications of such situations are horrifying to contemplate!

Unauthorised alteration or destruction of information

The unauthorised alteration or destruction of computerised information for fraudulent purposes has been described and discussed earlier. However, there is an increasing incidence of what may be regarded as pointless or mindless destruction of, and interference with, large and small systems and the information within them by electronic means these days. In its wake another of the problems enumerated by the Law Commission (1988) may be encountered namely, that of denying access to an authorised user of a system because access routines have been damaged. And such acts may be engendered by a variety of motives – sheer vandalism, revenge, terrorism, or even blackmail. There are also examples of physical attack on systems and equipment.

186

At its crudest the problem may involve an unauthorised user accessing a system or network and then summarily erasing or amending files or programmes. The effect may be immediate or delayed, minor or devastating. More subtly the wrongdoer may employ less direct means of invading a system by, for example, distributing harmful material through magnetic media (a floppy disk) or by planting material by electronic mail in another location to be activated later. The harmful material may not stay in one system (or even one continent!) but may be designed to replicate and distribute itself as described below.

The problem has spawned its own (not necessarily standardised) nomenclature – virus, worm, Trojan Horse, logic bomb – which threatens to give a sensational, if not glamorous edge to what is at best a nuisance and at worst threatens not only operations in affected institutions but progress in the development and application of IT systems generally.

An extensive list of terms and definitions will be found in Hoffman (1990) who uses the generic term 'rogue programs' to describe the entire range of software devices which are aimed at subverting operations of computers. Hoffman provides a comprehensive description of such problems together with a discussion of relevant precautions and countermeasures.

However, the difficulty of agreeing on precise definitions in this field is illustrated by the several definitions of various rogue programs quoted by Highland (1992). A computer virus has many parallels with its biological counterpart in terms of its capacity for spreading harm throughout a community, an issue explored more fully by Reiss (1990). For the sake of simplicity I have chosen to use the descriptions provided by Hoffman (1990) for a virus and a worm:

> *Virus (pl. viruses).* A program that can infect other programs by modifying them to include a possibly evolved copy of itself. Note that a program need not perform malicious actions to be a virus; it need only infect other programs. Many viruses that have been encountered, however, do perform malicious actions.

> *Worm.* A program that spreads copies of itself through network-attached computers. The first use of the term described a program that copied itself benignly around a network, using otherwise-unused resources on networked machines to perform distributed computation. Some worms are security threats, using

networks to spread themselves against the wishes of the system owners, and disrupting networks by overloading them.

There are indications that examples of attack by rogue programs are widespread and increasing. The increase may be attributable to a greater willingness to report instances on the part of computer users, or indeed a higher incidence of the plague brought on by wider knowledge of computer use and vulnerabilities (and the techniques of misuse) in the general population. What is undeniable is that systems are at risk from such activities and appropriate precautions are vitally necessary.

CRIME AND THE COMPUTER

In addition to electronically committed acts, traditional crime poses an equally dire if perhaps more overt threat to IT systems and equipment within an organisation. Thus equipment and material are vulnerable to theft and wilful damage or destruction. Even buildings housing computer installations may be targets for attack, and organisations may be subjected to blackmail threats.

With regard to theft, much of the equipment involved in IT operations is expensive, is becoming increasingly portable, and is now used more widely. It therefore represents a valuable and generally marketable target for the thief. Personal computers appear to have ousted the videocassette recorder (VCR) as the most popular target for stealing on many academic campuses, for example. And it is not the intrinsic worth of the equipment or material that is necessarily at stake always. What of the information, representing valuable time and effort, which may reside on a hard disk inside a personal computer that is stolen, or the boxful of floppy disks which are pilfered? The author has only recently had occasion to sympathise and commiserate with a research student who, having suffered a break-in which resulted in the theft of a personal computer and associated disks, had lost much valuable data and results with a resultant impairment and delay to her work.

Wilful damage of equipment, material and entire installations either through mindless vandalism, or more directed wrongdoing from someone with a grudge against an organisation, or from terrorists all have to be taken into account. Acts may involve physical attack, or setting fire to, or flooding premises deliberately. Even relatively minor incidents of this kind such as disabling and locking an important machine and throwing away the key, damaging a disc drive or cutting a cable can have very serious (and expensive) consequences for the operations of an organisation heavily dependent on IT systems. Blackmail and similar activities may be directed at threats of action against installations, equipment and even personnel, or may involve the threat of disclosure of information (not necessarily of an embarrassing nature) to commercial competitors or to the general population.

There are also the more generalised problems of terrorism which are tending to increase in a society where more and more groups seem to emerge with a grievance that they are unable or unwilling to articulate by more rational means. Allied to this is the problem of hoaxers and sensation seekers whose aim is mainly to cause disruption rather than damage. Many managers will have experienced bomb hoaxes which have involved the troublesome and costly evacuation of buildings and shutdown of systems.

THE COMPUTER MISUSE ACT 1990

Mention was made earlier of the Computer Misuse Act 1990 as a recent component in the endeavour to combat IT crime and misuse. Whereas in the past legal sanctions for misuses relied on conventional approaches such as theft, trespass, and the like (which were sometimes difficult to establish) the new Act prescribes specifically for IT related wrongdoing. The Act defines three criminal offences for misusing computers:

- unauthorised access to computer material (s. 1)
- unauthorised access with intent to commit or facilitate commission of further offences (s. 2)
- causing unauthorised modification of the contents of any computer (s. 3)

A person commits the unauthorised access offence if 'he causes a computer to perform any function with intent to secure access to any program or data held in any computer' (s. 1(a)) and that 'the access he intends to secure is unauthorised; and he knows at the time when he causes the computer to perform the function that this is the case' (ss. 1(b) and (c)).

The offence attracts a liability of imprisonment for up to six months and/or a fine of up to £2000 (s. 1(3)). Furthermore, the target of the offence need not be a specific programme or data or a particular machine (ss. 2(a), (b) and (c)).

The second offence of unauthorised access with intent to commit or facilitate commission of further offences is clearly more serious and the maximum penalties available increase to five years imprisonment and/ or an unlimited fine (ss. 3(5) (a) and (b)). It is immaterial whether the further offence is to be committed on the same or any future occasion as the unauthorised access offence (s. 3 (3)). Moreover, a person may be guilty of the offence even though it may be impossible to commit the further offence intended (s. 3(4)).

The third offence involves doing 'any act which causes unauthorised modification of the contents of any computer' when the person so doing has the requisite intent to cause a modification, and knows it to be unauthorised (s. 3). Again, the target of the wrongdoing does not have to be a specific nor the modification of any particular kind (ss. 3(3) (a), (b) and (c)).

Further detail in the Act, in Section 17, provides comprehensive definitions of the terms employed to describe offences. Thus terms like access, using programs or data, program, unauthorised access, and modification are described fairly precisely.

It is perhaps too early yet to assess the impact of this legislation in combating computer misuse. It does however promise to provide the manager with an additional mechanism for combating wrongdoing. Nevertheless, it is no substitute for proper and adequate regard to security in the IT environment.

In particular, systems must be sufficiently well protected to counter any claim of accidental or inadvertent access from those who have broken into systems; and the limits of authority to those using systems must be made very clear to avoid any ambiguities about authorised or unauthorised behaviour.

MANAGEMENT RESPONSES

For the library and information services manager viewing the entire perspective of crime with and against the computer the truism that prevention is better than cure has never been more apt. Adequate security precautions in terms of facilities and personnel are vital. Moreover, an organisation with a visible and positive approach to security will be less attractive to the wrongdoer, especially the casual or opportunist one. However, there can be tensions and the need for compromises between ideal security and user convenience in an open general access operation such as a library and information service. Moreover, as resources are not limited, (especially in the public sector) the price of security has to be matched against the risk. Even the best organised and regulated environments may succumb to a sophisticated and planned attack so a contingency procedure for such eventualities needs also to be in place. There are many general approaches to security and crime which will not be discussed in detail here but certain aspects specific to IT will be looked at.

The managers's approach to computer security needs to be systematic and thorough. This entails observing some preliminaries. Firstly, the threats that exist to premises, systems and equipment need to be established and analysed. The evaluation needs to be comprehensive but realistic, neither assuming too little and thus a carefree (or careless) attitude, nor too much to engender paranoia! Secondly, some assessment of the value of potential losses both direct and indirect needs to be made. In addition to the replacement costs of the more tangible items such as computer hardware, equipment and premises, other factors also have to be taken into account. These include the cost of lost data and its regeneration, the expense of disruption and dislocation of operations and services with costly provision of alternatives and redeployment of staff, the value of lost goodwill to patrons and even paying clients, and in extreme cases costs and penalties incurred if laws and contracts are broken. Finally, a strategy and mechanisms for controlling the organisation's vulnerability to computer misuse and crime, based on the assessments of threats and potential losses need to be worked out. In doing so, both preventative measures to combat the problem and palliative measures to minimise the impact on the organisation need to be addressed and a view of the costs and benefits of different approaches has to be retained

The factors involved in computer security are many and varied and range from the area in which an operation is located to its clients and suppliers. To these may be applied, possibly in combination, what may be described as physical, technical (or systems), and behavioural (or managerial) measures. Put in more basic terms, they involve locking away, coding or encyphering, and controlling or directing the components in IT security to secure maximum protection. At a further remove, organisational measures involving insurance, and stand-by recovery facilities may be featured in any computer security plan. The factors to be protected and the appropriate measures are examined more fully below.

Area

The obvious message is not to locate an operation in what may be regarded as a high risk area. This implies avoiding neighbourhoods where there is a history of vandalism or theft in general. More specifically, it means perhaps avoiding isolated locations, or conversely buildings bordering onto busy roads which provide a rapid means of getaway for wrongdoers. But the library and information services manager is rarely in a position to choose a location and even where this is possible, perhaps in commissioning a new service point, economic constraints and service priorities dictate far more its location!

Site and buildings

Wherever possible the layout and design of the site and buildings should incorporate general security with few or no vulnerable features such as outside doors and windows in secluded corners. Even shrubberies which have become overgrown or are poorly sited may offer screening and concealment for the wrongdoer. Adequate site and building illumination after dark can also contribute to protection.

Controlling access to sites is clearly important. However, it is more easily accomplished in private or semi-private sector organisations with a discrete boundary than for others. The public library in a busy shopping precinct or the resource centre in a large urban campus offer different problems.

Access control to buildings and even areas in buildings, can be more easily accomplished. No one should be able to reach a location without good reason for being there. Implicit in this is that buildings in general, and IT areas in particular, are properly secured with adequate locks, bolts and bars on doors, windows and other openings. Inevitably the task becomes more difficult when the IT environment permeates the building with equipment in almost every working area.

Hardware

Security measures for hardware must combat its vulnerability to outright theft, interference with its operation, or damage. If it is moveable, and especially if it is portable, it must be locked in place. There are several proprietary devices available which are designed to clamp or fix equipment in place but still allow removal when necessary for relocation or servicing. In addition, locks and other devices on equipment, which switch off machines, effectively disable keyboards or shut off disc drives are available. Many are standard features on equipment and should be used whenever items are left unattended. Moreover, keys should not be left around or kept in obvious top drawers. Neither should numbers for combination locks be left on display.

Software and data

Electronic information requires protection both within and outside of the machine. Networks create an extra level of vulnerability but they will be discussed later. For large installations employing minicomputers or mainframe machines, physical access to equipment should be sufficiently inhibited to prevent direct tampering with, or removal of, material or information. For the more widespread personal computer, information residing on the hard disk can be protected against unauthorised access by a password control system. Some machines now incorporate password protection as a standard memory resident feature.

Material on storage media such as magnetic disks and tapes, or optical disk needs a secure environment, the level of security being appropriate to the value or sensitivity of the information stored and the risks it faces. Large scale operations involving tape and disc libraries require a very strict and secure regime of storage and access control. This entails good locks on the room in which the library is housed, and secure shelves and cabinets in which material is kept. More modest collections of material require locked cupboards and boxes. Even a locked disc storage box in a desk may deter the opportunist thief or eavesdropper. The more important and vulnerable material in an operation should reside in a fireproof safe as an additional protection against the vandals, as well as against natural calamities.

A secure environment implies not only appropriate physical arrangements but other elements as well. Thus, where necessary, information can be stored in cipher or encrypted form on a disc or tape with the keys to deciphering the data being held separately. Password access to particular files can also be introduced. Proprietary software to introduce these measures can be acquired without too much expense and difficulty. Less sophisticated but equally effective may be the approach of employing simple codes to describe information and providing a look-up key for interpretation when necessary. Needless to say the key must be kept securely!

Measures and procedures to counter threats from viruses and other rogue programs which may be introduced from electronic media are very necessary. As a general rule, unauthorised loading of software or data into machines, large or small, should not be permitted – not only for reasons of preventing infection, but also to avoid intellectual property problems. The provenance of any imported media should be clearly verified before it is allowed near an operation. Ostensibly free or cut-price material from unfamiliar suppliers should be viewed with suspicion. Pirated material should never be acquired. Material from reputable suppliers should give the library and information services manager little cause for anxiety provided it is carefully handled and subjected to adequate security. Much proprietary software is now supplied in a sealed package to ensure that it has not been tampered with between vendor and purchaser. A reputable supplier can in any case be expected to stand by any guarantee of quality offered. Public domain and shareware material may have to be judged a little differently.

Software utilities exist to check material and equipment and, should the worst happen, help decontaminate infected items to recover the situation.

Back-ups

To mitigate the consequences of any loss of information by accident or design it is imperative that systematic and regular back-up of all appropriate information is undertaken. In general, in the larger operations with a manager specifically responsible for IT matters a strict regime will ensure adequate back-up practices are being observed. It is when operations are on a smaller scale or migrate onto the desktop that things may be less formalised and the attitude towards back-up procedures not so vigorous unless the library and information services manager is diligent. Moreover, back-up copies having being created, their physical safe storage is important. Copies should be located away from the original information also. Otherwise the practice simply provides the thief or vandal with two copies instead of one to attack!

Communications and networks

IT applications which involve communications links between machines inevitably extend the parameters of risk from wrongdoers. The more public and accessible the links, either in systems or physical terms, then the more vulnerable they become to interception. Without adequate security they provide opportunities for eavesdropping, or for misusing and damaging information. Rogue programs and viruses can also be spread through insecure networks.

Networks of all kinds are becoming more widespread and familiar and are no longer the preserve of the computer, telecommunications or information specialist. Local area networks such as those on academic campuses or research organisations are plentiful. Wide area networks offering opportunities to link across a country or even from continent to continent are also widely employed. The Joint Academic Network (JANET) is one successful example which serves the academic community in the United Kingdom. The commercial public telephone utility offers yet another avenue (or several avenues) of communication for computer information.

The majority of systems which the typical library and information services manager employs will embody basic access security measures designed-in by the vendors such as identity codes and passwords. It is clearly important to treat the details of such controls with care and more will be said about this later. Some systems may incorporate means of providing different levels of access and network use, and these may be determined either by the network provider or the local user node.

Circumstances may arise where added protection in the form of encryption of transmissions is deemed necessary for particularly sensitive information. It is unlikely however that the library and information services manager will need to employ highly sophisticated systems involving, for example, radio frequency hopping techniques, unless working in very sensitive and secret fields of information activity.

An important component of network security is of course the physical integrity of the machine at the heart of the network, together with the means of access to the network – the terminal. These, being so plentiful, provide considerable scope for problems. The measures which have been rehearsed already under the heading of equipment apply to these circumstances.

A further control on systems integrity can be applied through call logging techniques which record attempts, successful or otherwise, to access machines or networks. Their surveillance provides a picture of what is going on in the system and their existence may be sufficient to deter some potential wrongdoers who are not anxious to have their activity identified during or even after the event. Propagating the knowledge that call logging is in use may limit or deter much misuse.

Conventional media and records

It is easy to overlook the importance of maintaining proper security over conventional material in the IT environment. The extensive measures taken to protect electronic machines, networks and information will count for nothing if print on paper material is not accorded equal attention. Sensitive printout and documentation associated with systems should therefore receive appropriate storage and treatment, and its distribution should also be controlled. The manager needs to ensure that this area of operations does not suffer through its apparent lack of importance alongside the more obvious aspects of IT security.

Personnel

A range of people have a significant part to play in the security of IT systems in the library and information service. They include, as well as systems operators directly running tasks and managing systems, those who operate equipment, or who utilise the output from systems, or who regulate access to areas and services. Nowadays virtually every member of a library and information services staff will have contact with IT in some shape or form, whether it be through the catalogue, circulation control, acquisitions and budgeting, word processing, local and remote databases or various other systems. People's performance is clearly critical to the success of any security regime. Their honesty, knowledge, vigilance, skill and commitment contributes as much as any technology to the integrity of operations.

The library and information services manager must therefore ensure that relevant staff (and that means virtually everybody!) are properly trained and adequately supervised with reference to IT security. Instructions on operating systems and providing services should also incorporate clearly the security measures that are required. Moreover, the effort must be sustained by continuous updating and refresher sessions to take into account the introduction of new systems and methods, and even the discovery of new threats and risks!

Clients

Few, if any, library and information services managers are able to choose their clientele so it is not helpful to suggest that potential users should be screened to assist IT security. Nevertheless it is important to emphasise to users that they too have obligations regarding the security of the IT systems upon which they and many other users rely. Regulations for the library and information service should include strictures against misuse of systems. It should be made clear that wilful misuse of systems is a breach of any regulations (as well as perhaps the law) and could be subject to sanctions and penalties. On a more positive note emphasis should be placed on users taking sufficient care over passwords and confidential data released to them in the course of providing services.

GENERAL MANAGEMENT CONSIDERATIONS

Overarching the secure management of IT operations are some general considerations involving supervision, control, planning and anticipation. Much of this is simply good management practice but it needs reiterating.

The need to know principle

The strategy for control and supervision of access to equipment, systems and information in various formats has to be determined at the highest level in the library and information services organisation. Criteria must be established to identify who needs to know what, and who needs access to where, for any particular context and such decisions must be documented to avoid ambiguities.

Audits and spot checks

Regular audits of security measures and their effectiveness need to be conducted. Otherwise how will the manager know whether they are working or not? In addition, spot or random checks on operations and procedures should be periodically carried out to test the integrity of the system. Care must be taken however to present such practices in a positive way to staff to avoid impairing goodwill and commitment to security and the wider objectives of the service.

Inventory

The manager must know what equipment, systems and information are available and are part of his or her responsibility. This points to proper and accurate documentation and maintenance of inventories. If the inventory is itself machine readable then obviously it must have appropriate safeguards against misuse and loss.

Insurance

The manager must take a realistic view of security considerations and recognise that although prevention is better than cure, the burden of rectifying a breach of security is lightened somewhat if financial underwriting of the consequences is available. Equipment and material can be insured against loss or damage. Less tangible information products may be harder to value and thus insure adequately but it may be desirable to do so. In commercial information contexts it may be prudent to insure against lost business as a result of security failures. Insurers may impose their own strict conditions of storage, access and control on systems where the risks are thought to warrant them. This may be regarded as a further spur to the organisation to attend properly to security matters. Further information regarding insurance cover can be found in chapter 11 by Parsons.

Contingency and disaster planning

The manager is well advised to have a plan which anticipates a partial or total failure of IT security. Such failure may occur not only through wrongdoing but through natural events also. Reacting and adjusting to such problems may involve using alternative systems and equipment on site, or even the transfer of operations to other locations, depending on the scale of operations and degree of failure. Some commercial organisations provide this kind of contingency support – at a price.

The plan should allocate responsibilities and prescribe actions to be followed. In short, who does what and how! Its objectives should be, in the first place, to minimise the damage and/or loss to the operation together with limiting impairment to the service, and then to enable operations to be restored as fully as possible and as quickly as possible. It is in these circumstances that the quality of security training and back-up procedures come to the fore. The time to discover that a contingency plan does not work properly is not when the first disaster strikes but in the calm of a trial situation. Hence the plan should be tested and refined. The plan should be dynamic and evolve with change and events also.

Passwords

Arguably, any password protection on a system can be overcome given sufficient time and resources, but in general, poor password protection derives more from behavioural than technical shortcomings. Some staff still fail to use passwords effectively and intelligently despite the advice that is perennially provided from organisations and managers. The basic tenet is that a password should not be accessible to the potential wrongdoer. There are some fairly simple precautions to follow.

Where a password can be specified, it should be chosen with a view to making it difficult to discover or even guess at. Thus, one's initials, telephone number, date of birth or a relative's name should be eschewed in favour of a far less significant code. This raises the problem of memorising a password, of course, but noting it down too conspicuously and accessibly is also to be avoided. A password has little function if it is emblazoned upon the keyboard or screen of the machine for which it is intended to be effective! The number of people who know a password also needs to be strictly limited. In addition, a password should be routinely changed to overcome any possibility of its having been compromised without knowledge of the operators of the system. Clearly, if a known breach of password security takes place then a change should be effected as soon as possible. Passwords are a vital link in the chain of security which protects IT operations and should be managed as such.

INFORMATION AND ADVICE

The manager would be advised to become well briefed on this area of operations by relevant reading and, where appropriate, by seeking information and advice from specialist agencies. In addition to the items already cited, reference could also be made to Hruska and Jackson (1990), Schweitzer (1990), and Stuart *et al.* (1989). There is a growing literature and the topic is rapidly changing through the problems posed and the countermeasures available, so the manager should make every effort to consult newer sources as they appear. Also mentioned below are relevant programmes and initiatives of value.

UK Information Technology Security Evaluation and Certification Scheme

The cause of IT security has been advanced recently by the introduction of a new initiative for certification of security products from the government. The UK Information Technology Security Evaluation and Certification Scheme which became fully operational early in 1991 has, according to the official documentation (*UKIT...*, 1991), 'been established to evaluate and certify the level of confidence which may be placed in the security features of Information Technology (IT) products and systems'. The Scheme's objectives are further described as being 'to meet the needs of government and industry for the security evaluation of IT products and systems and to provide a basis for mutual international recognition of evaluation results and certificates'.

The scheme is designed to assist, on the one hand those responsible for selecting and specifying IT products with security features, and on the other, manufacturers who are seeking to substantiate the quality of their products. Products are independently tested and evaluated according to established criteria and those which are certified are listed in a regularly updated *Certified products list*. This represents a valuable source of reliable information for the manager, upon which to base judgements about acquiring security products. As support for the Scheme grows and the range of products certified extends so its usefulness will increase. Information and advice about the Scheme may be obtained from:

> Senior Executive of the Certification Body
> UK IT Security Evaluation & Certification Scheme
> Room 2/0804
> Fiddlers Green Lane
> Cheltenham
> Gloucestershire GL52 5AJ

The IT- Security Awareness Campaign

The IT Security Awareness Campaign sponsored by the Department of Trade and Industry provides a valuable information source for managers seeking enlightenment on IT security matters. The Campaign, which is managed by the National Computing Centre, was launched in February 1990 at the IBM '90 exhibition with a view to raising awareness of IT security issues and it is planned to run for three years. A great deal of valuable and informative material has been prepared and distributed under the auspices of the Campaign. Publications include a regular newsletter, *Password*, which appears twice a year, a series of case studies in which real examples of security problems are described and discussed, and a series of very useful *Factsheets* covering major security topics succinctly yet comprehensively. Events such as seminars to raise security awareness also take place. Information about the Campaign is available from:

> The IT Security Awareness Campaign
> Customer Service Desk
> National Computing Centre Ltd
> Oxford Road
> Manchester M1 7ED

The National Preservation Office

The National Preservation Office, based at the British Library, was established in 1984 to provide a focus for all aspects of preserving library collections. In addition to the more conventional aspects of material preservation, such as the durability of paper and bindings, the Office's parameter of interest extends to security matters in libraries in the broadest sense including threats from flood, fire, theft and vandalism.

The Office has established *Security guidelines* (included as the Appendix to chapter 12 by Jackson) which deal comprehensively with the issue. In addition, the office operates a free referral and information service, publishes a range of guides and leaflets and organises training courses together with a major annual conference on preservation issues. It thus represents a useful source of information and advice to the library and information services manager seeking to enhance security.

REFERENCES

Hearnden, K. (1990), Computer-linked crime – what is happening? in Hearnden, K. (editor) *Handbook of computer security 2nd edition.* London: Kegan Paul.

Highland, H. J. (1990), *Computer virus handbook.* Oxford: Elsevier.

Hoffman, L. J. editor (1990), *Rogue programs: viruses, worms and Trojan Horses.* New York: Van Nostrand Reinhold.

Hruska, J. and Jackson, K. (1990), *Computer security solutions.* Oxford: Blackwell Scientific.

Law Commission (1988), *Computer misuse.* London: HMSO. (Law Commission Working Paper No 110.)

Reiss, M. (1990), Computer viruses. *School Science Review*, vol. 72, no. 258, (September), pp. 65–68.

Schweitzer, J. A. (1990), *Managing information security: administrative electronic, and legal measures to protect business information 2nd edition.* London: Butterworths.

Stuart, R., Mitchell, C., and Jackson, K. (1989), How to stop computer fraud. *Which Computer*, (October), pp. 30, 31, 33, 37, 38, 41, 42, 44, 46.

Survey indicates growing threat of viruses (1991), *Password*, (Spring), p. 1.

UKIT Security Evaluation & Certificate Scheme UK Certified Product List (1991), no. 1.1, (1 June).

11

Insurance implications of crime and security

JOHN PARSONS

The main purpose of this chapter is to provide an insight on the many facets of insurance cover which impinge on the responsibility of the library manager. As the role of libraries and indeed the role of the librarian change to meet social and economic demands, so does the need to consider the problems, catastrophes, difficulties etc. which might befall the premises, the property, the public, the staff, and the liabilities which attach. When the risks have been assessed it is possible to transfer many of them by purchasing insurance cover.

As libraries differ as to the nature of their activities so their insurance requirements will differ. The insurance market place is a vast and ever changing environment. For peace of mind it is advisable that expert advice is sought from a professional insurance intermediary to ensure adequate protection is obtained.

The responsibility for placing of the insurance covers will differ widely from the owners (of private libraries)/Council officers and administration/ University Boards/librarians. However, one of the most important people in the insurance equation is the library manager, for he or she is the person who has responsibility for ensuring the library functions as intended. The library manager should be involved in ensuring that all aspects of covers and liability are catered for. They have invaluable knowledge and expertise to impart to the insurers in conjunction with those who may be arranging the covers and mindful of the cost element – it is teamwork.

The following are the salient aspects which it is believed will be common to most libraries, with some thought and comment on how certain insurance covers might be approached. It should be appreciated however that the list is not exhaustive:

- material damage
- business interruption
- theft
- commercial all risks
- money
- theft by employee
- personal accident
- professional indemnity
- liabilities
- motor vehicle cover

MATERIAL DAMAGE

By material damage one means the actual objects capable of damage or destruction and these can be further addressed under sub-headings of buildings, equipment, and stock.

Buildings

Ensure whose responsibility it is to insure the buildings and for what value, read carefully the terms of the lease or rental agreements. Check the extent of cover others may impose under the terms of the lease and be satisfied that such enforced covers meet the requirements of the library. For example, lease or owners may effect or insist on limited or specific covers being arranged such as fire/aircraft/explosion, though as a minimum such covers would do little to compensate the library in the event of loss or damage by storm.

When arranging buildings cover it is essential to ensure the insurance value selected is accurate, and more important, adequate. It is normal practice to insure buildings for their reinstatement value i.e. replacement as new, hence the sum insured must be sufficient to meet such reinstatement cost and care must be taken to ensure account is taken of the inflation factor during the reinstatement period. The sum insured must also be sufficient to cater for site clearance, architects fees and public authority requirements. Obviously as libraries are housed in many and varied buildings it is important to consider, at the outset, the practicalities of reinstatement of one's particular buildings. A modern concrete and glass building can be valued quite easily on a reinstatement basis and adequate provision provided to cater for site clearance and architects fees but for a library housed in a 14th century castle reinstatement would be impossible: consideration must be given to the type of building the library would accept in the event of total loss and agreement reached at the outset on precisely how and sometimes where the library could be re-built, taking into account the laws applicable to listed buildings. The alternative to reinstatement cover is indemnity cover and this effectively is the reinstatement cost less an amount for depreciation but it is important to remember the sum insured is the maximum liability therefore one can readily appreciate the importance in arriving at a realistic and adequate sum insured at the outset.

Insurers often use such jargon as 'catastrophe perils only' – ensure you know in plain English precisely what perils you require cover against and what covers you are being quoted for because one person's idea on catastrophe perils can differ from another's; generally catastrophe tends to infer cover against fire, lightning, explosion and aircraft. Insurers use the expression fire and full perils which is a contradiction in terms because the term limits the cover to the normal range of perils i.e. fire, lightning, explosion, riot, civil commotion, malicious damage, earthquake, storm, flood, burst water pipes, impact and subsidence – the widest range of cover is however all risks which in addition to the full perils adds accidental damage. It should be noted that theft is not treated here as a peril for it is dealt with in a separate section below. Obviously the wider the cover taken the more costly the insurance premium. However, it is possible, dependent upon the financial status of the library to bear some of the cost of each and every claim (called a deductible or excess) and in return the premium is discounted.

It is worth noting that there is usually a compulsory excess of £250 in respect of the perils, malicious damage, storm, burst water pipes and impact and accidental damage and with regard to subsidence £1,000.

Equipment

Computers are fast becoming an every day tool of trade and so it is imperative that specialist computer cover is sought immediately one thinks of purchasing the equipment for one needs back-up of hardware/ software and to ensure cover for the recovery of important data stored. One needs to consider catastrophe planning should one's operations be suddenly curtailed to ensure that the additional costs of working are fully catered for.

Appropriate cover – fire and perils or all risks – should be considered for all general contents (other than books) such as furniture, shelving, typewriters, fax machines, and photocopiers, but see also the section on commercial all risks below.

Stock and services

These are the lifeblood of any library and again only the librarian can say with any certainty the make up of the books and the impact damage or destruction will have on their services.

It is essential therefore that consideration be given to providing and regularly updating an inventory of books. Certain books and manuscripts will be more difficult to replace than others and some may be irreplaceable. Hence it is imperative that all parties to the insurance contract (librarian/intermediary/insurer) agree at the outset the method and extent of cover thus avoiding needless acrimony in the event of a claim. It is suggested that the bookstock might be allocated to differing types of cover possibly as follows:

- routine: fiction which is easily replaceable and can be insured on an indemnity basis (current replacement value less an amount for depreciation)
- valuable books replaceable only with difficulty: such books would be insured on a reinstatement value (current replacement value as new)
- valuable irreplaceable books: such books would need to be covered on an 'agreed value' basis and an authenticated valuation provided at the outset to avoid problems in the event of a claim

Libraries now offer a wide variety of different services incorporating community centres with provision of creche, cafe or restaurant facilities; exhibitions; craft and trade fairs. It is imperative that the contents and stock of all these are covered with responsibility for their safety and that insurance cover is clearly laid down at the outset i.e. in the case of craft fairs ensure that traders extend their insurance cover for the period of the exhibition. If however the library has to accept liability then insurers/ brokers must be advised before the event.

The covers discussed so far relate to the premises risk i.e. static at the risk address but many items (books, manuscripts and other library materials) by necessity are loaned out and consideration therefore needs to be given to covering such goods whilst away from the premises – stock in transit – and again expert advice needs to be sought.

BUSINESS INTERRUPTION

The covers outlined relate to the more tangible aspects of insurance namely buildings, contents, and stock but equally important is the loss of revenue and increased cost of working suffered by the library in the event of loss or damage. Again the key figures in arranging the covers are the librarian, the accountants and financial directors, for thought has to be given to how the library would (or would not) function and consideration ought to be given to catastrophe planning covering such aspects as:

- – provision of temporary premises
- – supply of books
- – hiring of machines i.e. fax, photocopiers, typewriters, computers
- – cost of advertising
- – provision of telephones
- – provision of stationery
- – redeployment of staff
- – honouring of outstanding contracts and functions

This list is not exhaustive but is intended to provide food for thought.

The accountant and financial director will be able to assess the existing income derived from library activities and the costs emanating from the provision of the library. Income, for example, would include that from leasing activity (craft fairs, exhibitions, cinema complex, cafe etc.); fines; the cost of loans in respect of certain research manuscripts; the portion of local authority grants for provision of the library facility. Expenditure would include rent (still to be paid in the event of damage); water rates; salaries of staff; redundancy payments in the event of certain staff by necessity being laid off.

It is most important to consider the length of time it will take the library to fully recover from the damage or destruction and this period is known as the 'indemnity period' and the insurance policy will indemnify the policyholder during this period for loss of revenue and increased cost of working but the sum insured has to be adequately assessed at the outset.

Obviously the longer the indemnity period selected the higher the premium, and similar to the material damage aspects – buildings, contents and stock – cover can be arranged against a variety of perils or all risks. It must be appreciated that the range of covers (i.e. perils insured) arranged for the business interruption cannot be wider than the covers arranged in respect of the material damage section. The reason for this is that business interruption insurers require the knowledge that material damage insurance monies are available to assist in the recovery of the business as quickly as possible.

It is also important when considering business interruption to consider the effects of future trends of the business during the indemnity period to ensure the sum insured adequately reflects this.

THEFT

The standard form of theft insurance is essential for businesses of this nature and the same considerations in arriving at a sum insured, particularly on books, apply as on the fire and perils cover. Careful security measures both in the sense of electronic and physical protection will clearly reduce the risk of loss through theft but do not always prevent the more determined thief. It should be understood at this juncture that the standard cover provides protection against the following circumstances:

- loss of, or damage to, stock and general contents following forcible and violent entry to, or exit from, the premises
- loss of, or damage to, all insured property other than stock and materials in trade whilst temporarily removed from the premises and situated in other premises. This must follow forcible and violent entry to, or exit from, the premises and the cover is usually written subject to a limit of 10% of the sum insured or £5,000, whichever is the less

- damage to the premises as a result of theft
- the cost of replacement locks in the event of theft of the keys to the premises, safes or strongrooms. This is again written subject to a limit, usually £500

It is not usual to provide cover for books stolen by the users of the library either whilst the library is open or in the event of non-return of books. The difficulties in monitoring books and security procedures make this a difficult risk to underwrite.

COMMERCIAL ALL RISKS

Many libraries possess a range of expensive equipment such as computers, photocopiers, coffee machines and fax machines and should therefore appreciate the need to obtain cover against accidents, which all too easily occur, in addition to the basic fire and perils normally insured. The policy covers all types of loss or damage to the property and may include loss or damage away from the premises. The policy cover is usually written subject to an insured's contribution and contains the following exclusions (which may be modified on occasions):

- consequential loss
- wear and tear
- mechanical or electrical breakdown or derangement
- theft from unattended vehicles

MONEY

Libraries will have money on the premises from various sources and this will always be a target risk. All businesses are well aware of both the current scale of break-ins and armed hold-ups, where the thieves are primarily after the cash whether on the premises or in transit. Unlike the theft of goods, robbery involves physical violence and as a result personal accident cover for employees should be considered.

The definition of money is wide and includes cash and currency notes, cheques (but excluding pre-signed blank cheques), postal or money orders, postage and revenue stamps, bills of exchange, luncheon vouchers, gift tokens and unused units in franking machines.

The standard money policy offers wide cover and provides indemnity for loss of, or damage to, money in the following situations:

- at the insured's premises
- at the residence of directors or employers
- in transit
- in a bank night safe until at the bank's risk

The policy also includes a personal accident benefit in the event of bodily injury to employees as a direct result of robbery or attempt thereat. The benefits are capital sums for death, disablement, loss of limbs or eyes or other permanent total disablement from any gainful employment and a temporary total disablement weekly benefit.

THEFT BY EMPLOYEE

Theft by employee insurance, or fidelity guarantee, is designed to protect an employer against losses as a result of employees abusing their positions of responsibility and using the knowledge vested in them to steal from their employer. When it was reported in 1988 that British companies lost a staggering £2.75 billion each year through employee theft and fraud, one can appreciate that this can be a very real risk.

The policy provides an indemnity against direct loss of money or goods caused by an act of theft by an employee. It also covers any other act of fraud or dishonesty by an employee, provided that this was committed with the clear intent of obtaining improper personal gain either for themselves or some other person or organisation. The term 'employee' under the policy shall mean any person under a contract of service or apprenticeship with the proposer and includes trainees under Government Training Schemes, directors under a contract of service who have only a minority shareholding, and retired employees who continue to perform work as consultants. A feature of the policy is the minimum standards of control required in respect of supervision, accounting procedures and for checking the security of money or goods. These minimum standards of cover are straightforward and tailor-made to the circumstances of the risk. The cover can be written either as a catastrophe cover with a high limit of indemnity, substantial insured's contribution, and a limited system of check, or a low limit of indemnity, no excess and a more detailed system of check.

PERSONAL ACCIDENT

The most important asset a library has are its employees. There is a wide range of personal accident and annual business travel covers which will:

– provide an important extension to the employee benefits portfolio
– protect the business against the financial cost of an injury to an employee
– meet the business travel insurance needs of the business and its employees
– provide illness insurance as an extension to the personal accident cover if required

The aim of the policy is to provide each in the event of directors or employees sustaining accidental bodily injury which results in death or disablement, regardless of any legal liability that may be involved. The policy benefits will provide:

– a lump sum payment following injury that results in death, permanent inability of the insured person to return to his or her usual occupation in the insured's business, or permanent total loss of: one or more limbs (including permanent total loss of use); sight in one or both eyes; hearing in one or both ears; speech
– income, being an amount normally paid at monthly intervals in the event of inability to work because of injury or illness; the income is usually payable for up to 2 years but can be adopted to meet any reasonable business need

Employers with employees who travel abroad can effect a business travel insurance to meet their needs. The cover is usually written on an annual basis with the policy providing personal cover for the traveller for medical and emergency travel expenses plus legal expenses, illness contracted abroad, personal baggage, personal money and credit cards and personal liability and cover in respect of the journey for cancellation, curtailment and change of itinerary (including replacement expenses), travel delay and hijack. The premium is dependent on the level of cover required and the number of journeys undertaken.

Visitors personal accident

Various disasters that have occurred in recent years such as Abbeystead, Zeebrugge and Kings Cross, caused the insurance market to introduce a new cover to the range of contracts available. Called visitors personal accident insurance it is a 'no fault' compensation policy which provides an inexpensive and speedy means of providing some compensation to bona fide visitors who suffer accidents on the premises. The cover does not take away the injured parties right to take action should the library be legally responsible for the injury but, as can be appreciated, legal proceedings can take time and the policy is there to provide immediate compensation to alleviate any financial hardship the injured party may suffer. The role of libraries makes consideration to this type of cover self evident.

Cover is normally purchased in units e.g. £25,000 and provides a benefit for both death and various specified personal disabilities.

PROFESSIONAL INDEMNITY

Following the income generating schemes that libraries are now undertaking the question of professional indemnity insurance becomes relevant. In a situation where the library is providing a service for a fee then the professional indemnity risk should be considered. The policy will provide indemnity against legal liability to pay damages and claimants costs and expenses as a result of a breach of professional duty. Claims can arise in the following areas:

- delays
- lost instructions from customers
- typographical error
- libel and slander
- dishonesty of an employee
- inaccurate advice
- misunderstanding clients requirements

As the activities of a library diversify in order to generate extra income the increasing exposure to claims from these sources should carefully be considered.

LIABILITIES

By liability one means the library's legal responsibility to others, either third parties or employees and/or the library's legal responsibility to the properties of others. These can be addressed under the subheadings of employers liability and public and products liability.

Employers liability

As a result of the Employers Liability (Compulsory Insurance) Act 1969 all businesses with an employer/employee relationship must take out an approved policy with an authorised insurer.

Employers liability insurance protects the employer against liability at law to pay damages to an employee who is killed, injured or contracts an illness or disease, whilst working in connection with the business.

How does the legal liability arise? Well, an employer has a duty of care to his employees as evolved from common law. Negligence in particular, has been, and continues to be, consolidated and extended by statute e.g. the Health & Safety at Work etc. Act 1974 and the Control of Substances Hazardous to Health Regulations 1988.

Apart from those under employment or apprenticeship contracts, there are others who are deemed to be employees. These include labour masters and persons they may supply, the self-employed, a person hired or borrowed and even people working under a work experience scheme.

How can employers liability claims arise? Some risks are obvious and immediate – employees working at height or operating dangerous machinery. Some are less obvious such as exposure to harmful substances or excessive noise (albeit doubtful that this could arise in a library). Other risks are more common (but no less real): an employee injured whilst lifting or carrying, hit by a falling object, or one who simply slips and falls.

However safe you consider your business, there will always be the risk of injury for which you may well be legally liable as you are required by law to provide a safe place of work at all times.

The law stipulates a minimum indemnity limit of £2 million. However, market practice is to provide cover which is an unlimited amount.

Other than injuries arising from certain types of nuclear radiation to which the Nuclear Installations Act applies, there are no exclusions in the employers liability policy.

The premium for employers liability insurance tends to be based on staff salaries and wages. It is important that the insurer is aware of the full range of activities of the library.

Public and products liability

This cover protects your library against liability at law to pay damages to those who are accidentally killed or injured (excluding employees) or whose property is accidentally damaged as a result of your business activities.

The majority of these covers available today extend beyond this by also including legal liability:

- for the false arrest, imprisonment or eviction of a customer
- for any nuisance or trespass you may commit on any rights such as right of way which may interfere in the course of your business

Your duty of care stems from common law – for example negligence, nuisance and trespass. These duties have been developed by many significant legal cases and further extended by statutes like the Supply of Goods (Implied Terms) Act 1973 and the Fire Precautions Act 1971. The Consumer Protection Act 1987 is one of the most significant changes in legislation to affect the extent of the common law duty of care in recent years.

Public and products liability claims can arise from a range of situations – customers may slip on a greasy floor, or be struck by falling masonry whilst visiting your premises, or water may overflow and damage property below. Alternatively, your customers may be injured or property damaged because of faulty products you supply e.g. injury may be caused by a chair collapsing, or food you supply could cause poisoning.

The need for adequate cover under this heading has never been greater. Only you, together with your insurance adviser, can decide upon the amount of protection you require. But remember that the level of damages awarded by the court continues to rise steadily.

As I have stressed, the choice is yours but it is vital that you make the right one as your insurance policy might not fully meet your total legal liability. For guidance, £1 million should be regarded as a realistic minimum level of protection but the majority of insurers these days can provide cover up to at least £5 million in the majority of circumstances.

MOTOR VEHICLE COVER

Motor insurance, like employers liability, is compulsory. Under the Road Traffic Act 1930 any person using a motor vehicle on the public highway has to have motor insurance with an authorised insurer. Since 1930 various pieces of legislation have added to the compulsory requirements of the cover.

Cover can be arranged for private cars, and goods-carrying vehicles including mobile libraries. Where the total number of vehicles owned by the library is relatively small i.e. up to 4, the insurance will probably be on a no claims discount basis with each vehicle having its own entitlement. A number of vehicles can be insured together on a fleet basis where one overall fleet discount would be allowed.

Consideration will have to be given to the type of cover required. Nowadays the minimum cover one can effect is third party, providing cover for your legal liability for injury to other road users including passengers and pedestrians and for damage to third party property. Third party fire and theft cover can be purchased but comprehensive cover is probably desirable and it is important to realise that this provides cover for damage to your vehicle in addition to providing protection against liability to third parties.

In order to assess the risk, an insurer will require:

- full details of all vehicles to be insured
- where garaged
- the accident/conviction record of each driver
- existing no claim discount levels

Should you decide to bear the first £50 or £100 of each claim for damage to your vehicle this will be reflected by a discount in the premium required.

CONCLUSION

The chapter started by stressing that a great deal of thought is necessary when arranging insurance cover to ensure that adequate protection has been purchased. I hope I have given the reader an insight of the type of covers that may be considered but as mentioned it is important to consult your professional insurance advisor when seeking cover as the above list of covers is not exhaustive. All interested parties should contribute to ensure no aspect of the library's activities has been overlooked and the insurance programme should be regularly reviewed to ensure it still meets the needs of the library and information service.

12

The national framework: the role of the National Preservation Office

MARIE JACKSON

Question: Is theft a problem in your library?
Answer: Yes, user's belongings – particularly money – are stolen regularly
Question: Do your users fail to return books?
Answer: Quite often, but they don't mean to be difficult...
Question: Have you any library books at home which you've had for quite a while?
Answer: Yes, books, tapes ... the lot!

The National Preservation Office has been working on library security since 1988; intensive research to produce the 1990 video *Library security: who cares?* included informal talks with all kinds of librarians and street interviews on camera with members of the public. This was not pure research, of course, but the insights gained were invaluable and the general tone of answers was both consistent and troubling. The questions and answers shown above reflect clearly the key messages which were impossible to ignore. Firstly, most librarians did not immediately equate words like security and theft as pertaining to the collections in their care. Secondly, most librarians were unwilling to believe wrong of their users. Thirdly, the public did not consider the non-return of library books (and other material) a matter of concern.

Although many librarians still do not admit the extent of library book theft and mutilation in libraries, there was enough concern as far back as 1987 for the British Library to host a seminar on the subject of library security. Part of the impetus was the completion of the British Library's own security review – a detailed, lengthy piece of work which took many months of investigation. The seminar drew high level attendance. All the copyright librarians were present or represented. Senior public and academic librarians were there. Papers were given by librarians and security experts. No proceedings were published. Those who attended recall startling honesty, a rich sharing of experience and an underlying feeling that the problems being discussed could no longer be ignored.

Ratcliffe (1983) had led to a call for a national focus – a central point for information, for advice, for arranging conferences and training. The 1987 security seminar led to a similar call. There was no particular lack of experience, or expertise. Many librarians, indeed, had a wealth of experience in combating problem patrons. There were some good security products on the market. But there was no central focus for sharing and channelling existing knowledge. The need for raising awareness was clear. A national office would be the ideal tool to get library security high on the librarianship agenda.

NATIONAL PRESERVATION OFFICE AND LIBRARY SECURITY

The security of collections found a natural home at the National Preservation Office. The Office was already experienced in increasing awareness of preservation issues; security of collections is closely related. Little point spending large amounts of money each year on conserving material for the future if they are not to remain part of the collections.

The remit given to the Office was to concentrate on the security of collections. The Library Association already gave advice on the safety and security of librarians in the workplace. The third accepted area of security – that of buildings – would be covered by the Office but to a lesser degree.

On a day-to-day basis, the Office attempts to answer enquiries itself or refer callers to other areas of expertise. Office staff keep up to date with literature on the subject and with new developments in security equipment. Many callers require advice on what systems will best suit their particular needs. Others have heard of publications they wish to trace. Specific furniture information – what cabinets for instance are preservation and security recommended? – is also required.

The long term aims of the Office involve a major shift of attitude on library security. To this end, the Office is embarking on a training and conference programme and attempting to encourage research into book loss in this country.

COST OF LIBRARY CRIME

The lack of facts on library crime is understandable. The librarian of the 1990s is far less likely to have the time and resources to do regular stock checks. In large libraries books may only be found to be missing if they are required by other readers. Mutilated books are even more difficult to spot, especially if colour plates only have been removed.

Formal statistics on crime in this country give librarians no help. Theft is classified simply as theft. Crime of all kinds rises annually by about 6% and there is little doubt that library crime figures are growing apace. But there is little proof (for further information see chapter 2).

A survey on crime and disruption in Great Britain's libraries was conducted in 1987 by Lincoln with the support of the Centre for Library and Information Management (CLAIM). Three hundred libraries, of a variety of sizes and in a variety of locations, were sampled. Lincoln found a book theft rate of 3500 incidents for every 100 libraries and, overall, the results showed:

- mutilation of books was common; 85% of the libraries reported episodes of intentional damage
- vandalism on the outside of the library buildings was common
- book theft occurred regularly
- theft of reference material was chronic
- half the sampled libraries had petty theft problems

Chief among recent useful written work on library security problems is Keele (1987). This work includes studies of loss rates from a variety of libraries and gives good advice on how basic good practice in layout and policy can affect loss rates.

Keele argues that two libraries side-by-side can experience totally different loss rates depending on the layout of their collections, training of staff and use of electronic equipment. He dismisses to some extent that the geographical position of a library, in an intercity area versus, say, a small country village, need massively affect loss rates.

Loss rates quoted by Keele and others are usually between 1% and 40% but higher rates have been recorded. Law libraries usually have high loss rates. This is probably explained by the high price of law literature and the pressure, particularly on students, to get information quickly.

What is an average loss rate in UK libraries? And what does this translate to in financial terms? Certain calculations can be made to present what may be the best scenario: there are 150 million books in UK libraries (there are more); there is a 2% loss rate (lowest conceivable); the replacement cost of a missing book averages £20 (it has to be more given the costs involved). This scenario has theft and mutilation costing UK libraries £60 million each year. This should be seen as an absolute base figure.

Keele is adamant that the pattern of loss in all libraries is similar. Recent acquisitions are far more likely to be stolen or not returned than older stock. This has obvious implications for library finances and the real cost of poor security practices. It is often unrealistic to take an average book price on which to base your financial losses.

The British Library's recent work on life cycle costings in the library environment (carried out as part of Enright's *Selection for survival: a review of acquisition and retention policies* (1989)) points to the real cost of library operations and is relevant when considering replacement costs of stolen or missing library stock. An item of information in a storage system has an initial cost, a time dependent cost and a usage cost. Reducing these into their component parts allows an equation to be formulated. Put simply and used for a security argument, life cycle costing shows the price of a replacement volume on a library shelf to be the initial cover price, plus the accessioning cost, any preservation cost, first handling cost, cataloguing cost, storage cost, etc. Of course, to benefit fully from such costings, the individual costs of operations must be broken down but even a recognition of the elements shows how careful librarians must be when quietly allowing their material to walk away from their shelves.

Keele believes that layout and electronic security systems can do much to alleviate loss rates. He also, importantly, stresses the role of library staff in reducing theft, non-return and mutilation of stock.

LIBRARY CRIME, CRIMINALS AND THE LAW

Nothing will be achieved in the UK without a major change of attitude from two groups: librarians and those involved in legal processes. Just as the general public does not see book theft as a crime, so the punishments meted out to those found guilty of library related crimes are rarely severe. It has not always been so. The Reverend Charles Burney became a noted classical scholar and the owner of the famous Burney collection purchased by the British Museum. In his younger days at Cambridge, however, Burney was discovered to be a book thief; despite his father's eminence, he was expelled. The perceived gravity of the offence is reflected in several contemporary letters.

It is undoubtedly true that library-related crimes carry far more stringent punishments in the United States than they do at present in the United Kingdom. A British Library reader convicted in 1989 of stealing from both the Reading Room at Bloomsbury and the Newspaper Library at Colindale and who had used false names for admission to the former, was sentenced to 100 hours community service. A random browse through the American journal *Conservation Administration News* finds a sixteen year old boy being ordered to undergo psychiatric evaluation and treatment for stealing a valuable book (as well as paying a substantial fine) and a librarian sentenced to fifteen years imprisonment for stealing manuscripts and rare books (as well as paying a very substantial fine).

Few library offenders in the UK reach court. Most librarians do not prosecute, for a number of reasons. Some have no faith in the legal system for redress in such cases. Some consider attendant publicity to be a bad thing. Many are overruled by, say, university or college authorities. Many are simply unwilling to go through the necessary work and aggravation.

Successful prosecutions of book thieves are rare enough to create major publicity. The trial of Rastafarian Seymour McLean in the mid-1980s was made into a Channel Four play, *The Book Liberator* and shown in December 1989. McLean 'liberated' more than 2000 items from libraries, claiming his right to return such items to Ethiopia (though they seem only to have got as far as his London flat). His philosophical arguments did not sway the court. He got a nine month sentence. The expense to the libraries involved was extensive. Probably the most famous book mutilator was playwright Joe Orton, who, with his lover Kenneth Halliwell was arraigned for stealing 72 library books and 1653 plates from art books. His book defacement is now legendary. He pasted female nude figures in a book of etiquette; he stuck monkey heads onto roses and added his own disgusting blurbs to library books. He and Halliwell both got a six month sentence.

To emphasise, then, the position of security in UK libraries which the National Preservation Office's first research painted:

- there is little published research on book loss and mutilation
- there is a tendency in UK librarians to dismiss issues of security
- there is little hope of severe punishment for those who abuse library services
- in the present financial climate, there is less and less probability of full stock checks, therefore little hope of painting a full picture of library losses
- there is little general, good advice available
- security is not a high profile discipline in most libraries

NATIONAL PRESERVATION OFFICE AND CRIME PREVENTION

The National Preservation Office published its *Security Guidelines* in 1989. These, available free of charge from the Office, are a handy 'do's' and 'don'ts' of library security with an introduction to some useful reading matter. The *Guidelines* aim to encourage librarians to think about their own situations and how they might develop security awareness about them. 'Call theft theft and thieves thieves' it says, loud and clear. The *Guidelines* went out widely and have been used extensively. They are included as an Appendix to this chapter.

Initial work in the National Preservation Office required making contacts with others involved in security issues. The Library Association has already been mentioned. As representatives of the majority of librarians in the UK, the LA has professional responsibility to advise its staff and does so on aspects of personal safety within libraries.

The National Preservation Office was initially charged with a feasibility study of whether a database of missing books for the library world was a realistic aim. It soon became clear that the launch of a new database for this purpose was not possible. To work well, librarians would need access to an online system virtually every hour of every day. No small office could man a database to that extent. The financial constraints were also beyond the purse of the Office. Most importantly, a database already existed, though it was not used as widely as it might be.

The National Database of Stolen Books is a joint initiative of the Antiquarian Booksellers' Association and the Provincial Booksellers Fairs Association. The database operates from the latter's premises in Cambridge. The database aims to inform booksellers, librarians and others of missing books. A librarian or bookseller suffering a loss or theft can ring either of the two organisations. Anyone suspecting that they are being offered stolen material can check the database, which is divided into four subject areas – books, manuscripts, prints and atlases. A hard copy of the database is issued monthly and distributed to members of the associations. Though the National Preservation Office encourages librarians to take advantage of this scheme, there is little evidence that many do so.

The National Preservation Office's previous experience on preservation issues was helpful in planning its awareness drive for security. Videos have always been a useful tool both for publicity and training. The possibility of producing a video gained weight when the British Library gave the Office a sum of money for training purposes. The video was produced in Liverpool, where a variety of libraries (public, university and polytechnic) exist within a small area. Library staff were prepared to help and allow the Office to use their rights and wrongs as an example to others. First and foremost the video is intended as the first stage in a training session for a librarian and his staff. It raises the main issues, suggests some correctives and shocks (hopefully) with statistics.

The cooperation of 3M Security Systems allowed the Office to issue with the video a set of four posters which highlight four library 'baddies' and exhort the public to report and not condone such users. The package – a video for librarians' use and a set of posters for display in libraries – worked well. The posters had an additional purpose in reinforcing the video's messages to the librarian.

A series of three security seminars was organised in association with SCONUL in late 1989 and early 1990. SCONUL members had for some time shown concern over various aspects of security and the three days had as their themes security and buildings, security of collections and security of staff. The response to these was good and the papers were published in 1991 (Quinsee and McDonald). A national conference on the subject of library security became the obvious next step. This took place in March 1991 at York University and drew together speakers and delegates from both the library and archive worlds.

The work of the Office will be much aided by publication of the first major survey of theft and losses from UK libraries (*Theft from UK libraries*, 1992). Funded by the Home Office Crime Prevention Unit, the six month research gathered theft and loss information from 1000 libraries and summarised good security practice.

REFERENCES

Keele, H. C. (1987), *Preventing library book theft*. Access Keelaway.

Quinsee, A. G. & McDonald, A. C. (1991), *Security in academic and research libraries*, proceedings on three seminars organised by SCONUL and the British Library, held at the British Library 1989/1990. Newcastle upon Tyne: University Library.

Ratcliffe, F. W. (1983), *Preservation policies and conservation in British Libraries: report of the Cambridge University Library Conservation Project*. British Library and Information Research Report No. 25.

Theft from UK libraries: surveying losses and preventive actions (1992). Home Office Crime Prevention Paper.

APPENDIX: NPO SECURITY GUIDELINES

Introduction

Ensuring the security of any library or archive collection is a problem. Collections are at risk from theft, vandalism and negligence, as well as from disasters such as fire and flood. The issue of security affects the entire library community, from the largest institution to the smallest public library.

First – know your problem

What sort of security risks are you running? Carry out a thorough survey of your existing arrangements. Look at the layout of your building. Where do you keep the most valuable items? What areas are open to the public? How obvious are your detection systems if you have them? Once problem areas have been identified, look at possible solutions:

Your building

- Ensure that there are adequate locks on all doors and windows.
- Door frames should be metal or if made of wood have reinforced hinges.
- Hinges should be on the INSIDE of doors or covered and strengthened.
- Take extra care with areas which present easy access, for example skylights or gratings.
- External alarm systems and lighting are both good deterrents.
- Make sure that the outside of your building is visible and not obscured by foliage and fences.
- Try not to keep any cash in the building and display notices stating that cash boxes are emptied each evening. Secure any valuable equipment, mark it and keep serial numbers in a safe place.
- Avoid 'hidden areas' in the building. Stacks should be arranged for maximum visibility and staff-only areas must be secure.

Your collection

You cannot secure a collection if you do not know what you have and where it is! Keep adequate, up to date shelf lists and, where possible, items should be catalogued. (This is also essential should a disaster occur). Make regular stock checks so you know quickly if material disappears.

- Consider an ownership stamp or other ways to mark the items in your care.
- A record of all stamps should be kept. Similarly, a cancelling stamp should be used if an item is to be discarded.
- Store valuable items in secure areas. Make sure the procedures for issuing such items are clear and safe.
- Books (especially rare books, manuscripts, unbound papers and prints) should be checked before being issued and on their return.

- Adequate proof of identity and address should be required before a pass is issued, renewed or replaced.
- Whenever possible, prohibit bags from reading rooms. Provide cloakroom facilities wherever possible. If no facilities are available, check bags as readers leave.
- Electronic tagging of items is effective in reducing theft and may be appropriate for your collections.
- When loaning items for exhibition purposes, make sure the borrower has adequate security arrangements.
- Exhibition cases must be secure, with strong locks and where the item is very valuable the case should be alarmed. Insurance cover, transportation and security arrangements in closed hours should all be examined. Conditions under which the case can be opened and by whom must be clarified.

Staff

The ultimate security of your collection rests with the staff in charge of it. Staff must be properly trained and be encouraged in their awareness of security issues.

- If reader passes are required, check them carefully.
- Challenge unknown persons found in closed areas. In a large institution it is an advantage if staff wear some kind of identification card or badge .
- Remember that staff are vulnerable to abuse and attack. Measures must be taken to minimise the likelihood of such incidents e.g. staff should not be left alone in the library at night.

Managers at all levels must discuss the problem with their staff. They must also be aware that those members of staff who become victims of violent or abusive attacks need skilled counselling and help.

The Library Association is particularly concerned with the safety of library staff and has produced a leaflet entitled *Violence in Libraries*. This leaflet and further help and advice can be obtained from The Library Association, 7 Ridgmount Street, London WC1E 7AE.

REMEMBER – YOUR LOCAL CRIME PREVENTION OFFICER IS ABLE AND WILLING TO HELP YOU SECURE YOUR LIBRARY.

Every institution is different and has its own specific problems. This leaflet cannot provide all the answers. However, the National Preservation Office exists to give advice and information on all aspects of library preservation and security. It acts as a forum for debate and attempts to keep preservation and security issues in the public consciousness.

Please ring or write to

The National Preservation Office
The British Library
Great Russell Street
London WC1B 3DG
Telephone: 071-323 7612

Worth thinking about?

Mount a display of mutilated books. As well as focusing on the damage done, make it clear how expensive it is to repair or replace.

Declare an amnesty on overdue or stolen books.

Good photocopying facilities can reduce the risk of pages being torn out. More than one copy of an item in demand may deter the user who steals from frustration .

Vandalism encourages further vandalism. Try to repair damage quickly.

Call theft theft. Call thieves thieves.

The National Preservation Office exists to promote awareness, provide information and encourage debate on all aspects of library security and preservation.

The Office provides

An information and advisory service on what to read, names of conservators, manufacturers and suppliers and details of products and services.

A range of promotional material, some free, some charged for.

Training courses and seminars on preservation and security issues.

A focus for debate, advice and information.

Suppliers of security equipment

Automated Library Services Ltd
Vector House
Brownfields
Welwyn Garden City
Herts AL7 1 AN
0707 336251

DDD (Security Systems) Ltd
Mile Lane
Coventry CV1 2NL
0203 525525

Knogo (UK) Ltd
Harleyford
Marlow
Bucks SL7 2DY
06284 6414

Plescon Ltd
Hall Farm
Chattisham
Ipswich
Suffolk IP7 5EJ
0473 87633

Senelco Ltd
Dormey House
Upton Road
Slough
Berks
0753 37722

3M United Kingdom P.L.C.
3M House
PO Box 1
Bracknell
Berkshire
RG12 1JU

Some further reading

Security for Libraries: People, Buildings, Collections.
Marvine Brand (editor).
American Library Association 1984

Protecting Your Collection. A handbook, survey and guide for the security of rare books, manuscripts, archives and works of art.
Slade Richard Gandert.
(Library & Archival Security 4 (1/2) 1982)

Museum, Archive and Library Security.
Lawrence J Fennelly.
Butterworths, 1983

Library Vandalism and Textual Mutilation.
Susan Lacey.
Birmingham Library School Cooperative
Occasional Publications 1976

Crime in the Library: a study of patterns, impact and security.
AJ & CZ Lincoln.
RR Bowker Company 1984

Library Crime and Security: an international perspective.
AJ & CZ Lincoln.
(Library & Archival Security 8 (1/2) Spring/Summer 1986)

Planning Academic and Research Library Buildings.
KD Metcalf.
2nd edition. P Leighton & D Weber (eds)
American Library Association 1986

The Protection of the Library and Archive: An International Bibliography.
Martin H Sable
(Library & Archival Security 5 (2/3) Summer/Fall 1983)

Study on Control of Security and Storage of Holdings: A RAMP study with guidelines.
DL Thomas.
UNESCO, Paris 1987

Collection Security.
SPEC Kit 100
Association of Research Libraries 1984

Security Bibliography
National Preservation Office 1989

Violence in Libraries: preventing aggressive and unacceptable behaviour in libraries.
Library Association 1987

Burglary, Protection and Insurance Surveys
by D E Bugg ACII and C Bridges FCII

Handbook of Security
Kluwer Publishing Ltd

Basic Museum Security
Museums Security Survey
International Council of Museums Security Council 1977

13

The community approach to crime and security

JOHN HINKS

This book is concerned with a wide range of behaviour and security problems in libraries. The choice of measures aimed at the alleviation of these problems must be similarly wide-ranging. There is no single course of action which will meet effectively the different challenges of, for instance, damage to the exterior of the building when the library is closed and behaviour problems inside the library during its opening hours. However, although a total solution is not to be found in specific measures, a particular approach, which has been tried and tested, is a powerful starting point for an effective response to the problems. Such an approach – the community approach – is suggested in this chapter.

Two points need to be stressed before proceeding. Firstly, the community approach is a way of dealing with wide-ranging problems in libraries. Although certain measures are described here, they are to be regarded as examples of the community approach in action, rather than as a package of instant wisdom to be applied to local problems. Secondly, while the measures described have been tested mainly in the context of a public library service, the community approach is recommended for consideration in other types of library, subject to the general proviso (which applies equally to public libraries) that solutions must be geared to local problems. There is no universal cure for behaviour and security problems in libraries.

So what is meant by the community approach? First and foremost, this is a positive and creative approach. It is positive, in offering a framework for both the prevention and reduction of crime in libraries, and creative in attempting to tackle behaviour problems at community level, rather than simply excluding problems from the library, content that the trouble has moved elsewhere.

The community approach is therefore ideally also a shared approach. Responsibility for the problem and the solution are, in a sense, shared by the provider of the service, its users and the community as a whole. The service provider who is unwilling to accept a share in the responsibility should consider some of the points made elsewhere in this book, such as the need to design safety and security into library buildings and the need to ensure that staffing structures and training programmes take account of crime and security factors. Managers of libraries and information services should not place all the blame for their problems on their customers or on a 'sick society'. One major difference, incidentally, between public and other types of library is that, by and large, in the non-public library it is outsiders who threaten its safety and security, whereas many of the public library's problems result from inappropriate behaviour by a minority of its customers, who have a legitimate right to enter the library and to use its services.

THE COMMUNITY PARTNERSHIP

Whoever is to blame for the worrying range of problems now faced by the providers of most kinds of library and information service, the community approach to tackling those problems is one of partnership. The manager of the service is the most obvious, and should be the most active, member of the partnership. The manager for this purpose is defined as the person nearest to the customer interface who has overall responsibility for service delivery in a particular location. In public libraries, this will probably be an area librarian or a branch or group supervisor.

There is nothing new in the manager being held responsible for tackling problems in the local library. What is innovative about the community approach is that the response to local problems is shared with a number of other participants. What is shared is not just responsibility for crime prevention and remedial action, but also the thinking, the caring and the stress, which should never be borne by the library manager alone.

The nature of the partnership will vary according to the type of library (public, academic etc.), the management structure of both the library and its parent body, the make-up of the community, and not least the scale and nature of local behaviour or security problems. Other partners typically include senior library management, representatives of trade unions and of non-union employees, personnel and training advisers from within the parent body and, most importantly in the community approach, some or all of: the police, teachers, youth leaders, other social and community workers as well as representatives, elected or other, of the library's user community.

The potential contribution of the various participants in the partnership will depend on a number of factors. The policy, and sometimes the politics, of the organisations involved may impact upon their commitment to helping the library cope with its problems. The attitudes and approaches of the individuals involved, whether or not as representatives of organisations, may vary. Organisational representatives, especially in some communities, may move on quite frequently, resulting in a somewhat disruptive lack of continuity. However, despite all these factors, it is suggested that the community approach nevertheless offers the library manager the most effective means of tackling behaviour problems.

Those involved in the partnership may have particular strengths to offer. One may be a highly skilled trainer, another may have detailed knowledge of the make-up of the local community, another may have particular understanding of relevant minority cultures and appropriate language skills. A teacher or youth group leader may be in a position to impose some kind of sanctions, outside the library context, on habitual troublemakers. A police representative will be able to offer a unique range of remedial action but may perhaps need encouragement not to be over zealous.

Whoever is involved, and whatever roles they assume or are assigned, it is essential that the shared approach to the library's problems is tailored, as closely as possible, to the particular local situation. A generalised response is seldom appropriate. The nature and scale of behaviour problems will inevitably vary widely in two important ways:

a) between different communities (and for this purpose a 'community' can be a very small unit, sometimes just a few streets or blocks)

b) at different times within a single community

The latter point is very important. Problems of this kind can come and go very quickly and it is all too easy, unwittingly or unthinkingly, to pour costly resources into a particular programme of action long after the problem has diminished, moved elsewhere or been eliminated altogether. This is perhaps a particular problem for those libraries which are part of a large and bureaucratic organisation, such as the more traditional type of local authority. Here the formal process of defining the problem, identifying the possible solutions, securing approval for a course of action and obtaining the necessary resources, may be inordinately slow. There could be a real risk of the problem having changed significantly in the meantime. At best this may result in a waste of resources as a solution is implemented for a problem which has gone away; at worst it could place library staff and customers at risk in a situation which has escalated from being a nuisance to being potentially or actually violent. In any case, having secured the resources and perhaps having employed people specifically for this purpose, it may prove very difficult in some bureaucratic organisations actually to stop the remedial action once it has been successful, or to implement a different strategy in response to a changed situation.

The community approach stands a better chance of success where the library's parent organisation has a creative style, capable of delivering action quickly and positively in response to an urgent need. In a more forward-looking local authority, for example, sufficient power may already be delegated to the director of the library service to enable resources to be diverted into an appropriate action programme without the delay of reference to elected members.

It is of course the responsibility of the local library manager to monitor and assess the changing nature of behaviour or security problems, keeping senior management informed and exercising judgement in deciding when to seek help. On the other hand, senior library management have a duty to create and maintain a caring organisational structure and climate, in which no local manager or front line staff member feels isolated or remote from support or advice.

Any course of action initiated within the library will have to comply with the policy of the parent body, be it a local authority, academic institution or other organisation. Many local authorities, for instance, are striving to align their policies and practices with a more open and user friendly public image. The introduction of the Public Service Orientation (Clark and Stewart, 1985) based on the process of 'getting closer to the public' (*Getting closer...*, 1987), will have the effect of creating a policy framework particularly hospitable to the community approach advocated here. A number of local authorities are also active in promoting an awareness in the community of crime and its prevention; the community approach fits well into such a climate. However, where the ethos of the parent body is of a more traditional nature, it may prove more difficult to sell the community approach to dealing with behaviour problems

It will seldom be the case that the library service is the only part of the organisation troubled by behaviour and security problems. There is a strong case for a corporate strategy, involving all relevant departments of the parent body in a shared approach to solving these problems. Where there is a corporate response, it is important to ensure that remedial action remains relevant to the library's specific problem, albeit within a broad common policy. It is all too easy for a corporate strategy to become so bland as to be ineffective. On the other hand, library managers should be willing to learn from relevant experience in other parts of the parent organisation and to take advantage of suitable skills available in-house. Many local authorities, for example, have a wealth of talent on hand in such departments as education and social services, which can be a positive source of support for library staff training and other activities.

The community approach is, by definition, a positive one. Its aim is to offer a creative solution to existing problems in libraries and to minimise as far as possible the risk of future problems. The shared nature of the community approach encourages a responsible attitude, which aims to eliminate the problem from the community, not to transfer trouble out of the library into another location. If it is to achieve its aim, the community approach needs to be carefully planned and structured, but it probably works best if it is not excessively formal. A regular discussion forum is desirable but formal meetings, with agendas, reports and minutes, are probably not the best way of implementing the community approach. However, much depends on the nature of the community and the extent to which it already works together in other ways. The decision on which road the community partnership is to take depends not only on where it hopes to go but also on where it is coming from. Some of the participants in the partnership may already be known to one another. Existing relationships, assumptions and prejudices will affect the way in which the partnership works, as will previous experiences of working together in other contexts.

PLANNING REMEDIAL ACTION

Once a community partnership has been formed, and an informal structure agreed for the way in which it is to operate, attention must turn to planning a course of action. As was explained at the outset, the community approach is precisely what its name implies: an approach rather than a set of specific measures. The community approach offers a platform upon which specific remedial action can be established in a shared attempt to rid the library, and the community as a whole, of crime. Each local partnership will need to decide on a course of action which is judged appropriate to the particular community and its problems. The positive nature of the community approach is likely to result in the adoption of a package of imaginative measures. A few possibilities are described below but it must be remembered that they are only examples. None of what follows is intended to be prescriptive. Local problems require local solutions. However, the measures described, although not intended as a model, have all been tried, tested and found helpful.

The problem of criminal damage (vandalism) to library buildings, stock and equipment is discussed elsewhere in this book. The community approach offers a positive framework for measures aimed at both the prevention and reduction of such problems, based on shared concern and support within the community. It is, however, in the area of behaviour problems, occurring during library opening hours, that the community approach is particularly appropriate. Sadly, few library managers and front line staff members are unfamiliar with the difficulties caused by a minority of library users, usually at the younger end of the age range, who indulge in inappropriate behaviour. In many libraries, the problem is sporadic and relatively easily handled, but elsewhere behaviour problems can result in a seemingly endless battle of wits between library staff and troublemakers. Where there are such persistent problems, staff are likely to suffer from the effects of stress. Groups of young people indulging in horseplay, even when they mean no harm, can be very intimidating to staff and to other library users.

The primary aim of remedial action is to find ways of helping library staff to cope more effectively with this kind of situation. Concomitant problems, such as adverse publicity or a decline in library use, are important and must be addressed, but the priority is to provide quick and effective support for front line staff. Imaginative support measures will enable staff to react appropriately to behaviour problems, minimising both personal stress and risk to their own and their customers' safety.

Practical measures may be simple ones, like installing a panic alarm system or an additional telephone extension, or may be more complex, such as a complete re-arrangement of the interior of the library or an improvement in lighting levels. Such improvements need not be prohibitively expensive and will often have an immediate impact on behaviour problems. Staff will certainly feel safer and more comfortable if such measures are taken as appropriate. Basic action of this sort is an important component of an overall strategy but it is not enough on its own.

The community approach was introduced above as a package approach. It is very unlikely that any one measure would be effective in combating behaviour and security problems in libraries. The potential success of the community approach rests, perhaps equally, on both its positive nature and its composite structure. Ideally, the package of remedial action will be planned and implemented as a total programme. In many libraries, however, there will be a history of both behaviour problems and remedial measures. The library manager would be unwise to ignore what has gone before.

The first step in designing a new programme of remedial action should be an audit of past and present measures which have been introduced in response to security and behaviour problems. Typically, these may be found to include some of the practical measures mentioned above, together with a particular pattern of curtailed opening hours, various procedures and instructions (for example on methods of summoning assistance), as well as various staffing measures, such as an increase in staffing levels or the employment of a part-time security attendant. A thorough audit of existing measures will involve an assessment of their effectiveness and their cost. Wherever possible, account should also be taken of measures which have been attempted in the recent past and abandoned, for whatever reason. When the picture of past and present action is complete, a new set of measures, which may well incorporate some elements of existing practice, can be planned. Where the community approach has been adopted, this planning stage is one in which the partnership has a key role. Members of the partnership may be able to share valuable experience, gained in contexts other than the library, but perhaps still within the local community, of successful and unsuccessful measures.

It may sometimes be necessary to implement action very urgently, where a new or escalating behaviour problem suddenly gives cause for concern. In such a situation, it may be felt that the planning process outlined above is too cumbersome. However, if the costing element is deferred, an audit can be conducted very quickly indeed; it need not result in a lengthy written report. The best course of action in response to a particularly pressing problem may often be the implementation of some temporary measure, such as a short-term increase in staffing levels or the redeployment of a security officer from elsewhere in the organisation. If this is clearly understood as a temporary response, it has several advantages. It re-assures staff that speedy action is being taken and it allows for an audit to be conducted along the lines suggested. Perhaps most importantly, it makes time available for consultation with library staff, union representatives and the community partnership.

At the planning stage, it is essential to identify precisely the nature of the problem, including any potentially sensitive aspects, such as racial abuse or sexual harassment. Where behaviour problems have a clearly identifiable racial dimension, this must be recognised and dealt with carefully. It is equally important not to make the mistake of perceiving a racial dimension where none exists. The library's parent body, particularly if it is a local authority, may be able to offer guidance on sensitive issues; there may also be official policy documents or guidance relating to racial and sexual abuse or violence in the workplace (*Violence...*, 1988, 1989). Where a community partnership exists, it should be relatively easy for any ethnic or cultural dimension to be dealt with openly and positively.

The community approach has already been identified as being essentially creative and positive. This rather takes for granted that the ethos of the library service is positive and customer oriented. A library manager who is content to offer a service which is less than user friendly would probably be unlikely to consider the community approach to behaviour and security problems. The approach aligns well with forward-looking service delivery policies and with an imaginative approach to marketing the library and its services. The customer care approach is gaining increasing acceptance in libraries of all types (Hinks, 1990), and users may already be accustomed to regarding the library as a friendly place, with helpful staff and a relaxed atmosphere. This informality is to be welcomed but it should be noted that the noise level in this kind of library may be rather higher than in a more traditional one; this may occasionally make it more difficult for staff to spot minor behaviour problems.

STAFF TRAINING

Staff need to be constantly vigilant and aware of potential problems but on the other hand they need to establish, probably tacitly, a tolerance threshold beyond which a minor distraction or nuisance becomes a real behaviour problem. Staff should have ample opportunity, probably during training sessions, of discussing what kind of behaviour is and is not acceptable. Problems in libraries can sometimes be exacerbated by a widely varying level of tolerance between different staff members. A number of factors may affect an individual's response to behaviour problems, including previous experience, health and personality traits. The library manager needs to be aware of any members of staff who might tend to over-react to behaviour problems, as well as any who might tend to be excessively tolerant. Training and discussion, in an open and friendly climate, should normally even out any major differences in the tolerance levels of staff members.

Training, of one kind or another, is a key part of the community approach. Where a partnership exists, training skills (and perhaps costs) can be shared. Library staff can benefit greatly from mixed group training, in which they learn that other community workers experience similar problems. Members of the partnership who have particular skills in dealing with young people, such as teachers or youth leaders, can make a valuable contribution to the library's training programme and should be encouraged to share their expertise. They will often be particularly skilled in two important areas:

a) knowing the appropriate behaviour and language to use in defusing a potentially difficult situation
b) creating positive relationships with young people which will reduce the risk of behaviour problems occurring in the first place

Their input to the training process can make a very real contribution to boosting the confidence and morale of library staff.

The staff training programme needs to be geared specifically to local behaviour problems, although it should be set in a broader context. A customer care training framework is especially suitable and enables the problem of dealing with difficult customers to be placed in a positive context. Opinions vary on the extent to which attitudes can be changed by training. It is very doubtful whether underlying prejudices can be eradicated through training, although it should be possible, by giving staff a structured opportunity for reflection and discussion, to modify certain attitudes. What is achievable through training is a change in behaviour. Many customer care training programmes encourage professional behaviour at the public interface and are less concerned with trying to change underlying attitudes.

Training programmes aimed at enabling library staff to cope more confidently with behaviour problems should not be excessively formal or highly structured. Experience in many libraries has proved the potential of informal, relatively low key training in small groups. Whatever its structure, this type of training must allow ample time for staff concerns and fears to be expressed openly and dealt with honestly. A trainer who is thoroughly aware of the local problem, and is prepared for a really open dialogue with front line staff, will make a valuable contribution to equipping staff to deal with difficult situations. A standardised off-the-peg training programme stands little chance of acceptance or success. Inappropriate training can actually make things worse.

A key role for the trainer is to act as a catalyst, who encourages staff to analyse the local situation and suggests possible solutions. A simple, but very effective, exercise involves giving a group of staff a set of cards with a note of particular aspects of the problem. They discuss each card very briefly and then assign it to one of three categories:

a) those I could do something about
b) those which the local library management could deal with
c) those that need a policy decision at senior management level

Group members are usually very surprised at the size of the first category and sometimes the second. Exercises like this can help staff to realize how much power they themselves have to modify a seemingly intractable situation. Senior management should, of course, also be prepared to look at the (probably small) third pile of cards and to consider taking appropriate action. Senior and middle management should play an active part in the training of front line staff, if only to show that they are concerned and prepared to take action.

Where behaviour and security problems continue over a period of time, some thought will have to be given to top-up training, probably moving from general to more specific areas of concern. Whatever training is carried out, it is essential that it is reinforced by clear written instructions. Procedures should be brief and clear, with a view to their being memorised. Should a difficult situation break out, staff should not have to start fumbling through a large file full of instructions! No member of the library staff should be in any doubt as to what to do if a problem occurs, including when and how to summon police assistance. (Local police advice should be sought on which method to use.) All staff need total familiarity with the library building: the location of alarms, exit doors, keys and telephones.

Where violent situations are a real possibility, staff should know how to retreat, as a last resort, to a secure part of the building from where they can telephone for help. Knowledge of this kind is as important as being aware of fire and first aid procedures; it is a priority need for new and temporary staff members. Where there is a serious risk of violence towards staff, they should be offered appropriate training, using specialist advice and assistance. The police will advise on whether training in self defence is appropriate; they may advise against it.

MANAGEMENT SUPPORT

Other measures to complement staff training include systematic management support. Front line staff will usually be reassured by the knowledge that they can contact a senior colleague, should the need arise, outside normal office hours. Options include a list of senior staff home telephone numbers or a duty manager rota. The duty manager in a multi-site library operation should be accessible by mobile telephone or pager. Libraries at risk of serious trouble should be equipped with a panic alarm; experience shows that although it may seldom be used, it will help staff to feel less isolated. The value of peer group support, as a complement to management support, should not be under-estimated. Opportunities should be created for library staff to share problems and ideas with each other and, where a partnership exists, with colleagues in other community services.

The authority to close the library in the event of serious trouble, should always be delegated to a staff member on duty at the individual library. It is unfair to expect staff under threat of violence to have to telephone elsewhere for permission to close. The relevant staff must obviously be well briefed, so that closing is regarded as an absolute last resort, which may be subject to subsequent investigation by senior management. There should be clear instructions to local staff about record keeping and reporting procedures. Library managers will need regular information to assist them in monitoring behaviour and security problems. Where there is a partnership, its members should give some time to monitoring the situation across the community. Management information is often the key to effective remedial action.

Library management should accept responsibility not only for the wellbeing of staff while they are on duty but also for getting them home safely. If staff are worried about leaving the library late in the evening, a lift should be arranged. Where there is a community partnership, some cooperative action on transport may be feasible. If a taxi is the only solution, the library should consider bearing the cost of the fare. Staff who walk home should, if they wish, be issued with personal attack alarms; police advice should be taken on which type to use.

Staffing levels

The purpose of most of the measures already mentioned is to enable staff to deal with problems themselves, with the help of appropriate support systems. In smaller libraries, staff numbers on duty at particular times may need to be increased beyond the level required for straightforward service delivery. As a general rule, no member of staff should have to work alone in a library which is vulnerable to behaviour problems. Apart from the obvious risk to their personal safety, one person alone will find it impossible to deal effectively with a behaviour problem. Where two staff members are on duty, one can call the police from a back room while the other tries to cope with the situation. Library users will sometimes offer assistance when a problem arises but this should not be relied upon.

Staffing levels must be sufficient to allow staff to feel as safe and confident as possible and should enable them to respond to any problems which arise. Where the cost of increased staffing cannot be found, one solution is to restrict opening hours. Providing service on, say, two evenings per week instead of four, should enable staffing to be doubled. Where this solution is adopted, the effect on public relations may be more positive than might be expected. Library users, especially those who have witnessed the staff dealing with difficult situations, can be quite supportive of such measures, even though service availability is reduced. Even where staffing levels are adequate, evening hours of opening should be kept under review. The demand for public libraries to remain open late into the evening seems, in many areas, to have reduced in recent years. The impact on customers of closing thirty minutes or an hour earlier, even in an academic or other non-public library, may be acceptable, especially if the reason for the change is made known. In some locations, earlier closing can effect a marked reduction in the level of security and behaviour problems in the library.

Security staff

It is essential that the basic level of front line staffing is maintained at an appropriate level if a serious attempt is being made to reduce behaviour problems. In addition, it is often considered that the employment of certain special categories of staff is necessary. The decision on the number and type of staff necessary in a particular library is one which can be made only in the light of local circumstances. In certain types of library, it may be felt that the employment of one or more security attendants is appropriate. Past experience is a valuable guide in this as in other considerations. If an audit has been carried out, as suggested above, of the effectiveness of present and recent past action, the value of employing security staff may be clearer. The presence of uniformed attendants may be found helpful in a large library, such as a university main library or a central public library. The patrolling or policing function may be necessary in the large library, but may be considered less appropriate in the less formal setting of a smaller library.

Where the decision is taken to employ security staff, their role should be absolutely clear, both to them and to other library staff. It is preferable for security staff to be under the control of the library manager, so that they are seen as a key part of the library's team, sharing in training and briefing sessions as necessary. If security services are provided by a private firm, the contractor must be well briefed on the library's needs. The kind of security measures which are often hired in other situations may not be appropriate for a library. The same caveat applies where the library's parent organisation provides the security staff. Whoever provides the uniformed presence, the library manager must be quite clear on

243

what their role is to be. The traditional job of a security attendant is to patrol the library, admonishing anyone found behaving unacceptably. Where the problem persists, an attendant is usually authorised to remove the offender from the library.

This may well be the approach that the library manager wishes to implement; if so, the uniformed presence is probably as good an option as any. One word of caution, however: expert advice should be taken on what powers security staff have within the law. It is very easy for an over-zealous security officer to overstep the mark; it is only fair to them to explain exactly what the law allows. Because of the legal limits to the powers of security staff, some police forces will advise against their employment; advice should be sought locally. The senior management of the library, and/or its governing body, may decide that the uniformed attendant (or the non-uniformed bouncer) is incompatible with the welcoming, positive image that should be the aim of the library service.

Employment of youth workers

How is the library manager to achieve this more positive image for the library? Up to a point, suitably designed training for library staff will achieve this end, given that the right kind of staff have been recruited in the first place. Another way, which has been used with great success by at least one public library service (and is being considered by several other local authorities) is the employment of youth workers, to work alongside the library staff at times when behaviour problems are likely to occur.

The youth worker option was the one eventually chosen by Leicestershire Libraries, after long experience of only limited success with other courses of action. Staff training had been carried out, using external expertise, clear instructions had been issued to all staff, and good working relationships were maintained with the police, both at top management and community level. In addition, those libraries considered most at risk benefited from increased staffing levels, the installation of panic alarms, review of opening hours and various other measures. Problems persisted, however, and during the winter of 1982/83 had escalated in a few libraries to an unacceptable level.

Discussions between senior management, front line staff and trade union representatives resulted in a formal request from the union that uniformed attendants be employed. Library management refused this request, disliking its negative approach; the advice of the police supported the management view. Further discussions were held between the trade union, the staff, elected members and library management. Agreement was finally reached on a pilot scheme for the employment of youth workers in two libraries, on a sessional basis in the late afternoon and evening. The trial period was a great success and, when resources permitted, this approach was extended to a number of other libraries. The Leicestershire experience has been recorded elsewhere in more detail (Hinks, 1989).

Where youth workers are employed, it is important that they and other library staff are clear on their role. The aim must be to make use of their specialist skills in dealing with young people in a variety of situations. Their expertise should also be shared with other library staff through training and in less formal ways. They should never be regarded as non-uniformed security officers or as bouncers, although as a last resort they may have to ask someone to leave or, very occasionally, attempt to prevent a known troublemaker from entering the library. In Leicestershire Libraries, the youth worker role is clearly defined. They are there to support other library staff and to establish, as far as possible, a friendly relationship with young people using (or abusing) the library service. They are expected to share their expertise with other staff, thereby encouraging a positive approach to behaviour problems. They have made a major contribution to the reduction of behaviour problems, simply by talking to young library users and organising occasional informal activities. Virtually all of their work is library based, making use of the library's full stock of books, records, board games and magazines.

Youth workers employed in libraries require training specific to the library situation, which builds upon their more general knowledge and experience of dealing with young people elsewhere. Their training should ensure alignment with library policy on, for example, support for GCSE students. Librarians specialising in services for young people should support and assist youth workers in their library-related activities. The library manager must also decide what youth workers are to do when the library is quiet; they are usually prepared to help out with routine library work but this requires the goodwill of other staff and union representatives. The relatively high turnover of part-time youth workers can be rather a nuisance but is a small price to pay for the success which good youth workers can achieve quite quickly. In a local authority the education department may be able to offer advice on the recruitment and training of youth workers. There are standard service conditions and rates of pay for both qualified and unqualified youth workers employed by a local authority.

It is acknowledged that the youth worker approach is not a universal remedy for behaviour problems in libraries, although its success in Leicestershire has been considerable. This approach may be most suitable in a public library but managers of other kinds of library may wish to consider some similar means of harnessing specialist skills which are not possessed by most library staff. It is important to recognize that the employment of youth workers is only one component, although a key one, of a total strategy for dealing with security and behaviour problems in libraries. Many of the other measures described in this book will need to be used alongside specialist staffing. Where the community approach has been adopted, there may be scope for sharing youth workers between libraries and other establishments within the framework of the community partnership. Even where this is not practicable, the positive and creative approach typified by the use of youth workers is well worth trying. A short-term trial period may be facilitated by the use of short-term contracts for youth workers or other specialist part-time staff.

CONCLUSION

As was explained at the outset, there is no single course of action which will eliminate security and behaviour problems in libraries. Specific problems demand specific, tailor-made, solutions. The community approach discussed in this chapter is offered as a positive framework within which the individual library manager may consider solutions to local problems. It is a shared approach, which accepts the premise that the community as a whole has the ability, if it has the will, to make a real contribution to the reduction of crime in libraries.

REFERENCES

Clarke, M. and Stewart, J. (1985), *Local government and the public service orientation: or does a public service provide for the public?* Local Government Training Board.

Getting closer to the public (1987). Local Government Training Board.

Violence to staff: report of the DHSS advisory committee (1988). HMSO.

Violence to staff (1989). Health and Safety Executive. (A practical booklet aimed mainly at employers but also of interest to employees and trade union representatives.)

Hinks, J. (1989), Behaviour problems: the youth worker option. *Assistant Librarian*, vol. 82, no. 2, (February), pp. 29–31.

Hinks, J. (1990), Customer care in libraries: taken as read? *Library Association Record*, vol. 92, no. 2, (February), pp. 109–114.

14

Countering crime: a model training programme for managers

COLIN BADDOCK

Various other chapters in this volume have alluded, in varying degrees, to the need for training. The requirement for it is not doubted and normally it will be built into the strategy arising out of the stated objectives of the organisation. It has already been noted that although violence is not considered as the major crime in libraries, and the chances of encountering it are statistically remote, there is, nonetheless, a very real perception of fear which can, and often does, have an adverse affect on individual motivation and productivity. The particular importance of providing training to deal with violence, aggression and abuse is therefore considered as extremely important. This chapter therefore concentrates on the identification of a model programme and the factors surrounding its formulation; by doing so it is intended to raise the awareness of library managers to this important issue.

The problem with running a training course on violence and aggression in libraries is that, done properly, it involves separate training courses on a host of related topics, all of which justify at least one day to themselves. These topics, which can be divided into communication techniques and knowledge needed, include:

Communication techniques

- customer care including image and ambience of the library, problem customers, etc.
- public relations and marketing

- – non-verbal communication (body language)
- – listening skills
- – memory training
- – mentally disturbed readers
- – dealing with racism

Knowledge

- – law relating to public order, sexual harassment, racism etc.
- – coping with stress
- – self defence
- – first aid
- – detection of alcoholism, drug abuse, glue sniffing, etc.

Ideally, these courses would be logically planned to give the new recruit to our service an introduction designed to make him/her capable of dealing with most situations and the ability to cope with most incidents that are likely to arise. Unfortunately, few library staff will be able to attend more than one or two such courses, and those that can may not receive them in a planned and logical order.

When attending an interview for the post of library assistant at the local library many candidates profess a 'love of books' and a liking for 'meeting people'. Young prospective assistant librarians, fresh out of their Schools of Librarianship and Information Studies, usually say the same thing wrapped up in more sophisticated terms – 'helping the public to achieve their leisure, information and educational needs'.

Though many assistants will be disappointed that a love of books features relatively low in the requirements for a successful member of the library staff, meeting people and the interpersonal skills necessary to achieve a satisfactory outcome to that meeting (however brief) is essential. The new assistant soon realises that readers come in all shapes and sizes. They also come in different moods and with different attitudes and expectations. The majority are extremely pleasant in their demeanour and reasonable in their demands. Others exploit the service to the full and expect us to be able to do the impossible NOW. Occasionally readers enter our library for purposes other than that for which it was intended.

It is unfortunate that the ability to deal with all kinds of aggressive and anti-social behaviour has become one of the necessary skills required by many library staff who have direct contact with the general public. It is also an area where staff feel least skilled and most concerned. The aim of this chapter is to suggest training methods that may help to reduce the effect that such customers may have on other library users and on our own staff.

IS THERE A PROBLEM?

When I have asked this question on violence and aggression training courses I am frequently assured, especially by librarians from small branches, 'No – all our readers are lovely'. During subsequent discussion it frequently emerges that 'Well, yes, we did have an incident three months ago when two teenagers had a knife fight'. It is almost as though admitting that an unsavoury occurrence took place on library premises will result in a black mark against the assistants on duty – perhaps a feeling that the Chief only wants to hear good news about his/ her library.

The other frequent reaction to minor incidents is that it is the society we live in and what can anyone do about it? If an incident is reported it gets lost in the administrative jungle in City Hall so it is all a waste of time!

It is true that, so far, UK journals are not peppered with the headlines that can be seen in some American library journals:

> 'Knife-wielding youth slays public library staff member'
> 'Librarian grapples with killer as seven are slain in library'
> 'Librarian stabbed at desk'
> 'University of Fla. Library Director shot by former employee'

Nevertheless, Chiefs should heed the warning signs. Indications are that minor incidents (e.g. noisy behaviour, swearing, etc.) are becoming commonplace and more serious incidents (e.g. knife fights) may happen occasionally. At the very least many staff have a very real fear of a problem occurring in their library and that they will be unable to cope. A frightened assistant, no matter how able, is unlikely to give of his/her best until the cause has been removed.

So the first step towards establishing whether a problem exists is to communicate with the staff. If you have a supportive work climate your management team are probably aware of any problems. They will encourage incidents to be reported. They will ensure that staff are not made to feel inadequate if the incident that occurred in their library was not handled too well. They will be sensitive to the feelings of staff who feel vulnerable in their workplace.

However, this approach is unlikely to be successful if the management style is austere and autocratic. If all other management decisions are taken without consultation, staff will have no reason to believe that the approach to the problem of violence and aggression will be any different. The change from an austere work climate to a supportive one takes time and cannot be isolated to target specific problem areas at the will of management. The real problem here is that there are very few Chiefs who think of their style as austere and autocratic. If the Chief has not heard of problem customers in his/her libraries (apart from those arising from letters, telephone calls etc. where they cannot be hidden) then he/ she may fall into this category. A start may be to set up a survey, perhaps allowing respondents to remain anonymous, to find out what is really happening out there and what the staff feel about it.

QUESTIONNAIRE

The questionnaire could be issued to staff working in the field. It is suggested that it be along the lines indicated below. The example given may be suitable for a small branch library but could be adapted for the larger library. Part 1 should be completed by the branch manager, Part 2 by all staff.

The branch library and its location

  a) what time does the library close in the evening?
  b) how far is the library from the nearest police station?
  c) what track record do the police have in responding to urgent calls from the library? Fast? Medium? Slow?
  d) is it situated close to community facilities that attract youngsters (e.g. swimming pool, youth club, etc.)?
  e) is it situated near to an organisation helping the socially ostracised (e.g. alcoholics, mentally disturbed, etc.)?
  f) is it isolated from other buildings?
  g) can individuals or groups approach the library without being seen? If 'yes', have you any recommendations for improving this situation (e.g. cutting down or removing shrubs, taking posters off windows)?

h) are the exit facilities satisfactory (e.g. when you leave the library on winter evenings are you in darkness)?

i) are car parking facilities safe for staff leaving the library on winter evenings? How could this be improved?

The staff

a) does the library have periods when only one member of staff is on duty?

b) is there a clear management policy on minimum levels of staff in your library?

c) do you have problems with misbehaviour from:
i) individuals
   adults; teenagers; children
ii) groups
   adults; teenagers; children
please specify the problem(s)

d) what facilities do you have for fast communication for assistance if necessary (e.g. a sufficient number of telephone extensions)? How could this be improved?

You may find it convenient to develop a matrix to help pin-point the major problems, an example of such being given in Figure 14.1.

The form should also give staff the opportunity to express their feelings, such as:

'I've been lucky so far, but how long can it go on?'
'I was shaken and trembling for half an hour afterwards.'
'The police didn't come as quickly as I thought they would.'

When the form is analysed for training purposes such obvious expressions of anxiety, stress and fear should be taken into account.

Every encouragement should be given to staff to complete these forms. Of course, duplication of incidents will occur, but only by giving *all* staff the chance to participate in the exercise and to express their concerns will you be able to gauge the extent of the problem. Management will have to judge whether common, but less serious, problems (e.g. noisy chatter) should be given preference over serious, but relatively infrequent problems (e.g. sexual harassment of female staff).

	Children 5–14 years	Teenagers 14–18 years	Young adults 19–25 years	Adults 26–64 years	Elderly 65+ years
Noisy chatter, shouting					
Swearing					
Dumb insolence					
Drinking/eating					
Smoking					
Spitting					
Threatening/abusing staff					
Racial abuse					
Sexual harassment/ offensive suggestions					
Glue sniffing					
Drunkenness					
Scuffling/fighting					
Graffitti					
Damage to stock, furniture, buildings					
Obscene telephone calls					
Others – please quote					

Figure 14.1: matrix showing areas of concern to librarians

DESIGNING A TRAINING PROGRAMME

Having analysed your forms you will be in a position to decide whether you need to proceed any further. Assuming that the indications are that you do have a problem you will be able to identify the objectives of the course based upon the most pressing areas of concern. The difficulty may be twofold:

- all staff who deal with the public need the training course; ideally, a two day course is desirable, but for a hard-pressed service, struggling to maintain its high standards, a one day course for everyone may be all that can realistically be afforded
- no clear pattern emerges from the survey, so a general one day course is indicated

If it is decided to run a general course on violence and aggression I believe the following elements should be included:

a) course members should be able to express their problems and anxieties to each other
b) identification of anti-social behaviour
c) the incident – before, during and after – are we guiltless?
d) authority: a look at relevant Acts, library bye-laws, regulations and procedure instructions
e) an opportunity for staff to consider their own working environment, think about their personal safety, and how it can be improved
f) problem customers at the counter or enquiry desk (angry and rude readers, mentally disturbed readers, etc.)
g) coping with eccentrics
h) practical exercises on basic self-defence techniques
i) a talk by the local Crime Prevention Officer

The inclusion of all these elements would make a very crowded day and the course organiser should be aware that the nature of this course will lead to a lot of discussion.

The training programme that emerges could have the following objectives:

- to outline techniques that will enable staff to diffuse potentially dangerous situations

- to make staff aware of the Acts, bye-laws, regulations and procedure instructions relating to abuse of the library and its personnel
- to consider ways in which we might make our working environment safer
- to develop techniques for dealing with angry, rude or mentally disturbed readers at the counter or enquiry desk
- to introduce elementary techniques of defending oneself against possible attack

A sample timetable for the programme is presented below but this of course will be tailored to any specific local requirements:

0930	introduction: delelgates identify examples of anti-social behaviour and difficult situations from their own experiences
1000	defusing an incident
1045	coffee
1100	Acts, bye-laws, regulations
1130	staff safety: staff devise a checklist of points that could improve their own safety at work
1245	lunch
1345	problem customers at the counter/enquiry desk: skills of handling angry, rude or mentally disturbed readers
1415	eccentrics (case studies): dealing with the less normal members of society
1500	tea
1515	personal safety: elementary techniques of self defence
1630	close

Police involvement

The police may or may not be able to provide a speaker or they may or may not attend at your preferred time. Ideally they should attend from the beginning, hear the problems identified by the course members and be available for comment, before launching into their own talk.

CONTENTS OF THE PROGRAMME

In this section each of the timetabled elements is discussed in detail. I do not suggest anyone attempts to cover all the topics mentioned in a one day course, but your survey will indicate areas for special targeting.

Course members identification of difficult situations

From this, the following is likely to emerge:

- aggressive gangs of youths
- drunks
- teenagers on motorbikes
- tramps
- dumb insolence from schoolchildren
- incidents upon leaving the library

Many of these will have emerged from the survey and you may have designed your course to take care of them, but the occasional one might throw you. If you were not prepared for 'My library is located near an open prison from which there has been a recent spate of escapes; I am very worried about this', you might be very grateful to have a policeman beside you to give the necessary reassurance. (An answer could be that known violent criminals are unlikely to be placed in open prisons, and escaped prisoners will normally put as much distance between themselves and the prison in the shortest time, so they are unlikely to hang around surrounding towns and villages.)

Defusing an incident: the six As

The first step that the librarian needs to take is to ensure that their own situation has been examined and is relatively blameless. True, an unattractive library and a poor staff attitude is no excuse for violence and aggression on the part of our customers, but an effective customer care training programme will enable staff to diffuse potentially explosive situations. We should consider what effect the six 'As' may have on our more hot-headed readers. The six As are:

ambience
attitude
appearance
approach
assertiveness
anxiety

It will be seen that the first three are concerned with the pre-incident stage while approach, assertiveness and anxiety are concerned with the incident itself.

Ambience and environs of the library

What does our library convey to the reader entering the building for the first time? What about the approaches to the library – does the new reader have to kick his way through Coca-Cola cans and read graffiti scrawled on the walls? Does the library itself give a warm friendly, welcoming image? Or is it run down, with bits of 'Blu-tack adhering to the notice board? Has the shelf guiding been picked off or reassembled by our less enthusiastic customers?

If we give the impression that we don't care about our library, how can we expect anyone else to?

Attitude

Having considered the ambience of our library we must next consider the attitude of our readers and of ourselves. It takes two to make a problem reader – the reader and the librarian: problems devolve around our perception of them and their perception of us. We, though, have no control over the attitude in which the reader enters our library. We can only control our own attitudes.

Our attitude is affected by our:

a) moods: the disposition of our readers and ourselves – 'which side of the bed we got out of'

b) personal problems: all readers are entitled to our best attention all of the time; it's not their fault that we have a cold coming on, or we are having problems with an elderly relative, they are still entitled to the very best help we can give

c) hidden motives: some assistants (hopefully only a few) actually approach readers with a confrontational attitude of mind – a kind of 'them and us' syndrome, perhaps believing that we should do unto them before they do unto us; the problem here is that they do not appreciate that no-one ever won an argument with a customer

d) experiences: one bad experience with a gang of teenagers sporting the latest in hair styles or 'jewellery' may colour all subsequent encounters with similar groups; this is natural enough, but letting our necessarily limited experiences become a role model for all similar situations leads to stereotyping

e) media manipulation: unfortunately stereotyping is reinforced by the media – often in a humorous way, but we need to be aware that stereotyping may soon turn into prejudice

f) prejudices: it is obvious to everyone that prejudice has no place in the library. Unfortunately, we are surrounded by it. We all suffer from prejudice of some form or another – some totally irrational and idiosyncratic dislike of some group of people. It does not have to be (though it often is) national, racial, sexual, religious or political. A friend of mine has assured me on several occasions that he would like to shoot all football referees and cyclists. Few of us are free from our own version of my friend's prejudices

A combination of these factors will colour our visible behaviour – the behaviour that other people see. Like an iceberg – Figure 14.2 – people only see a fraction of what goes to make up our behaviour. Most of the time there are hidden factors that combine to make us the person that our colleagues and the public see.

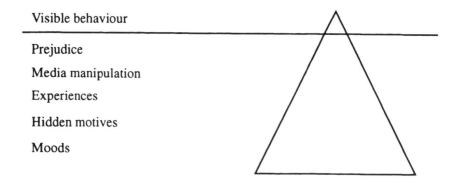

Visible behaviour

Prejudice

Media manipulation

Experiences

Hidden motives

Moods

Figure 14.2: Iceberg model of factors governing behaviour

Appearance

'You never get a second chance to make a first impression.' Everyone makes a judgement of you when they first see you. This may be done subconsciously, but it is based initially upon appearance. Their judgement may change as they get to know you better, but first impressions are often difficult to alter. The following points may be considered in relation to appearance:

a) we should dress appropriately for the job we are doing. What is appropriately?

b) are we able to suppress our prejudices against the foibles of others – bizarre hair style, vagaries of modern fashion, accents?

c) do not judge people by their appearance – at least, no more than you can help; be aware that the appearance of others may create prejudice

d) dress is a form of uniform: it makes a statement about a person and their beliefs; it identifies young people as following a certain code of ethics. Similarly, OUR dress also identifies us: if we follow the normal pattern for people in excess of 25 years of age our dress will identify us as 'conventional' and it may be seen, along with our position as 'librarian' as representing an authority figure, the *status quo* and , as such, a target to be challenged

Approach

The way we approach readers will determine the likely reaction that we will receive from them. When customers are behaving aggressively our approach needs careful consideration because *behaviour begets behaviour*. If we approach even a placid reader in an aggressive or brusque manner, their response is likely to mirror our approach. Similarly if readers approach the staff aggressively the temptation is to snap back in kind. However, it does not have to be so – we can choose our own behaviour: we can use our choice either to help or to hinder a transaction. If we respond to aggression with aggression an incident of no importance is likely to be blown up into a major incident. At the very least a smooth transaction will be hindered.

The Video Arts video production *If looks could kill* covers this aspect of customer relations very well. If you, or your organisation, can afford a copy you will find it a very useful acquisition for all customer care courses.

When coping with aggressive behaviour that could become violent (e.g. a gang of youths) our approach is particularly important, as the correct approach can defuse a potentially dangerous situation. Different approaches will achieve different results:

    a) aggressive ('You're a damn nuisance – get out'). This approach may work with some groups of teenagers, but it is more likely that their leader will respond to aggression with 'Who's going to make me?'

    b) submissive or hesitant ('I'm terribly sorry, but – er – I'm – er – afraid you'll have to – er – well – er – leave the library. I have mentioned this – er – four times already this afternoon. I really – er – don't like doing this – er – and I'm awfully – er – sorry) An assistant using such an approach is asking to be dominated by the group. Again, 'Who's going to make me?' may be the retort. Another response from the group may be a further assurance that they will keep quieter, but make no attempt to do so.

    c) assertive ('I suggested five minutes ago that your behaviour is not acceptable in my library. Since it has not improved please leave!') The assertive request should be made pleasantly, but firmly. State the position and what you wish to happen.

Assertiveness

The assertive approach is not a cure-all for this type of situation, and may elicit the response 'No!', in which case you will respond 'Then I will contact the police.' – AND DO SO.

    a) *body language (non-verbal communication).* Assertiveness is not only concerned with the words we use but with communication generally. In our case it is face-to-face communication. Researchers in this field claim that face-to-face communication comprises:

        55% body language
        38% tone of voice
        7% words used

    This means that though the words used may be assertive, they will not be taken seriously unless the body language supports the assertive approach and the tone of voice is firm. Beware that your body language does not contradict the words you use.

b) *listening skills*. Assertiveness means making our point of view known without violating the rights of others. This means that if we expect people to hear our message, we must be prepared to listen to them. But listening *and hearing* what customers are saying is difficult if we have got ourselves into an emotional state. While the emotional states of frustration and anger are going through your mind it is impossible for you to listen. However, it is important that you do listen to the reader as he unburdens himself. You may miss the important point of his anger and the error may be repeated on a subsequent occasion.

c) *touch*. Avoid being over familiar with readers and don't touch a reader unless it is really necessary (e.g. someone in distress). Never touch someone who is being violent or aggressive – you might get an elbow in the face!

d) *manner*. Assertiveness means treating everyone with respect as you would wish to be treated yourself. Don't let the routine of your job allow you to develop a casual or sloppy manner as a behaviour pattern: it can cause negative reactions from customers – 'Don't worry about it – we're doing this all the time!'. Avoid being patronising. Even if you have answered the same question fifty times this week, it is the first time this particular reader has asked it.

The subjects of assertiveness techniques, listening skills and acquiring a knowledge of non-verbal communication should be treated as training courses in their own right. Only a cursory mention of them can be included on a one day violence and aggression course.

Anxiety and stress

Do librarians work in a stressful occupation? Surveys indicate that librarians work in a placid and serene environment. Clearly, we do not have the stress of some occupations – police force, miners, hospital workers, etc., but we do deal with a particular client group, which for many librarians is the public with all their irrational and idiosyncratic wants, needs, attitudes and behaviour.

Coping with anxiety and stress is a course in itself, and there are many books, leaflets and other information available. If you wish to introduce this topic on a violence and aggression course I suggest confining yourself to the basic questions 'How do we recognise anxiety?' and 'How do we alleviate anxiety?'.

Acts, bye-laws, regulations and procedure instructions

It is important that the course members understand the legal framework which governs our libraries. They should be introduced to the Public Order Act 1986 and, depending on the results of the survey, the Sex Discrimination Act 1975.

When did course members last read the bye-laws and regulations of their library authority? Are they familiar with their contents? (e.g. is there any stipulation as to how long a customer may continue reading a newspaper or periodical when another customer has notified the librarian of his/her wish to read the same item?) Do staff appreciate the difference between bye-laws and regulations? Finally, are there procedure instructions, staff manuals, or any other guides that may be helpful when dealing with disruptive members of the community?

Staff safety

So far the course has been controlled by the course leader. True, course members' identification of problems will have been largely the delegates themselves, while the session 'diffusing an incident' will have generated a degree of discussion. The section on the Acts will have been largely informative with little opportunity for discussion except to clarify any enquiries.

This session can profitably involve a high degree of group work. Course members could be asked to consider and devise a safety checklist for libraries. Three groups could break up the checklist as follows:

> Group 1
> a) the building and its environs – the characteristics of the community in relation to the location of the library (e.g. where is the library in relation to the nearest police station)
> b) the exterior of the building – e.g. is the car park easy to reach and well lit at night
> Group 2
> a) characteristics of the library: what distinguishing features

in your library may be likely to increase the risk of crime (e.g. it houses desirable items such as video recorders and compact disc players)

b) internal control of the library: how well do staff protect themselves and their property when at work? (e.g. do all staff have lockers which are locked when they contain valuables?)

Group 3

a) personnel factors: what part does or should the Personnel Department play in helping us to achieve a safer work place? (e.g. are management seen to be too lax in pursuing adequate safety policies?)

b) entrance and exit procedures: attention should be paid to entering a building and especially leaving a building on a dark night. (e.g. do staff leave by a secluded back or side door?)

Course members should then be encouraged to think about their own library. Can they relate their findings to the greater safety of all?

Problem customers

I feel that it is necessary to advise staff on the correct way to handle customers who may turn violent themselves, or who are likely to produce an angry reaction within the staff. The angry reader may turn violent if the assistant not only fails to diffuse the anger but also adds fuel to the flames by reacting angrily back. It may be the natural thing to do (behaviour begets behaviour) but by not responding in a professional manner it will turn a minor incident into a major one.

Advice on handling rude customers is necessary. Such customers are unlikely to turn violent as offensiveness is their normal attitude of behaviour. They can, however, get under our skin. While we may be capable of keeping our words in check, our body language can easily betray our emotions. It is also tempting to be mildly sarcastic often because of their outrageous claims: 'My staff know what they're doing; they don't make mistakes.'; 'Well, sir, if you run a firm that never makes mistakes there's a job waiting for you as Prime Minister of Britain!'

Haughty or arrogant readers can produce adverse reactions from our staff. No one likes to be made to feel small or inadequate, but some readers seem to enjoy this particular form of one-upmanship. Such a reader delights in finding an inexperienced assistant who is perhaps lacking in the knowledge that he/she should have. The tempting, though unprofessional, approach is to respond by falling back on the use of library jargon or abbreviations: 'Surely you know what an ISBN is: I thought everybody knew that!'

The above are just three of the types of difficult customers that our staff need to deal with. They are not violent, but they can produce anger, frustration and stress within our assistants as easily as the gang of youths that invade our premises for nefarious purposes.

Other types may also be identified. You may need to discuss the mentally disturbed, or how to handle customers identified by our staff as 'creepy, but I'm not sure why!'.

The use of trigger videos may be used to good effect in this session. They can be a stimulating way of getting your message across. My chief reservation with their use is that they rarely give enough information to give the course members the opportunity to make a genuine response.

Eccentrics

The problem with dealing with less normal members of society is that their abnormality will show itself in so many different forms, many of which can be discounted as being so improbable as not worthy of attention – until it happens to *you*. Examples of this form of behaviour could be voyeurism, exhibitionism, Tourettes syndrome (uncontrollable swearing) and loiterers.

I suggest that, using your survey and file relating to such behaviour, you identify three or four examples that are relatively common, but where the methods of handling the problem may be unclear or the staff reluctant to follow procedure. Examples are dumb insolence from youngsters, molesting of a young librarian, kleptomania, handling drunks, obscene telephone calls, etc.

An interesting and profitable way of handling this section of the programme is to turn your selected examples into case studies and let course members decide how best to handle these problem customers. With most of the above there is no easy answer because:

a) we are reluctant to add to the troubles of someone who is mentally disturbed (e.g. the kleptomaniac or the sufferer from Tourettes syndrome)

b) the member of staff may be reluctant to follow procedure or get the police involved (e.g. young librarian being molested)

   c) some forms of behaviour take time to trace and apprehend (e.g. obscene telephone calls)

   d) some forms of behaviour are difficult to prove (e.g. dumb insolence, voyeurism, loitering)

A well designed case study will bring out the points that you wish to raise and initiate profitable discussion as to how best the problem can be tackled, with the course leader summing up and adding any points of his/her own that need to be emphasised during the de-briefing session.

Assuming a class of 10–20 course members, my suggestion would be to divide into three groups. Each group could have a different case study, thus allowing three different forms of misbehaviour to be explored. Given a sufficiently large class you could, of course, provide any number of case studies, but then time becomes a problem during the discussion period afterwards.

Personal safety

The personal safety of staff concerns all library authorities. This is obviously true when the member of staff is working on the premises, or in transit between their home and their place of work. It is equally true that an authority should consider the well being of staff at all times. Leaving aside concern for the physical and emotional well being of staff, the organisation will suffer in terms of effectiveness and efficiency of the service if staff are absent through injury – irrespective of where the injury is sustained. It follows, therefore, that it is in the interests of the organisation to give staff some training in self defence.

There are many self defence actions that any of us can undertake given a short training session. My own preference for tackling this session is to obtain one of the many videos available on this topic and encourage the course members to follow the instructions given. It is necessary for the course leader to be *au fait* with the video and available to give advice on performing the moves as they come up. Some moves may be so dangerous that they should only be viewed on the screen (e.g. forming your fingers into a V shape and attacking your assailant's eyes). Most movements though, are perfectly safe to try out in slow motion. The leader must be vigilant for any over enthusiasm by course members – the credibility of the course would go down if two or three members reported absent through injury the following day.

The main problem is that attacks are mercifully rare (figures suggest that the average person will be attacked about once every 100 years). This means that for most of the participants this particular session will never be applicable, and for those to whom it will apply it will probably be several years before it will be needed.

However, I do believe that this final practical session is necessary. It builds confidence and course members should be encouraged to practice moves that appeal to them regularly with their spouses.

CONCLUSION

Many librarians may have different ideas concerning training to combat the growing menace of violence and aggression in libraries. Some authorities will invite experts in various fields to give a series of talks (e.g. a probation officer, a psychologist, a security expert, a legal advisor). The problem here is that a day's (or even half day's) programme consisting solely of talks can soon become boring. Furthermore, it is rarely possible to guarantee the quality of the speakers.

I have suggested that one outside specialist will suffice – the policeman. Beyond that, rely on your survey to guide you when formulating your programme.

Should time or expertise be unavailable from within your own staff consideration should be given to contracting a training consultant specialising in this type of activity – it can be an efficient and effective way of proceeding.

15

Security policy formulation

ANDREW McDONALD

Security planning and policy making is an essential but regrettably neglected area of the management of libraries and information centres and one which has implications for virtually all aspects of library operations. In contrast with the USA, security policy has not received the attention it deserves in the United Kingdom but now that libraries all over the world are at risk from an increasing number of threats, international interest in this dilemma is growing. As society changes so does the nature of security problems and many are regarded as endemic with complex socio-economic and even political bases, but their importance cannot be underestimated. As Metcalf (1989) reminds us, no library is immune even from the more innocuous outlets for human emotion. The modern library manager must take full responsibility for security and develop policies and a coherent strategy in relation to the crimes and misdemeanours which threaten the survival of our libraries.

Whilst total security is unattainable and probably unworkable in a service organisation, all steps should be taken to prevent or deter crime and reduce the security risks to which the resources under our care are exposed. These resources are often worth millions of pounds; they may be irreplaceable, and their absence would certainly render our parent organisations much less effective, less competitive, or even inoperable. In protecting and preserving library resources, effective security measures can also be seen as contributing to the quality, efficiency and availability of the service provided.

POLICY INTERACTIONS & CONFLICT

In developing policy the library manager must recognise not only the nature of the threats concerned but also that security cannot be treated in isolation. Decisions regarding security, whether taken explicitly or implicitly, interact with virtually all other areas of policy. The way in which our buildings, collections and staff are organised fundamentally affects security and conversely security policy decisions have implications for the use and operation of our services. This conflict can be illustrated by a number of examples.

Access and the library environment

Libraries have developed as welcoming and informal places where the emphasis is on access to collections, the encouragement of use, customer care and meeting the needs of users with the minimum number of rules and regulations. Unfortunately as Quinsee (1991) observes, the popular open door policy to a wide range of readers from different cultures and social backgrounds makes libraries vulnerable in the face of increasing anti-social behaviour. Resolving the inherent conflict between the needs of security and conservation and making material readily available to readers is one of the greatest challenges facing the librarian (British Library, 1981). Regrettably it has to be recognised that higher degrees of security may also diminish, to a greater or lesser extent, the readers' freedom to enjoy the library (Thompson, 1989) and in some cases may even add to the recurrent running costs of providing the service. Readers often behave in a far more relaxed and trusting way in libraries than they would in other public places. Providing an environment in which the genuine reader feels comfortable but the criminal is deterred by effective security measures may prove a formidable challenge for many libraries.

Internal arrangements

The internal arrangement of the library has a considerable effect on security. Some libraries have established a policy that all areas of the stack should be within sight of staffed positions and have even arranged ranges of shelving in parallel rows to improve visibility. Whilst, as Metcalf (1989) concedes, this may seem extreme and unattainable, especially in a large library, effective surveillance or visibility enhancement is one of the most basic and important preventative measures. A reasonable level of staffing and supervision will deter much anti-social behaviour. However, the understandable tendency to arrange shelving for maximum storage and convenience, the overcrowding resulting from increases in stock and numbers of readers, and changes in the use of accommodation, all contrive to make supervision more difficult. Although convex mirrors and mechanical devices such as closed circuit television can assist, effective surveillance relies on the presence of staff. It is a sad irony that the numbers of staff in libraries in recent years have been reduced just at the time when the security risks have increased.

Collection management

All aspects of collection management policy which directly affect the availability of books to those who require them will have an influence on security. Many librarians are convinced that recent savage reductions in book and periodical expenditure have restricted access to essential reading and have resulted in security problems. Smethurst (1991) suggests that there may well be a close relationship between book losses and policies for loan, especially for books in heavy demand. Certainly the non-return of books may be closely related to the fine system; it is often cheaper and easier for a reader to fail to return a book than to pay the fine. Indeed the penalty for non-return may be lower than the penalty for late return, since fines levied for books in heavy demand often exceed the initial cost of the book.

In setting regulations, Smethurst (1991) advises that librarians should be aware of the implications on security. A stringent fine system or a severe restriction on the number of books which can be borrowed may encourage a reader to consider borrowing the required books illegally. Certainly the removal of pages from books is common where books are restricted to use in the library and where no adequate photocopying facilities exist. Ironically, improvements in security such as the introduction of a book detection system, may also lead to an increase in the incidence of mutilation. Regrettably mutilation is almost impossible to prevent when readers have free access to books (Metcalf, 1989).

The need for security must be balanced against the convenience of users (Friend, 1991). The organisation of collections on open access is generally regarded as more convenient for users and less costly in operation, but the collections are less secure than those on closed access. In practice libraries normally adopt a compromise arrangement whereby the greater staff costs associated with closed access can be justified for certain collections, such as rare and valuable books or items in heavy demand.

Many libraries no longer have the staffing necessary to undertake thorough annual stock checks or even less regular selective ones, but these surveys can generate important information about the extent and patterns of theft and can be invaluable in developing remedial strategies.

Buildings

Often the nature of the building itself is in conflict with security. Deep, open-plan, flexible space found in many modern buildings may have helped to alleviate many of the security problems associated with older buildings, in which internal walls, rooms and corridors create nooks and crannies which are hard to supervise. But the modern approach can also contribute its own problems – planning for maximum confrontation between readers and library stock and services may increase temptation and heighten vulnerability. Fears have been expressed that open plan buildings offer little resistance to the penetration of flood water or blast damage and that air conditioning systems could even assist the spread of fumes and pollutants (Harrison, 1991).

Many of the security problems of libraries, whether situated in new or old buildings, are a legacy of the original design and so when planning or refurbishing buildings, security should be carefully considered and where possible potential security problems should be designed out. As Morris (1986) claims, 'of all the precautionary measures librarians can take against such crimes (as vandalism, theft and incendiarism) none is more basic than that of securing the building itself'. Indeed, the requirement for security should be stated explicitly in the brief for a building project and the librarian may have to firmly reject design features which, however attractive in aesthetic terms, will create security problems in the future. Apart from architects themselves, advice is freely available within the profession, for example from the National Preservation Office. The Architectural Liaison Officers in local police forces (or Crime Prevention Design Advisers as they are known in London) provide assistance at the concept stage of the building and throughout the planning, design and building processes on ways in which security risks can be reduced or eliminated. To achieve greatest benefit advice should be sought at the earliest possible stage in the planning process.

A refurbishment project in itself poses temporary security problems of a most unusual kind – the library effectively becomes the building site for a number of contractors' and sub-contractors' workmen. During a recent refurbishment of the Brotherton Library, University of Leeds, Carr (1991) reported no fewer than 40 security incidents within a six month period, ranging from fire alarms to windows being left open overnight. Libraries are similarly at risk when extending the building or when moving to new premises.

Safety

Even safety requirements can conflict with security. A safe library might, for example, be one amply provided with unlocked exit doors to facilitate rapid escape in an emergency but such a library would hardly be a secure one (Quinsee, 1991). Safety considerations are necessarily driven by current legislation and various legally enforceable regulations.

ELEMENTS OF POLICY FORMULATION

People-centred policy

It is quite mistaken to consider security only at the planning stage of a building or even to regard security as simply a physical building problem. Security policy presents a substantial management challenge because it is concerned with a complex interaction between people, buildings, collections and services. Successful policies recognise the central importance of human behaviour in the process, because it is people who commit offences, people who endeavour to prevent them and people who have to deal with the effects. The ultimate security of the library rests with all the staff who must be properly trained and fully encouraged in their awareness of security issues. A coherent strategy in which the manager confronts the problems in a professional and objective manner will assist in developing appropriate attitudes amongst the staff and give them confidence in dealing with unpleasant incidents.

There has been a marked deterioration in the standards of behaviour amongst library users in recent years and public librarians in particular face an increasing number of incidents involving abuse or even violence (Library Association, 1987). Such incidents can have an effect on the whole organisation and not just the particular staff assaulted. For many librarians these risks may seem unlikely and remote but for others, especially where personal risk is involved, the uncertainty and unpredictability can be very disconcerting and can have a profound effect on job performance. Uncertainty itself can cause anxiety and stress and indeed, as Houlgate (1991) notes, the fear of crime can often be as damaging as crime itself and can affect staff morale and behaviour.

Mission and costs

Although many libraries now have mission statements and aims and objectives, security is rarely explicitly mentioned and so it is not surprising that some libraries, library committees and their parent organisations do not perceive the development of policy and expenditure on security as a priority. The manager may need to raise the profile of security, but there is an unfortunate tendency in society to view libraries as somehow different from other organisations and to regard books as relatively inexpensive, disposable commodities which are everyone's property. Unfortunately even some librarians are reluctant to acknowledge book theft and other security problems in their libraries. As Lincoln (1984) confirms, 'librarians themselves are often too tolerant of behaviour that administrators/managers of other facilities would quickly label theft'. Smethurst (1991) suggests this could be due to a number of factors: ignorance of the full extent of losses; fear that the losses might reflect badly on library efficiency; concern that publicising theft might expose the lack of effective security measures; or a genuine, but often misplaced, belief that the culprit did not intend to steal the book but would return it at a later stage.

By no means all security measures are costly although some may be both expensive and inconvenient, but the cost of ignoring the risks, both in financial and political terms, can also be high. In assessing publicly funded libraries the Audit Commission (1988) will evaluate the effectiveness of security measures against expenditure on replacing stolen books. One university library has been asked to identify the cost of vandalism, theft and graffiti and to build the recurrent remedial costs into annual estimates (R. Davis, 1990, personal communication). The loss of rare and valuable items from special collections could result in embarrassing publicity. Newspaper stories reporting investigations into the disappearance of 2000 books each week from the public libraries in one London Borough may not inspire public confidence in the management of these resources (Rafferty, 1990).

Library regulations and the theft of books

A particular constraint which must be recognised is that the theft of library books is not only seen as somehow different from the theft of other commodities, but also that is has often proved very difficult and costly to establish in the courts that the culprit intended to permanently deprive the library of the books, which is the requirement for a conviction for theft under the Theft Act 1968 (Fox, 1991). Even where cases have been sufficiently strong and many stolen books recovered in the culprit's house, sentencing is often relatively light.

Fox (1991) suggests that carefully worded rules and regulations are needed for the library to have effective sanctions against those readers whose behaviour is unacceptable. These rules and regulations must make it clear that the use of the library implies a contract between the institution and the user whereby the user is granted certain privileges for agreeing to abide by certain conditions. In other words the use of the library is conditional upon the observance of the rules and regulations. These must be carefully thought out, logical, fair and above all capable of being enforced within the framework of the organisation in which the library operates. They should make clear to staff and users the penalties for behaviour not consistent with proper use of the library. In the case of stolen and mutilated books they should empower the library to either ban the reader or extract fines or charges sufficient to pay for the full cost of the repair or replacement of the item.

Librarians must resolve their own policy as to whether the main objective is the return of the books or the punishing of the reader. A mechanism often used by libraries to achieve the return of outstanding books is to declare an amnesty on overdue books and fines. One County Council received 10,000 books in a week by pursuing this course of action (Rafferty, 1990). The concept of Library Recovery Officers who attempt to recover stolen or non-returned public library books is a relatively new one in the United Kingdom, although Smethurst (1991) reports that as early as 1913 the New York Public Library appointed a special investigator to both recover stolen material and apprehend culprits.

Theft by library staff poses particular problems, and measures to counter insider theft such as identity passes or even bag searching for staff can be very damaging to working relationships in the library. Where required they need to be introduced with sensitivity and as sensible precautions rather than as over-restrictive, all staff are guilty, measures and as Smethurst (1991) warns us, these are strongly resisted by institutions and trade unions alike.

New technology

New technology is something of a mixed blessing as far as security policy is concerned. Modern sophisticated surveillance systems, intruder alarms and electronic locks can be of great assistance, although at some cost, but the introduction of increasing amounts of highly desirable portable computer hardware into libraries in itself creates a considerable security risk.

The display of security measures

There is some difference of opinion in the profession regarding the openness with which to display or advertise security measures and the approach depends to some extent upon whether the library seeks to deter and prevent crime or to catch and punish offenders. Since the psychology and motivation of the offender or forgetful reader are known to be complex, it is not surprising that this is not a straightforward matter.

Many libraries favour a discreet approach to security. Whereas some high street stores provide clearly visible tags on the goods which are removed when the goods are purchased, the triggers normally used for library books are permanent and virtually undetectable. Indeed some librarians, in seeking to provide a welcoming and accessible environment, may themselves find explicit security measures somewhat uncomfortable or even threatening and not consistent with their motives for entering the profession.

However, there can be little doubt that overt security measures can act as a substantial deterrent. A clearly visible closed circuit television monitor reminds readers that surveillance is in operation. It is probably also true that occasional false alarms of the book detection system serve to remind readers that a system is in operation, although too many false alarms would frustrate readers and library staff alike and only diminish confidence in the system. Some libraries set up exhibitions of mutilated books to focus attention on the damage done and the high costs of replacement and repair. Others argue that such a display may only serve to encourage this type of behaviour.

Response policy

A rapid and effective response to all security breaches is a fundamental part of the overall security strategy. *Ad hoc* reactions to particular events such as announcing the occurrence of thefts on notices or on a public address system, are important but insufficient in themselves. It is vital to repair damage and the effects of vandalism immediately to maintain the quality and functioning of the library. Incidents involving people should be dealt with confidently but sympathetically and many libraries have produced standard incident report forms to ensure that essential information is recorded. Victims of crime, whether users or library staff, may require considerable support and even skilled counselling. The motivation and performance of staff can be severely affected by the occurrence of serious incidents. It is important to provide an infrastructure which permits staff to express their concerns and discuss policy and which also facilitates the review of policy in the light of experience. The importance of adequate maintenance, especially for electronic intruder systems and book detection systems, should not be underestimated.

An approach to policy development

Responsibility for the planning and coordination of security policy must be held at a senior level in the library and in common with other areas of management, this should take account of:

- the aims and objectives of the library
- the nature of the perceived risks
- the regulations and culture of the organisation
- current legislation
- the resources available

SECURITY AUDIT

A useful approach is to conduct a security audit of the library, as if one were a newly appointed chief librarian or a security consultant charged with responsibility for identifying security risks, assessing the adequacy of security policy and making recommendations for improvements. Such an audit could examine the following questions:

a) does the library have a security policy?

b) what are the current security risks? Identify and assess the risks in relation to the building, its collections, and the staff and readers. Encourage library staff at all levels to do likewise, preferably on a standard reporting form

c) build up a profile of recent incidents and analyse trends. Discuss the crime profile of the area with the security men within your organisation and the local police

d) assess the adequacy of current security measures

e) examine current arrangements for responding to incidents and reporting procedures. Determine whether experience gained from incidents is satisfactorily fed back into policy discussion

f) identify who has overall responsibility for planning and coordinating security arrangements. Is communication regarding security amongst the staff satisfactory?

g) assess the extent of security awareness amongst staff and the effectiveness of staff training. Are staff manuals available, providing clear statements regarding security policy and procedures?

h) examine current library rules and regulations in relation to those of the organisation. Are they effective in dealing with unacceptable behaviour in the library?

i) how good are relationships with other professionals involved in security, e.g. the local police and security men? How adequate are the insurance arrangements?

j) what resources are currently deployed on security and what is the cost of dealing with the existing level of crime and misdemeanours? What priority is given to security in relation to other areas of policy?

Having conducted the audit, the librarian is in a better position to review security policy and make the required changes, bearing in mind that the support of the parent organisation is essential and the necessary resources must be available. The manager must decide upon the degree of security required and the priority accorded to it. In practice this is not easy and the approach may have to be selective, varying for different parts of the library, for example in the special collections area and in the computer room. Metcalf (1989) reminds us that many security problems change with time and it is very important to provide for a flexible response to security needs.

Although it is impossible to be exhaustive or prescriptive in relation to all types of library, there are a number of basic areas of security which might be considered in such an audit: location, site and access; the building envelope; building services; entrance and exit points; internal arrangements; collections; book detection systems; equipment; cash management; and personal security. Within each of these broad categories a variety of specific details should be examined and assessed.

Location, site and access

- neighbourhood – problems encountered in a city centre are very different from a green field site
- position in relation to main roads and public footpaths
- proximity to and accessibility from surrounding buildings
- quality of exterior lighting – tamper-proof exterior lighting especially in vulnerable areas is an excellent deterrent
- small perimeter bushes to keep people away from the building, but prickly to deter loiterers
- exterior cameras
- paths which generally keep people away from the sides of the building but which are logical and direct
- landscaping features – rocks, stones and young trees are an open invitation to some
- access for emergency vehicles
- facilities for car parking and surveillance of car parks

Building envelope

- vulnerability of the building shell to vandalism and intruders
- hiding places created by the shape of the building
- aspects of the building, its features and finishes which facilitate

277

climbing e.g. solid drainpipes, monumental sills and ledges, external metal roof ladders.
- where graffiti is a problem consider anti-graffiti coatings or even murals
- ground level windows, doors, air vents and other potential points of entry such as skylights, roof hatches and gratings etc.
- vulnerability of the book return chute

Windows

- windows representing an open invitation to vandals or intruders, e.g. unbarred windows with ordinary glass at ground level
- consider the type of glass used – laminated glass is preferred
- openable windows from which books can be thrown out
- the quality of locks on openable windows

External doors

- doors which open into vulnerable quiet areas or can be easily opened from the outside
- doors should be strong, tight-fitting and equipped with high security locks, hinges and glazing
- door frames should be made of metal or if made of wood should have reinforced hinges which should be on the inside
- emergency exits need alarms to signal unauthorised use, preferably a remote alarm to alert staff
- who has keys, especially non-library staff, such as cleaners and maintenance staff?
- are locks and keys up to modern standards? What are key suiting arrangements?

Building services

Fire

- detection system – is there an automatic detection system, either local or connected to fire authorities?
- suppression system – has an automatic system been installed in open stack areas, the special collections room or the computer room?

- identify fire risks e.g. the accumulation of rubbish and broken furniture in stair wells
- do arrangements such as escape routes conform to the Fire Certificate?

Flood

- is there an automatic detection system?
- what arrangements exist for getting rid of water?
- is the location of stopcocks known?

Other services

- does the library possess wiring diagrams, building services plans?
- assess the vulnerability of service control panels, ducting panels, fuse boxes etc.

Locks and keys

- review the quality of locks and keys – the technology of locksmiths has moved into the electronic age and high levels of security and flexibility can be achieved at a price. How easily can keys be copied?
- review levels of access and the system of masters, submasters and ordinary keys. Who can and should have access to where in the library?
- ensure that vulnerable areas such as external doors and windows and certain other areas such as computer rooms and special collections areas have adequate security locks

Intruder alarms

- has a system been fitted to detect illegal entry and/or readers who remain once the library has closed?
- is the alarm local or remote to a security firm or to the police?
- has the system been designed and fitted by an expert security company and what are the maintenance arrangements?
- consider the suitability of the detectors and sensors used and of zoning arrangements
- assess the authorities response time to alarms

Entrance/exit points

- the number of entrance and exit points; a single combined point is preferred
- control of those entering the library such as by a card entry system or by ticket checks; these systems can also provide valuable management information regarding users
- presence of a clearly visible uniformed porter or attendant to oversee readers either entering or leaving the library, who makes a security 'statement'
- is the entrance in clear sight of the main counter for ease of supervision?
- the flow of readers in and out – is it controlled by barriers and turnstiles and therefore easier to supervise?
- arrangements for checking those leaving the library and their books; is there a book detection system supplemented by manual checks by a porter?

Back door, delivery area

- review the supervision of this area and in particular the quality of the locks and the number of keyholders, arrangements for receiving and securing deliveries (books, consumables and equipment) and equally for dispatching materials

Internal arrangements

- the degree of natural supervision in the library
- do staff or porters make security patrols; do security staff or police 'drop in'?
- consider changing the layout of the shelving; for example, to run in parallel rows to improve visibility
- identify secluded areas and blind spots and consider improving the lighting levels and supervision with mechanical aids such as closed circuit television, convex mirrors and controlled entry and exit points
- arrangements for the supervision of high risk areas; consider using mechanical aids or security glass
- the vandal resistance of vulnerable areas such as the internal lift finishes, toilet cubicle finishes

- are graffiti removal procedures quick and effective?
- select tamper-proof furniture and equipment wherever possible
- can readers gain access undetected into non public areas?
- consider notices or door alarms to protect cataloguing areas, staff staircases etc.
- the security of staffrooms and storage areas

Collections

Collection management policies

- do you know what you have? All collections should be catalogued or listed
- basic housekeeping procedures – check ownership stamps and the cancelling stamp for discarded items
- the frequency of stock checks; what arrangements are made for recording missing items?
- consider the effects of the level of acquisitions, the fines system, loan periods and borrowing privileges, especially for materials in heavy demand; do the regulations encourage the reader to remove or retain required books
- the adequacy of photocopying facilities, especially the convenience and cost

Loss rate and mutilation

- is the current loss rate and the incidence of mutilation known? Many libraries no longer have the staffing to undertake complete annual stock checks, but selective stock checks or at least recording requested but missing items may be useful. Regular shelf checks will reveal temporarily misshelved books
- analyse reports of the incidence of theft and mutilation for discernible patterns or trends particularly incidents relating to particular courses, subject areas or groups of users. In some academic libraries high loss rates are reported in law and theology collections. Car manuals and books on health frequently go missing from public libraries

Responses

In addition to the security measures already discussed, a number of other strategies for dealing with the theft and mutilation of the collections have been developed in libraries.

- reconsider and if necessary change any aspects of the rules and regulations and the stock management policy, which either fail to meet the needs of users or create security problems. Try to discover the reasons why certain sections of stock are particularly vulnerable and formulate appropriate policies
- enhance the supervision of exits
- consider creating a cloakroom or locker area and make the depositing of coats and bags compulsory
- consider closed access for certain stock
- improve the checking of bags as readers leave, either randomly, regularly or for all readers
- employ Library Recovery Officers to recover unreturned books
- mount a public relations campaign to enlist the support of readers by, for example, posters, articles in newspapers, notices on the shelves saying 'this book has been stolen'
- declare an amnesty on overdue books and fines
- set up an exhibition of damaged books, although some librarians feel by advertising the problem you may also be encouraging it
- ensure mutilated books are swiftly dealt with by replacing damaged pages or the whole book. Many libraries which operate a book detection system also trigger replaced pages in case demand is such that other readers are similarly tempted to remove them
- install a book detection system (discussed in chapter 16)
- consider the difficult question of security measures for dealing with thefts by staff by introducing sensible precautions such as identity passes or even bag searching

Special collections

Because of the rare and valuable nature of some collections of old books and manuscripts, security may require special attention but unfortunately many approaches absorb a considerable amount of staff time and cost. Indeed most special collections are organised on a closed access basis. Experience has shown that such collections are under threat even from some of the scholars and researchers who consult them. Potential responses are:

- collections should be marked and adequately catalogued or listed
- store rare and valuable items under lock and key; very special items should be kept in a safe or strong room with appropriate fire and flood protection
- display areas should be secure and may require special cabinets with laminated glass, vibration detectors, weight sensors and motion detectors; closed circuit television and guards may be necessary in display areas
- the credentials of those consulting the collections can be checked and some libraries have key or card entry systems for the special collections area
- a supervised reading room can be provided for consultation, possibly also equipped with closed circuit television
- returned items should be checked; many libraries even weigh returned manuscripts
- losses can be reported to appropriate professional bodies who maintain databases and to interested antiquarian bookshops

Equipment

- do you have a full inventory giving the details and serial number of all your equipment? Equipment should be marked to enable identification. As with books it is essential to know and be able to identify what belongs to the library.
- some equipment can be secured in locked cupboards and made available to readers on request
- valuable equipment should be physically secured to stands or tables with security hardware
- consider electronic security and chain breaking security, sounding either a local or remote alarm
- portable computer hardware may be a particular risk – consider physical and electronic security measures
- surveillance may be necessary for the use of some equipment, e.g. closed circuit television

Cash management

- arrangements for dealing with cash may be subject to control under the parent institution's policy but it is preferable not to retain cash in the library, and some libraries even display notices that cash boxes are emptied every evening
- procedures for financial transactions and cash transfers should be reviewed. It may be preferable for money to be counted by staff other than those who empty the tills
- regrettably, experience shows that some thefts are by library staff and procedures must be carefully thought out to achieve a responsible, preventive, but not overly-restrictive regime
- also consider the security of cash equivalents such as photocopy cards, interlibrary loans vouchers and unprocessed library books

Personal Security

The Library Association (1987) offers advice to its members on personal security in the workplace and has produced a useful leaflet *Violence in libraries: preventing aggressive and unacceptable behaviour in libraries*, in which it is suggested that employees, trades unions and employers work together to identify and resolve problems.

- encourage staff at all levels to consider personal security and report on their concerns and experience. All incidents should be reported on a standard form
- ensure all staff have access to telephones, panic buttons or even personal alarms, which sound either locally or remotely. Consider making personal alarms available to readers at, for example, closing time
- identify the times and situations in which staff are left alone and might be vulnerable, such as working in small departmental libraries, shelving on a subject floor in the evenings, accompanying readers to a remote part of the library to answer a query, working in the evenings or on Saturdays with relatively few staff, and getting home, especially after late opening. Avoid these situations wherever possible
- adjust opening hours to ensure a sufficient concentration of staff

- consider using a public address system to close the library and reduce the need for staff to walk around at closing time. It can be also be used to announce any immediate security incidents such as theft
- assess the adequacy of numbers of staff on duty – staff presence is an effective security measure
- do you have a uniformed porter or attendant at the front entrance?
- assess arrangements for staff training to make staff aware of security problems and how they are expected to respond to certain situations. Encourage feedback and discussion which will help to improve confidence and morale in dealing with difficult and threatening situations
- publish an Emergency Manual outlining policy and procedures for dealing with fire, medical problems, security, theft, safety, police, structural problems, bomb threats, and other disasters
- staff and users who become victims of abusive attacks and violence may require skilled counselling and assistance
- in large libraries do staff carry some sort of identification or wear a badge? Are staff encouraged to challenge unknown persons found in restricted areas or check the tickets/passes of readers
- do workmen and maintenance staff carry identification and are they required to sign in and out? Consider security in your plant room
- how up to date are the library's membership files?

CONCLUSION

Security policy is an essential element in the management of libraries and information centres and many potentially damaging situations can be avoided or alleviated by effective forward planning and good management policies. The manager must decide upon the priority to be given to security and must ensure that the necessary resources are allocated. Although security policy can often be in conflict with other areas of policy, unless librarians themselves consciously place security matters high in their priorities for determined and cooperative action, progress will be limited (Smethurst, 1991). Many security risks can be designed out when planning new buildings or refurbishing existing ones, but once the library is completed it is probably true to say that good security costs money. However as Carr (1991) confirms, when the total real value of the library's assets are reliably calculated, the money spent on security can be seen to be a justifiable investment.

Most criminals are opportunists and can be deterred as a result of strong and effective security management. In practice it is the cumulative effect of a whole range of preventative or defensive measures which are important. Harrison (1991) observes that 'the strategy should be to place so many inhibitions in the way of the miscreant that the intended act is likely to be immediately observed or discoverable, or difficult to carry out'.

As social habits change, the security risks to which libraries are subjected will also change. It is, therefore, important to develop policies not only in relation to the existing level of crime and misdemeanours but also capable of providing a flexible response to changing patterns of risk. Libraries have already begun to experience politically motivated crimes and even armed robbery and it would be regrettable if such developments diminished the enthusiasm for freely available, open access library services. The Library Association (1990) has already reported the first known closure of a public library, ironically known as the fortress because of its mesh protected windows, as a result of vandalism and anti-social behaviour.

Security policy poses a substantial challenge for managers of all types of libraries and there can be little doubt that security concerns will continue to influence the shape of library buildings, the organisation of collections and arrangements for staffing and using library services.

> *And you all know, security*
> *is mortals' chiefest enemy*
> Macbeth
> Act III Scene V

REFERENCES

Arfield, J. A. (1991), Theft detection systems – some practicalities, in *Security in academic and research libraries*, edited by Quinsee, A. G. and McDonald, A. C. Newcastle upon Tyne: University Library.

Audit Commission (1988), *Performance Review in Local Government: A handbook for auditors and local authorities, action guide.* London: HMSO.

British Library (1981), *Annual Report 1980–81.* London: The British Library.

Carr, R. (1991). Problems of Security in Older Library Buildings, in *Security in academic and research libraries,* edited by Quinsee, A. G. and McDonald, A. C. Newcastle upon Tyne: University Library.

Cumming, N. (1987), *Security: The Comprehensive Guide to Equipment,* London: Butterworth.

Fox, P. (1991), Legal Process, in *Security in academic and research libraries,* edited by Quinsee, A. G. and McDonald, A. C. Newcastle upon Tyne: University Library.

Friend, F. J. (1991) Theft Detection Systems – Policies, in *Security in academic and research libraries,* edited by Quinsee, A. G. and McDonald, A. C. Newcastle upon Tyne: University Library.

Harrison, A. (1991), New Library Concepts and Security Problems, in *Security in academic and research libraries,* edited by Quinsee, A. G. and McDonald, A. C. Newcastle upon Tyne: University Library.

Houlgate, J. (1991), Building Design and Crime Prevention, in *Security in academic and research libraries,* edited by Quinsee, A. G. and McDonald, A. C. Newcastle upon Tyne: University Library.

Jackson, M. (1991), Where to get help, in *Security in academic and research libraries,* edited by Quinsee, A. G. and McDonald, A. C. Newcastle upon Tyne: University Library.

Library Association (1987), *Violence in libraries: preventing aggression and Unacceptable behaviour in libraries.* London: The Library Association.

Library Association (1990), *Trade Union News,* no. 28, (October). London: The Library Association.

Lincoln, A. J. (1984), *Crime in the library: a study of patterns, impact, and security.* New York: Bowker.

Lincoln, A. J. (1984), Protecting the library. *Library Trends,* vol. 33, no. 1. pp. 3–94.

Metcalf, K. D. (1986), *Planning academic and research libraries, 2nd edition,* by Deighton, P. D. and Weber, D. C. Chicago: American Library Association.

Morris, J. (1986), *Library disaster preparedness handbook.* Chicago: American Library Association.

Powell, J. W. (1975), Architects, security consultants, and security planning for new libraries. *Library Security Newsletter*, vol. 1, no. 5, (September/October), pp. 1a, 6–8.

Poyner, B. (1983), *Design against crime: beyond defensible space.* London Butterworth.

Quinsee, A. G. (1991), Introduction, in *Security in academic and research libraries*, edited by Quinsee, A. G. and McDonald, A. C. Newcastle upon Tyne: University Library.

Quinsee, A. G. and McDonald, A. C. (1991), *Security in academic and research libraries*, proceedings on three seminars organised by SCONUL and the British Library, held at the British Library 1989/1990. Newcastle upon Tyne: University Library.

Rafferty, F. (1990), Missing book costs libraries £100m a year. *Daily Telegraph*, October 16, p. 4.

Sannawald, W. W. and Smith, R. S. (1988), *Checklist of library building design considerations.* Chicago: American Library Association.

Smethurst, J. M. (1991), Library security: an overview, in *Security in academic and research libraries* edited by Quinsee, A. G. and McDonald, A. C. Newcastle upon Tyne: University Library.

Thompson, G. (1989), *Planning and design of library buildings, 3rd edition.* London: Butterworth.

Underwood, G. (1984), *The security of buildings.* London: Butterworth.

Wright, K. G. (1972), *Cost-effective security.* London: McGraw Hill.

16

Book detection systems

Andrew McDonald

Protecting the collections may be seen as the highest priority in many libraries where they are the most expensive resource in terms of accumulated value and replacement cost. At the same time, they may be seen as offering the most obvious value to readers. They may also be the most vulnerable resource particularly in open access libraries in which all readers are encouraged to handle unsupervised the various materials under our care. Rapid and easy access to the collections has not only promoted use by genuine readers but has also increased vulnerability to forgetful, anti-social and criminal behaviour. Chapter 15 considered a number of approaches to the security of the collections, the buildings housing them and the people using and managing the services. Many libraries have successfully installed one of the now well established electronic book detection systems on the market and there can be little doubt that a well managed and properly maintained detection system effectively reduces the loss of books and other materials.

It cannot be emphasised too strongly that a detection system is not a security system in itself but merely reacts when it detects books which have not been formally issued. As a security measure the systems are most effective when they form part of an overall security strategy within which the management policy for the detection system has been carefully planned and implemented. Whilst no system is foolproof, especially against the determined or professional thief, the detection systems are most effective in deterring casual theft.

Basically the systems are quite simple. A trigger concealed in the book will activate an alarm when the book passes through a detection field, normally a free standing sensing unit, situated at the exit point and arranged so that readers must pass through it before leaving the library. Unless the trigger has been desensitised when the book was issued (referred to as a full circulating system) or the book passed around the detection field by a member of staff (in the case of the less popular but cheaper bypass system), an alarm will sound to alert library staff and a gate or door will temporarily lock to prevent the reader from leaving immediately. The precise configuration is normally adapted to suit the local requirements of the library concerned.

Systems are available to suit small and large libraries and the choice of a particular system will be influenced by a number of factors including:

- cost
- reputation of the company and the system
- effectiveness of the system
- design and appearance of the sensing panels
- functioning of the (de)sensitising units
- range and convenience of triggers available for the materials to be protected
- compatibility with related equipment such as the issue system
- servicing arrangements

3M, Plescon and Knogo all currently supply electromagnetic book detection systems and Plescon also offer a radio frequency system. The experience of a good supplier and of other libraries with similar systems can be invaluable at the planning stage and the suppliers also offer professional advice on a whole range of security issues without commitment.

When planning for a system, there are four main areas of concern:

- justification for a system
- mode of operation
- triggering the stock
- operating the system

THE CASE FOR A SYSTEM

The relatively high capital cost of installing a system together with the recurrent maintenance charges and the cost of the triggers themselves can be justified against the total cost of replacing stolen books and the inconvenience suffered both by readers and library staff in searching for missing items. A return on investment can often be projected within a few years, or in some extreme cases, in a few months. It is a sensible precaution taken by a responsible library manager who recognises the importance of a book detection system as one of a number of desirable measures necessary to improve the availability of stock to the benefit of all readers and library staff alike. By promoting the availability of the collections, the system can be seen as making a significant contribution to the quality of service offered. Conversely, a high loss rate will almost certainly damage the credibility of the library, reduce staff morale and divert precious resources to the purchase of replacement copies.

MODE OF OPERATION

Although bypass systems are less expensive to purchase, they can prove less convenient and less flexible in operation. Because the triggers are permanently sensitised, a member of staff must be present at all times at the detection point to check that books have been properly issued and to pass them around the detector, and this process may slow the rate at which readers leave the library and may cause frustrating queues particularly at busy times. Every book must bypass the system, even books borrowed correctly on previous visits to the library which the reader has brought back into the building. Once permanently sensitised triggers have been securely fastened to the books the library cannot easily convert to a full circulating mode of operation which, in the case of the electromagnetic systems, requires different triggers that can be desensitised when books are issued and resensitised when they are returned. Unfortunately books from libraries with bypass systems will normally set off the alarm in libraries with full circulating versions of the same system and so the suppliers encourage customers to adopt the full circulating mode to avoid unnecessary false alarms.

In libraries with full circulating systems, readers with correctly issued books can move freely in and out of the library and only those in possession of an unissued volume will set off the alarm and require attention by a member of staff. However, the need to desensitise and resensitise books does add a stage to both the issue and return procedures and space must be found for the necessary (de)sensitising units on the main counter where it is essential for equipment to be ergonomically arranged. Some librarians comment upon the size, weight and appearance of the (de)sensitising units such as those supplied by 3M, but as the company will confirm, the units must be sturdy enough to cope with the number and weight of books issued and a number of books can be (de)sensitised at once. Furthermore, there is little chance of operating the units accidentally because books must be deliberately placed on the unit in such a way that a beam is broken before the unit operates. Flat units are also available with all the electromagnetic systems and these can be set on top of or into the counter. The status of triggered material can be changed merely by passing the book over the unit or in some cases by reading the bar code with the issue pen or scanner. Indeed there is considerable interest in units linked to computerised issue systems, offering the convenience of desensitising the book when it is issued. Non electric units suitable for cassettes are produced and also hand held units capable in some cases of resensitising a whole shelf or trolley of returned books at once.

By adopting a full circulating system, it becomes easier to physically separate the circulation function, which may be viewed as the responsibility of library assistants, from the task of security, which may be regarded as a porter's or an attendant's task. Some library staff prefer not to deal directly with security problems feeling that it is not consistent with the positive and friendly attitudes they seek to encourage with library users, but in reality security is the responsibility of all staff. The security desk is sometimes located some distance from the main counter and this can make a swift response to an alarm very difficult, especially in libraries where the security point is not permanently staffed and staff from the main counter are expected to respond by leaving their normal place of work. Some public libraries prefer the bypass system because there is no additional process involved in issuing and also because library staff are able to maintain close contact with readers as they pass through the security system. When combining the issue and security function, careful ergonomic design of the counter area is required to minimise the stretching movements involved in passing books around the detector.

The exit and entrance areas must be designed to ensure that readers leaving the library are forced to pass through the detection area and care should be taken not to site any equipment near to the detector which may reduce its sensitivity and effectiveness. Where this cannot be avoided, heavy shielding may be required.

TRIGGERING THE STOCK

A range of triggers is now available to protect the various book and non-book media collected by libraries. The triggers used for books in the electromagnetic systems are thin strips inserted down the spines or between the pages and are virtually undetectable by readers. Special triggers are also available for audio cassettes, records, compact discs, computer disks, videocassettes and ephemera. Security containers incorporating triggers are also provided for audiocassettes and compact discs. Triggers are available in a variety of lengths and widths and can also be purchased in the shape of labels for disks and cassettes and as bar codes. Some libraries use triggers to protect computers, headphones and other equipment. Microfiche remain difficult to protect and computer disks can suffer data corruption when issued in some systems. Libraries using the radio frequency system produced by Plescon report that readers rather more easily locate and sometimes remove the slightly bulkier tags normally concealed behind a bookplate. For this system to operate as a full circulating one, a due-date card must be physically placed over the tag so as to effectively screen it. The system is non-magnetic and therefore completely safe for audiovisual materials. It is in the availability of triggers suitable for the library's collections, especially for non-book media, that the systems vary and this may well influence the choice of supplier.

Whilst triggering 100% of the stock gives maximum protection, many libraries will take the advice of the system providers and initially at least aim to trigger 40–50% of the existing stock, especially when the cost of the triggers and the labour cost of inserting them is taken into account. Most libraries will selectively trigger the most vulnerable stock – new acquisitions, heavily used books, most recently borrowed books and books in subject areas which have suffered the greatest losses. Information from automated issue systems, short loan collections, stock checks and the judgment of the specialist staff are all extremely valuable in selecting priorities. Particularly vulnerable are current issues of periodicals but few libraries can afford to trigger all current parts and doing so may cause problems when the parts are bound. The binding of periodicals provides an opportunity to insert a well hidden trigger as does the lamination of materials such as maps. Triggered items should be unobtrusively marked in some way.

Finding the necessary manpower for triggering is especially a problem when retrospectively triggering a large existing stock and the librarian can consider utilising library staff or external labour for this formidable task, although some libraries prefer not to employ users in an attempt to maintain some discretion about how the system works. Estimates vary, but experience indicates that between 75 and 100 triggers can be inserted in an hour in libraries using the electromagnetic systems (Arfield, 1991). Library books suppliers will often trigger new acquisitions as part of pre-processing work.

OPERATING THE SYSTEM

The detection systems simply detect unissued books and normally respond by activating an alarm and temporarily locking a gate or door, depending on the configuration selected for the circumstances of the particular library. Their effectiveness as a security measure depends upon the library's security policy and in particular upon the speed and appropriateness of the response of library staff.

Whilst a permanently staffed exit point is preferable, providing for immediate response and enabling supplementary manual bag checks, not all libraries have the staffing resources to achieve this and instead rely upon the response of staff close at hand, for example at the main counter. The deployment of staffing effort inevitably reflects the priority accorded to security. Some librarians argue that a staffed exit point is not so essential and that would-be offenders are unlikely to risk the embarrassment of setting off the alarm in full sight of their colleagues or other readers. Others however suggest that the chance of being caught by a person as opposed to a machine is a far greater deterrent.

Good staff training is crucial for the chosen system to operate effectively. Staff should be clear in advance why the system was introduced, how it works and most important should have written instructions on the procedure to be followed when the alarm goes off

(Arfield, 1991). Confrontations with readers caught by the system can be difficult and the manager must make it absolutely clear how all staff are expected to deal with these situations and not only provide the necessary staff training and guidance but also be prepared to discuss experience and adjust procedures accordingly. Some libraries have effectively used role playing exercises for this purpose. The suppliers themselves offer staff training for their customers. False alarms will inevitably occur and so long as there are relatively few may even be regarded as valuable in reminding readers that the system is in operation.

The library must establish whether its policy is primarily to deter theft or in fact to catch and punish thieves. If the object is to prevent theft and encourage adherence to correct borrowing procedures, some publicity may be required, emphasising the positive reasons for the installation of the system, but at the same time making it clear to everyone concerned that action will be taken against persistent and deliberate offenders. Libraries have developed a wide range of policies to deal with readers who are caught by the system. Bearing in mind the difficulties of establishing theft in the legal sense, the sanctions imposed must be clearly stated within the rules and regulations and must be enforceable in practice within the environment in which the library operates. Readers may simply be asked to return to the counter to borrow the books correctly; details of every alarm incident may be recorded on a standard form; readers may be interviewed after each alarm or after an allowance of a small number of forgetful incidents; and the library may write to readers asking for an explanation of continued problems. Many libraries take a much more serious view imposing immediate or deferred punishments such as fines, the withdrawal of borrowing privileges, or even suspension of membership. Serious cases may be referred beyond the library to the parent institution for disciplinary action. Ultimately readers may be threatened with legal action, employees with dismissal and students with the withholding of degrees or sending down.

As with all electro-mechanical equipment the book detection system must be well maintained in peak performance, which in most cases is essentially a compromise between sensitivity and the number of false alarms. The operation of the system should be checked daily or at least weekly. Because a book detection system has been successfully installed does not mean that the library should no longer be concerned about the loss of books. Whether by complete or selective stock checks or simply by recording requested but missing items, the loss rate should be periodically assessed and compared with previous figures. Libraries which record alarm incidents will also have statistics on how many books they might otherwise have lost through forgetfulness or theft. Smethurst (1991) reports that the average loss rate in libraries is generally thought to be 1–2% per annum, although he concedes that many would argue that it is considerably higher. Should the loss rate be perceived as unacceptable, and it has to be said that this must be judged against the priority given to security and the level of expenditure on security measures, then arrangements should be reviewed. The operation of the system can be checked and if necessary the sensitivity increased, supplementary bag checks can be introduced, and other security measures outlined in the previous chapter implemented particularly in areas vulnerable to high loss rates.

A related problem is the mutilation of books and some librarians argue that improvements made to security can lead to an increase in the incidence of pages being ripped out of books and journals. Once again, if all such incidents are recorded trends in this particularly disagreeable behaviour can be assessed and preventative measures considered, which may well include arrangements for improving the availability of the literature in question to those who require it. In some libraries readers enjoy the freedom to move freely in and out of the building with their coats and bags but others insist that readers deposit such items in a cloakroom or locker area before entering the library. It is argued that coats and bags are a security risk and also unnecessarily clutter the library. However, cloakrooms take up valuable space and when supervised absorb recurrent staffing costs, providing not only a place to deposit coats and bags but also a left luggage facility. Coin operated lockers, far from generating income, can be expensive and inconvenient to maintain and will inevitably be used for storage of items not connected with library activities.

BIBLIOGRAPHY

Arfield, J. A. (1991), Theft detection systems – some practicalities, in *Security in academic and research libraries*, edited by Quinsee, A. G. and McDonald, A. C. Newcastle upon Tyne: University Library.

Friend, F. J. (1991), Theft detection systems – policies, in *Security in academic and research libraries*, edited by Quinsee, A. G. and McDonald, A. C. Newcastle upon Tyne: University Library.

Headland Press (1986/1987), Theft detection systems. *Library Equipment Reports*, (December/January).

Metcalf, K. D. (1986), *Planning academic and research libraries, second edition* by Leighton, P. D. and Weber, D. C. Chicago: American Library Association.

Smethurst, J. M. (1991), Library security: an overview, in *Security in academic and research libraries* edited by Quinsee, A. G. and McDonald, A. C. Newcastle upon Tyne: University Library.

Thompson, G. (1989), *Planning and design of library buildings, third edition*. London: Butterworth.

Index